THE
BIRDWATCHER'S
SITE GUIDE TO BRITAIN AND IRELAND

JOHN GOODERS

BLITZ

A GRISEWOOD & DEMPSEY LIMITED BOOK

This edition published in 1992 by Blitz Editions,
an imprint of Bookmart Limited, Registered
Number 2372865.
Trading as Bookmart Limited, Desford Road,
Enderby, Leicester LE5 5AD.

10 9 8 7 6 5 4 3 2 1

The text and maps in this edition were previously
published by Kingfisher Books in 1992 in The
Complete Birdwatcher's Guide.

ISBN 1 856050 39 4

Printed and bound in Italy.
Phototypeset by Rowland Phototypesetting Limited,
Bury St Edmunds, Suffolk.

Acknowledgements
Page 5 Mike Mockler/Swift Picture Library; 6
Martin King/Swift Picture Library; 7 Mike Read/
Swift Picture Library.

Maps: Jeremy Gower, Malcolm Porter
Senior Editor: Janice Lacock
Editors: James Harrison, Jonathan Elphick
Design: Terry Woodley
Picture Research: Sarah Donald

CONTENTS

The Site Guide

Any guide to birdwatching localities inevitably involves making choices and is therefore personal. Birds can, of course, be seen anywhere, but some places are better than others and are generally acknowledged as such. These sites may or may not be bird reserves. They may have particularly scarce habitats. They may, by virtue of their geographical position, have the ability to attract birds. Or they may be simply the best available area in an otherwise rather dull region. Many birders have their own small patch that they watch regularly and that by dint of hard work may produce all manner of species. It may be a local park, garden or open space – a sort of urban Fair Isle – but such places are seldom rewarding for the casual visitor. Thus this guide concentrates on the top birding spots in the British Isles, rather than on places where an individual or small group has managed to see a few interesting birds.

By and large the best birding spots are coastal, simply because coastlines have most of the habitats that are found inland as well as those that are not. Thus a good coastal site will have farmland, woodland, heath and hedgerow as well as shoreline, cliffs, marsh and estuary. Additionally, shorelines offer a haven to land-birds making lengthy sea crossings and duck migrants may, on occasion, appear in huge numbers. It is then not surprising that coastlines attract birdwatchers in large number.

Some areas have, over the years, built up a remarkable reputation for producing scarce or interesting birds. Fair Isle, Scilly and Cley fall into this category and the number of skilled observers that they attract tends to maintain their reputation. Other areas may be equally as good but, because they are not subject to such continual observation, fail to produce interesting birds. This phenomenon can be regarded as the geographical equivalent of the 'weekend rarity bias. There are, however, quite genuine reasons why these places maintain their reputation and any beginner could do a lot worse than make his first major outing to a place such as Cley.

There are, however, many other places that are worthy of attention and it should be a major aim to get to know them well and learn about the normal bird populations and their regular comings and goings. This may involve frequent visits to a particular area of woodland, marsh, reservoir or even heath or moorland. The most rewarding sites are usually at water because that is where the birds themselves are found in their greatest number and variety. In seeking such local 'hot spots' the Ordinance Survey Maps are invaluable.

When I lived in London I regularly visited the London hot spots, and evening visits to Barn Elms Reservoir and weekends trips to Staines were, for a while, part of my routine. I did, however, hanker after a spot of my own and by scouring the appropriate OS map discovered a miniscule, old-fashioned sewage farm along the River Wandle. Having cycled over to seek permission I was delighted to find a tiny settling lagoon, an overgrown dump area and a wet grassy field forming an oasis right in the middle of Merton's urban sprawl. Within weeks I was seeing Greenshank, Little Stint and Common Sandpiper right in my own backyard, so to speak. There were no other birdwatchers and it was a joy to watch what were otherwise 'coastal' birds in such an environment. Less anyone tries to find this little gem, I must inform you

The elusive Dartford Warbler is only found on a few heathland areas in southern England. Of the sites mentioned in this guide, the most likely are Arne, Brownsea Island and Studland Heath in Dorset (see pages 11, 21 and 98), the New Forest in Hampshire (see page 78) and Thursley Common in Surrey (see page 101).

that the area is now the industrial estate right next to Wimbledon football ground.

About the same time I also started scouring my local common every day. It, too, was surrounded by suburban London, but the comings and goings of small migrants were fascinating, even if the numbers were small. The best birds were far from outstanding – Wood Warbler, Pied Flycatcher, Redstart, Wheatear – but by urban London standards they were really very exciting. Quite recently a friend who still lives in the area managed to find a Pallas's Warbler, so even national scale rarities are not out of the question. Such local-patch birding may be immensely rewarding, but daily visits are really essential if the scale of migration is to be appreciated.

Inevitably, every birder will also develop his or her own favourite coastal location, too, that has the variety of habitats necessary to attract and hold a good variety of birds. For many years all of my weekends and holidays were spent on a particular stretch of the East Anglian coast. Eventually, however, the journey became somewhat tedious and I turned my attention to the Kent–Sussex border country where I now live. It is nowhere near as beautiful or as lonely as my East Anglian stomping ground, but it does produce some fabulous birds.

Some watchers never settle for a favourite spot at all. These gipsy-like birders flit from one spot to the next, partly on impulse and partly in search of reported rarities. Mostly they will be visiting places covered in this book but birds can and do appear at all manner of strange places and the gipsys will follow. Residents of a small Hampshire village once reported a strange nocturnal sound and were worried enough to call in the Electricity Board to investigate. Eventually, someone thought it might be a bird and contacted an experienced local. The sound turned out to be an off-course Scops Owl and the village was inundated by birders for several weeks. It is, of course, not listed here.

With so many birders now travelling the length and breadth of the country, it is easy for records to go unreported. Nevertheless, virtually the whole country is covered by a network of local recorders who are responsible for assembling the records of birds for the local bird report. The British Trust for Ornithology will be happy to put you in touch with the relevant recorder. Most importantly, if you spot a rare bird report it instantly to the warden (if there is one) or to the local society.

How to use the site guide
The sites detailed in this guide are arranged alphabetically rather than geographically. This makes it easy to find a site known by name.

Name
Each site is named and placed in its appropriate county or region. This is followed by the relevant map reference with OS for Ordinance Survey; OSNI for Ordinance Survey Northern Ireland; and IOS for the Ordinance Survey of the Irish Republic. The maps referred to are the modern 1:50,000 series except for Ireland where they are the $\frac{1}{2}$ inch series. Each grid square represents one square kilometre.

The Black-tailed Godwit can be seen at many freshwater marshes and estuaries around Britain and Ireland both during spring and autumn passage and when wintering. Large flocks winter at Gayton Sands, Langstone Harbour, Chichester Harbour, Studland Bay, the Exe Estuary and the Ribble Estuary (see pages 44, 61, 27, 98, 37 and 87) while many Icelandic birds regularly spend the winter on the Shannon Estuary, Co. Limerick (see page 91). The only place where large numbers of birds breed regularly is the Ouse Washes (see page 81).

The Site Guide

The Glen More Forest which surrounds Loch Morlich in Scotland (see page 25) contains many ancient Scots pine trees and is the home of the Scottish Crossbill, Crested Tit and Capercaillie. There is also a fair chance of seeing Osprey around the Loch.

Location
Under this heading a general indication of where the area lies is given, usually with the distance from the nearest large town or city. A good road atlas will then help you look in the right direction.

Habitats
In general the wider the range of habitats the greater the variety of birds that will use a particular area. The habitats found in each area are summarized, giving an idea of the sort of landform to be expected.

Birds
It is impossible to list every bird found in each area so this section is inevitably selective. The most interesting regular species are picked out along with the possibilities of seeing other scarcer birds, and particular attention is drawn to seasonal differences. Planning visits, for example, to watch waders is generally best in spring when all the summer visitors have arrived and when all the birds are singing.

Access
This section gives precise directions about how to get to the area, usually from the nearest large town, and certainly from the nearest main road. Details about footpaths, trails and hides are also incorporated.

Permits
Where necessary these are detailed, giving places and times where they may be obtained. Bear in mind that such information does tend to change quite rapidly, especially where small, largely voluntary organizations are involved.

I would be pleased to hear of major changes and developments to any of the featured sites c/o the publishers.

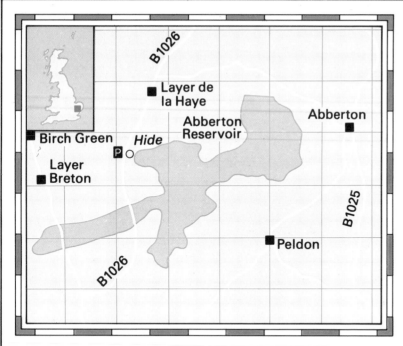

ABBERTON RESERVOIR, ESSEX OS 168

Location: 4 miles south of Colchester.

Habitats: this is one of lowland Britain's largest man-made waters; it has banks at the western end, large shallow bays and, in autumn, considerable areas of open mud.

Birds: one of the very best reservoirs in the country for divers, grebes, wildfowl, gulls and terns. Great Crested and Little Grebes are present throughout the year, and winter brings the scarcer grebes plus divers and ducks, especially Wigeon, Gadwall, Shoveler, Pochard and Tufted, with good numbers of Goldeneye. Smew, Goosander and Bewick's Swan are frequently present.

During spring and autumn passage periods waders are present, with Little Stint and Curlew Sandpiper turning up regularly, especially in autumn. Black Tern and Little Gull are also regular and it is a poor migration season that does not produce Garganey and Red-crested Pochard.

Access: much of the reservoir is visible from the B1026. After 5½ miles there is a parking area on the right. A turnstile (small charge) leads to a hide. The main causeway lies ½ mile south. Follow the B1026 and signs to Layer Breton for a secondary causeway.

Permits: not required.

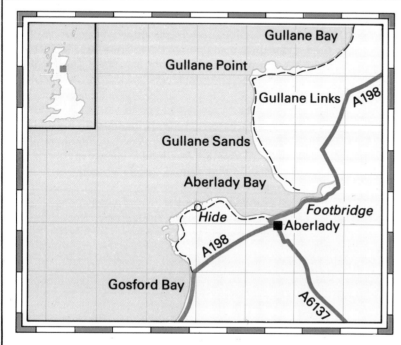

ABERLADY BAY, EAST LOTHIAN OS 66

Location: about 12 miles east of Edinburgh, on the south shore of the Firth of Forth.

Habitats: intertidal mud, backed by low-lying dunes.

Birds: winter is probably the best season, when there are flocks of Pinkfeet, Whooper Swans, and many seaducks, including Eider, Scoter, Velvet Scoter and Long-tailed. The sea also holds impressive concentrations of divers, as well as of Slavonian and Red-necked Grebes. Waders are abundant, with all the usual species plus Purple Sandpiper and, sometimes, Ruff. During passage periods, visitors regularly include Black-tailed Godwit, Curlew Sandpiper and Little Stint. Aberlady boasts one of the most important wader roosts in Scotland. In summer, terns are often present and Eider breed locally. Gannets breed nearby at Bass Rock (*see page* 14).

Access: leave Edinburgh on the A1 eastwards and turn left on the A198 to Aberlady. About ½ mile beyond the village is a car park where a footbridge crosses a stream and a footpath leads out along the eastern shore. This is best visited on a rising tide.

Permits: write for a car park permit to Department of Leisure, Recreation and Tourism, Brunton Hall, Musselburgh, Edinburgh EH21 6AF.

ABERNETHY FOREST, HIGHLAND OS 36

Location: this area lies to the east of the River Spey and north of Aviemore a few miles from Boat of Garten.

Habitats: a huge area of old Scots Pine forest, together with new plantations at various stages of maturity.

Birds: this area is best visited in summer. Although you will have to mingle with hordes of visitors to see the Ospreys at Loch Garten (*see page* 67), the forest specialities – Capercaillie, Black Grouse, Crested Tit and Scottish Crossbill – are best seen early in the morning, when few tourists are about. Additionally, there are Goshawk, Hen Harrier and Merlin. Redstart, Siskin, Dipper and Common Sandpiper should all be seen. Long-eared Owl is as elusive as elsewhere.

Access: access to this National Nature Reserve is freely available over many tracks and roads. The best areas lie to the south of Loch Garten and can be approached via the minor road to Tulloch just north of Auchgourish. Find Mhor Cottage for a Blackcock lek (communal display ground of male Black Grouse), but do not disturb the birds. Continue to Forest Lodge.

Permits: not required.

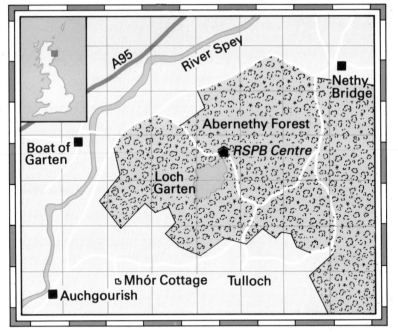

AINSDALE SANDS, LANCASHIRE OS 108

Location: this shoreline lies between Southport and Formby.

Habitats: the tide exposes considerable areas of intertidal sand, backed by an extensive area of dunes and dune slacks. There are also extensive plantations of pines.

Birds: this area is often overshadowed by other, more famous, locations nearby, but has always had its own band of dedicated devotees. It is best during spring and autumn passage periods, when the dune thickets hold many small migrants and the shoreline may be full of waders. The latter are more numerous in winter, when large numbers of both Black-tailed and Bar-tailed Godwits, Sanderlings, Turnstones and the more widespread species may be seen. Skuas and terns are usually present in autumn, often with a few auks. Even in summer exciting birds are possible at this site.

Access: from Freshfield Station in Formby walk northwards up the road along the landward side of the railway and cross to Fisherman's Path. This leads to Massam's Slack and the shore. To the north a road leads to Ainsdale-on-Sea for seabirds. Other areas are of restricted access forming part of a National Nature Reserve.

Permits: not necessary for casual birding.

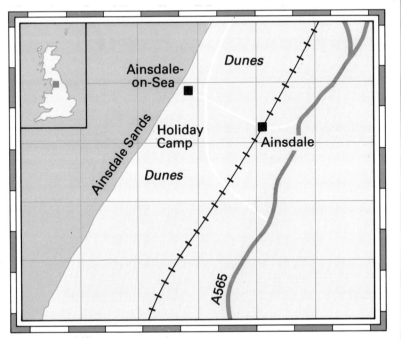

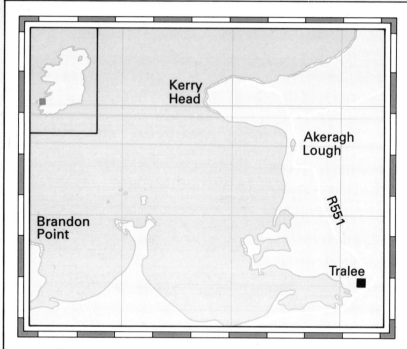

AKERAGH LOUGH, CO. KERRY, IRISH REPUBLIC IOS½ 20

Location: this small area of freshwater lies in northern Kerry just a few miles north of Tralee. The quickest route for visitors across the Irish Sea is by air to Shannon, then by roads N18 and N21 to Limerick and Tralee; or by air to Cork then by road N22 to Tralee.

Habitats: there are three fresh-to-brackish water pools here that, in winter, are joined to form a larger flooded area. This is the only stretch of permanent freshwater in northern Kerry.

Birds: the nearest stretch of freshwater to America, Akeragh's international fame rests on the extraordinary array of transatlantic vagrants that it attracts every year. It is difficult to predict what might turn up here in autumn, but Pectoral Sandpipers, Lesser Golden Plovers, one of the dowitchers and White-rumped and Baird's Sandpipers must be regarded as distinct possibilities. The Lough also holds the occasional American duck as well as the more usual European species.

Access: leave Tralee northwards on the R551 and view Akeragh on the left before Ballyheige village. Do not ignore the intertidal areas of Tralee Bay. Brandon Point, about 20 miles to the west, is a major autumn sea-watch station.

Permits: the area is private and permits are not available.

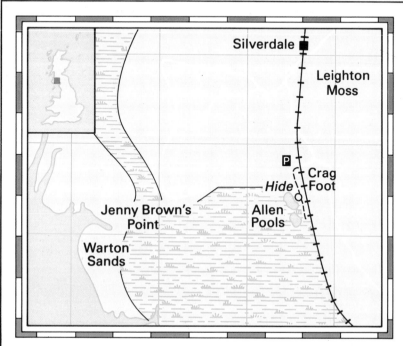

ALLEN POOLS, LANCASHIRE

OS 97

Location: a few miles west of Carnforth in the northeast of Morecambe Bay; part of the RSPB Morecambe Bay reserve.

Habitats: a huge area of intertidal sand and saltmarsh, where the RSPB has created two pools on the Carnforth Saltings, one of which is dedicated to the memory of Eric Morecambe – not only a very funny man, but also a bird-lover and dedicated conservationist.

Birds: Greylag Geese, Pintail and Shoveler are particularly fond of this area. The winter landscape is dominated by the huge flocks of waders, with Knot the most abundant. There are also many Dunlin, Oystercatcher and Bartailed Godwit, along with lesser numbers of Turnstone, Redshank and Sanderling. During spring and autumn passage periods other species occur, including large flocks of Ringed Plover, particularly in spring, together with Spotted Redshank, Black-tailed Godwit and Little Stint. Terns are often present in spring and autumn, and there is usually a good collection of the more common gulls.

Access: leave the M6 at exit 35 to Carnforth and take the road toward Silverdale. At Crag Foot take a left under a railway bridge to the car park and hides.

Permits: free access to the pools at all times.

ALTON WATER, SUFFOLK OS 169

Location: this relatively recent reservoir lies 5 miles south of Ipswich, between the estuaries of the Stour and Orwell.

Habitats: flooding a shallow valley has created a lowland reservoir with a highly indented and shallow shoreline that is particularly attractive to passage and wintering wetland birds. Its position, near many well-established bird resorts, makes it one of the best reservoirs in the country.

Birds: Alton Water has become one of Britain's major strongholds of breeding Great Crested Grebes. Greylag Geese, too, find it attractive and, in winter, they are joined by large numbers of ducks that regularly include marine species, such as Long-tailed Duck, Scaup, Goosander and Smew. Passage waders are often interesting, but the lengthy shoreline does make locating them something of a lottery. Snipe, as well as regular Jack Snipe, are present in winter.

Access: leave Ipswich southwards on the A137 toward Colchester and turn left towards Tattingstone. Before the village a causeway crosses the higher part of the reservoir. Beyond the village lies another viewpoint. Continue via Stutton to the dam, where there is a car park.

Permits: not required for access as detailed above.

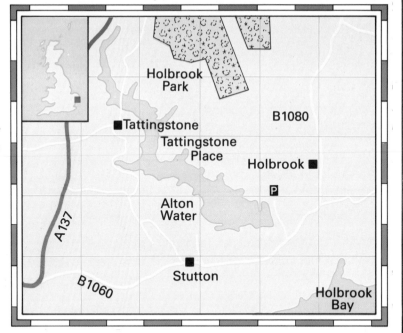

ARNE, DORSET OS 195

Location: the Arne peninsula lies on the south side of Poole Harbour, a few kilometres east of Wareham off the road to Swanage.

Habitats: sandy heath, covered with heather, ling, gorse and stands of pines with birch scrub. Also large areas of intertidal mud with reed beds and saltmarshes.

Birds: Arne's most famous bird inhabitant is the Dartford Warbler. More birdwatchers have 'ticked' this species here than at any other site. Other typical heathland birds include Nightjar and Stonechat. A good variety of waders may be seen on the mudflats and saltings, both in winter and on passage (*see also Brownsea Island, page* 21). Black-tailed Godwit, Spotted Redshank and Avocet winter here, and in autumn may be present in quite large numbers. They are joined by Curlew Sandpiper, Little Stint, Greenshank and often a few terns. Both Buzzard and Sparrowhawk breed in the area.

Access: leave Wareham on the A351 towards Swanage and turn left after ½ mile in Stoborough. Continue to Arne village and the car park and RSPB reception. There is free access to the Shipstal area. A nature trail starts opposite the church.

Permits: not required. Groups may arrange for escorted visits by writing to: The Warden, Syldata, Arne, Wareham BH20 5BJ.

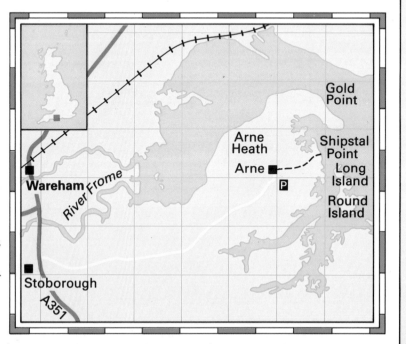

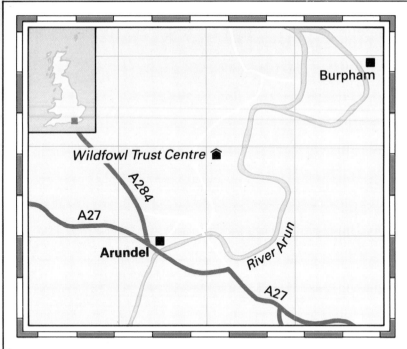

ARUNDEL, WEST SUSSEX OS 197

Location: this Wildfowl Trust Refuge lies just a ½ mile north of Arundel between Chichester and Worthing and is well signposted from the A27 roundabouts.

Habitats: a series of pools has been created alongside the River Arun to house a fine collection of captive wildfowl. There is also a more natural lagoon surrounded by an extensive growth of reeds.

Birds: the wildfowl collection here includes a fine and representative array of the world's ducks, geese and swans, including feral Canada and Greylag Geese and several species of seaducks not usually on view at such refuges. During passage periods scarcer waders, including Green Sandpiper, are often seen. In winter the 'natural' lagoon is frequently visited by other waders, as well as good numbers of Water Rails, Snipe and the occasional Bittern or flock of Bearded Tits. Only a short distance to the north lie Waltham Brooks at Greatham Bridge, and the new RSPB reserve of Pulborough Brooks.

Access: leave the A27 at Arundel and follow signs to the Wildfowl Trust Refuge. Park on the right after one mile.

Permits: there is an entrance charge, though Wildfowl Trust members are allowed in free.

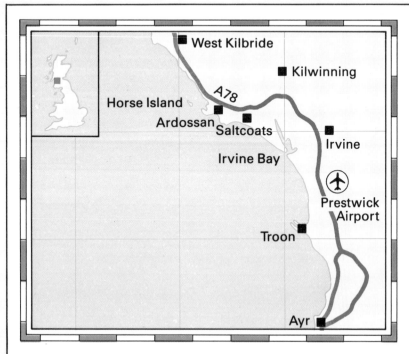

AYR, STRATHCLYDE OS 70

Location: 30 miles south-west of Glasgow at the mouth of the Firth of Clyde. The major bird areas lie between Troon and West Kilbride.

Habitats: the intertidal area is not huge, but still offers excellent opportunities to see a great variety of seabirds.

Birds: in summer there are good tern colonies on the RSPB's Horse Island to the north of Ardrossan. The birds can be seen easily from the town itself. Eider, Gannet and Guillemot are also present at this time. Spring and autumn passage brings a wider variety of species, but it is in winter that this coast really comes into its own. Divers are then plentiful and there is a sizeable herd of Whooper Swans at Irvine-Garnock estuary. Seaducks include regular Red-breasted Merganser, Scoter and Eider. Waders may be abundant and Purple Sandpipers are always present. The South Bay at Troon is a likely spot for this bird, as well as for Glaucous and Iceland Gulls among the roosting flocks. Another good spot is Doonfoot Bay, south of Ayr.

Access: leave Glasgow southwestwards on the A737 and turn right to Dalry on the A780 and again on the A781 to West Kilbride. The A78 coast road is excellent, with easy access to the seafront at Ardrossan, Troon, Ayr and Doonfoot Bay.

Permits: landing on Horse Island may be arranged with the RSPB, 17 Regent Terrace, Edinburgh EH7 5NB.

BALRANALD, NORTH UIST, WESTERN ISLES OS 18

Location: this RSPB reserve lies on the west coast of North Uist between the villages of Tigharry and Paiblesgarry.

Habitats: this is a harsh, crofting landscape surrounded by a rocky shoreline with huge dune beaches. There are areas of marsh and loch and flower-strewn coastal grasslands. Typical of the Outer Hebrides, these rich grazing lands have been built up on lime-rich shell-sand. They are called by their Gaelic name *machair* (pronounced 'mackar') and have a rich birdlife.

Birds: a typical range of Outer Hebridean birds that includes Corncrake and sometimes Red-necked Phalarope. The former is more often heard than seen, though Balranald is one of the best places for this declining species in Britain. Red-necked Phalaropes are often present in the second half of May. Other breeding wetland birds include several duck species (notably Wigeon, as well as Gadwall, Teal, Shoveler and Eider), while Arctic Terns are often abundant. Black Guillemot, Dunlin and Ringed Plover all breed.

Access: by air to Benbecula, then northwards across the causeways to North Uist. Follow the A865 westward and turn left to Hougharry. There is a visitor reception cottage at Goular.

Permits: access is free at all times, but keep to the marked paths.

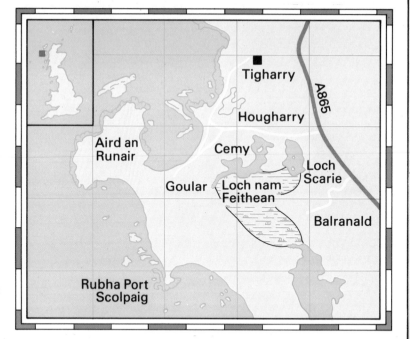

BARDSEY ISLAND, GWYNEDD

OS 123

Location: this island lies off the tip of the Llŷn Peninsula, which forms the northern arm of Cardigan Bay.

Habitats: Bardsey is a small island with areas of farmland, a conifer plantation, a few cliffs and a hill that rises to 170m.

Birds: though Manx Shearwater breed on the east side of the hill and Shag, Razorbill, Kittiwake and Chough nest on the cliffs, Bardsey is essentially a migration watch point. A bird observatory was established in 1953 and a succession of rare and scarce birds has been recorded since, especially in autumn. The lighthouse at the southern end of the island was for long a major killer of small migrants and, though the death roll has now been reduced, birds are still attracted during overcast conditions.

Access: there is a regular boat service (at present early on Saturday mornings) from Pwllheli. Accommodation at the Observatory, from March to November, is in dormitories. Inquiries (enclose s.a.e.) to The Secretary, Mrs H. Bond, 21a Gestridge Road, Kingsteignton, Newton Abbot, Devon. Contact Bardsey Trust, Tyddyn Du Farm, Criccieth, Gwynedd, for cottages to rent.

Permits: see above.

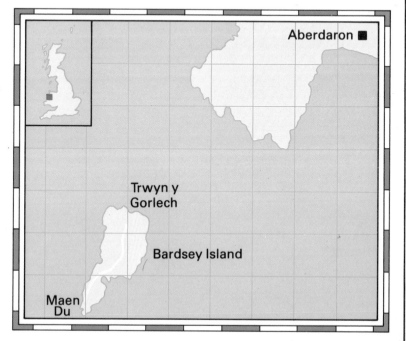

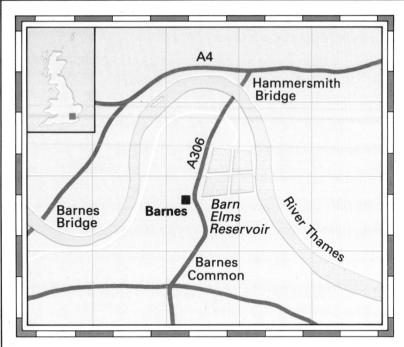

BARN ELMS RESERVOIR, LONDON OS 176

Location: West London, south of Hammersmith Bridge.

Habitats: four concrete-banked reservoirs in a suburban landscape only a few yards from the Thames. The banks offer little in the way of food, but still manage to attract a few waders on spring and autumn passage. In winter the waters offer a safe refuge and feeding opportunities to a remarkable collection of ducks.

Birds: in winter Barn Elms holds great rafts of Tufted Duck and Pochard, together with Gadwall, Goosander and Wigeon. The latter graze the grassy banks and nearby playing fields. Hard weather may bring in the occasional Scaup or even Long-tailed Duck. Great Crested Grebes are regular and occasionally one of the scarcer grebes or even a diver may also be present. Black and Common Terns are regular in spring and autumn and a few waders are often present. A complete redevelopment of the site is planned by the Wildfowl and Wetland Trust.

Access: from Hammersmith, cross the bridge and turn left at the traffic lights on the south bank into Merthyr Terrace. The reservoir entrance is 180m away, at the end of this road.

Permits: must be obtained in advance from Thames Water, New River Head, Rosebery Avenue, London EC1R 4TP.

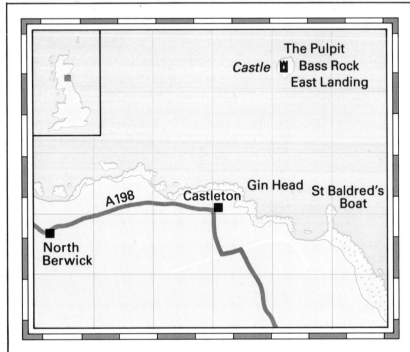

BASS ROCK, EAST LOTHIAN OS 67

Location: off the southern shore at the mouth of the Firth of Forth, about 3 miles north-east of North Berwick and some 20 miles east of Edinburgh.

Habitats: this is a monolithic lump of rock rising precipitously from the sea that offers a home to large numbers of breeding seabirds.

Birds: this is one of the most accessible gannetries in Britain, with over 20,000 breeding pairs of Gannets. To visit a large colony of this spectacular black and white seabird is a unique experience. The birds can be approached and photographed at close range, though the noise, smell and commotion are not to everyone's taste. Shag, Guillemot and Razorbill are also present.

Access: leave Edinburgh eastwards on the A1 and take the A198 to North Berwick. The boatman, Fred Marr, in North Berwick should be contacted in advance (Tel: 0620 2838) and much can be seen from his regular tourist boat trips. Landing is not allowed in the earlier part of the season, when serious disturbance to the breeding birds could result.

Permits: contact the Scottish Ornithologists' Club, 21 Regent Terrace, Edinburgh EH7 5BT (Tel: 031 556 6042) for details of their own excursions and for permitted landing times.

BEACHY HEAD, EAST SUSSEX OS 199

Location: on the South Coast, between Eastbourne and Seaford.

Habitats: sheer chalk cliffs plunge vertically 150m to the sea with only one break, the Cuckmere Valley. The cliff-tops offer a mixture of grassland, scrub, arable fields and a few areas with trees.

Birds: Beachy is a migration point offering excellent seawatching together with the chance of grounded migrants, including exciting rarities. Between Eastbourne and Seaford there is only one 'major' wood (90 square metres) and only a few sheltered hollows where birds (and their insect food) can escape the wind – Whitbread Hollow, Belle Tout, Birling Gap and Cuckmere Haven. Each area should be thoroughly searched during spring and autumn passage periods. In spring Pomarine Skuas are something of a speciality, while small migrants are often abundant.

Access: from the promenade at Eastbourne, the South Downs Way continues to Beachy Head and beyond. A coast road also offers access. Birling Gap is good for spring seawatching. There is a car park at Exceat Bridge and a track down the valley to the sea, though this is much frequented by trippers.

Permits: not required.

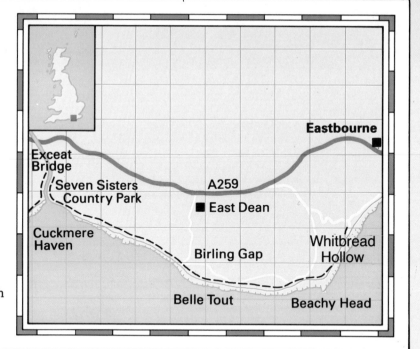

BEINN EIGHE, HIGHLAND OS 19 & 25

Location: 20 miles south-west of Ullapool.

Habitats: though Beinn Eighe National Nature Reserve, Britain's first, was created to protect one of the last remnants of the old Caledonian pine forests, it covers a huge area of mountain, moorland, loch and marsh.

Birds: this is a rugged landscape, boasting breeding Golden Eagle, Peregrine and Merlin, along with Red Grouse, Ptarmigan and Greenshank. Both Black-throated and Red-throated Divers breed, as do Dipper, Dunlin and Common Sandpiper. Both Crossbills and Scottish Crossbills may be found. Redwings breed among birches.

Access: start at Kinlochewe at the junction of the A896 and A832 at the head of Loch Maree. About 1 mile north on the A832 is the Reserve Visitor Centre, which offers advice and from which a pony trail runs westward into the highest part of the area. About 1 mile further north is a car park and the start of the Glas Leitire Nature Trail. The lower slopes here have Scots Pine with crossbills. Birders should take all the necessary precautions that wild mountainous country demands.

Permits: not required outside the deer-stalking season, currently between 1 September and 21 November (to check dates contact the British Field Sports Society, 59 Kennington Road, London SE1).

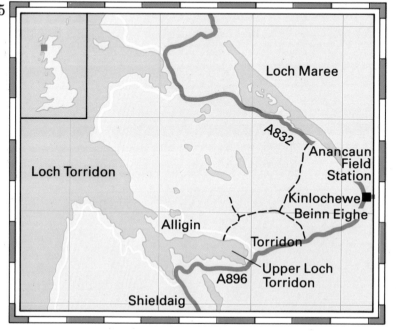

BEMPTON CLIFFS AND FLAMBOROUGH HEAD, HUMBERSIDE

Location: between Scarborough and Bridlington.

Habitats: vertical cliffs jutting out of what is otherwise a smooth and regular coast.

Birds: Bempton Cliffs supports tens of thousands of Kittiwakes, Guillemot, Razorbill, Puffin, Fulmar, Shag – and Britain's only mainland gannetry.

The cliffs at Flamborough are some 75m high, perhaps too high for perfect seawatching, but the Head's position makes it one of the top two or three seawatching spots in Britain. All four skuas occur every year, especially Arctic and Great Skuas. Manx Shearwaters are regular and even the Mediterranean race appears most years. Sooty Shearwaters are seen throughout the autumn and there are reports most years of both Cory's and Great Shearwaters. In winter there are divers offshore as well as gulls, seaducks and even the odd skua.

With small migrants, autumn is usually more spectacular than spring. All the usual warblers, chats, flycatchers and thrushes, including Pied Flycatcher, Whinchat, Redstart and Wryneck, are regular passage migrants. Semi-rarities such as Ortolan Bunting and Yellow-browed Warbler turn up annually. Most of these birds are found among the hedges that separate the small fields, or in the scrub along the coastal path.

Access: leave Bridlington northwards on the B1255 and turn left to Bempton after 2 miles. Continue through the village and follow RSPB signs. From the car park, walk to the cliff top footpath and explore. There are observation points, an information centre and daily boat trips along the foot of the cliffs from Bridlington.

Take the B1259 to Flamborough Head, from where a path leads down from the lighthouse to sheltered crannies. There are alternative routes to North Landing, South Landing and the southern end of Danes' Dyke.

Permits: none required.

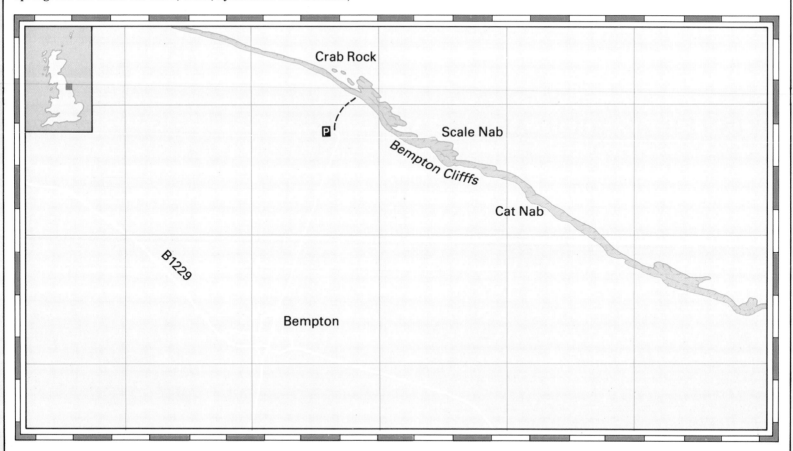

BENACRE, SUFFOLK OS 156

Location: on the coast a few miles south of Lowestoft.

Habitats: the large broad is separated from the sea by only a narrow shingle beach. The water is fresh and the inland part is densely overgrown with reeds. The broad's shoreline includes exposed mud. The whole area is surrounded by mature, mixed woodland. To the north is a series of disused gravel pits that are now flooded, providing more fresh water. An area of scrubby hedges frequently holds a good variety of small birds during spring and autumn passage. To the south is a line of crumbling cliffs.

Birds: the reed beds hold a good selection of East Anglian specialities, but there is no access. In winter the broad has a good collection of ducks and the odd harrier. During migration, there is often a good range of waders, and gulls regularly include Glaucous and Mediterranean. Terns regularly come to bathe and the occasional skua may do the same. The bushes hold chats, warblers and flycatchers, though rarities are surprisingly few. The East Anglian coast is poor for seawatching.

Access: leave the A12 at Wrentham, taking the minor road to Covehithe. Park beyond the church and walk north. There is a hide on the southern shore.

Permits: not required – but do not trespass on to the Reserve.

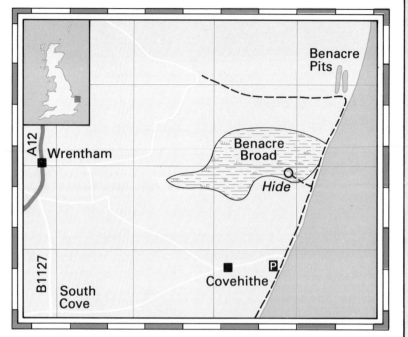

BIRSAY MOORS AND COTTASGARTH, ORKNEY OS 6

Location: one of the largest RSPB reserves, it lies in the extreme north of Mainland, to the east of Brough Head.

Habitat: rough, windswept heather moorland with large bogs as well as lochs and streams. Fortunately, much can be seen from the public roads.

Birds: with the dedicated help of the RSPB's local man, the late Eddie Balfour, the Hen Harrier survived here and has since spread back to the mainland. Many birds find conditions perfect here, including Short-eared Owls, Arctic and Great Skuas and Red-throated Diver.

Access: the B9057 crosses the moors between Dounby and the north coast, while a minor road runs from it north-westwards to Loch of Hundland and Twatt. The lochs are worth exploring. There is a hide at Lower Cottasgarth, reached by turning left just beyond the Norseman Garage, 3 miles north of Finstown. Another hide at Burgar Hill, near the wind generators, is approached from Evie. Further access is possible at Durkadale, reached by taking a rough track from the southern end of Loch of Hundland.

Permits: not required.

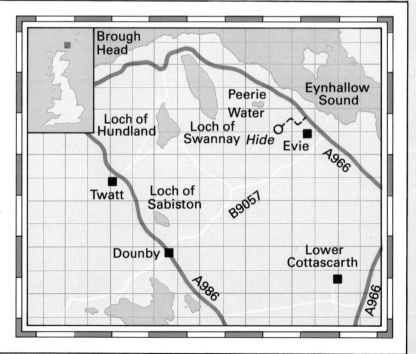

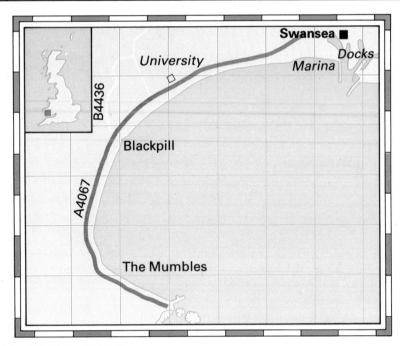

BLACKPILL, WEST GLAMORGAN OS 159

Location: this is no more than a seaside suburb of Swansea, lying to the south-west of the city and overlooking Swansea Bay.

Habitat: the intertidal area here is blessed by having a small stream entering the sea, providing freshwater in which birds can bathe. There are large areas of mud and sand, a promenade and a boating pool. All in all, it is not a place that would seem to have anything special to offer the birder – but it does.

Birds: the first ever Ring-billed Gull from America was discovered here in 1973 and Blackpill has been famous for rare gulls ever since. Ring-billed Gulls still occur here more regularly than at any other British site, with up to five present, mainly in March. The roost here attracts several thousand gulls, among which Mediterranean, Glaucous and Iceland may be found. There are also winter waders, including a good flock of Sanderling, plus the occasional seaduck and diver. Autumn passage produces a wider range of species, but Blackpill remains primarily a gull-watching spot, with other birds simply a sideshow.

Access: the A4067 southward from Swansea runs behind the beach to the Boating Pool, where most birders gather.

Permits: none required.

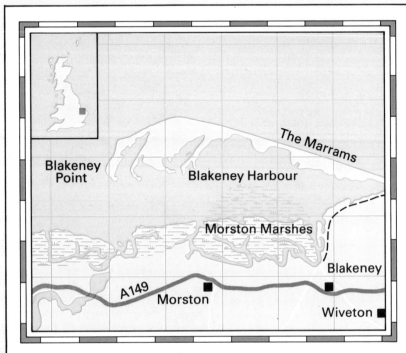

BLAKENEY POINT AND HARBOUR, NORFOLK OS 132

Location: the Norfolk coast offshore from Blakeney and Morston.

Habitats: the Point forms the climax to a lengthy shingle bar that extends westwards from Cley Beach. Areas of shingle and sand are overgrown, in parts, with dense patches of seablite (*Sueda*) and other low vegetation. There is a small plantation. The Harbour is a vast intertidal basin that exposes large areas of mud at low tide, with huge areas of saltmarsh.

Birds: Blakeney Point has a large colony of Common Terns, watched over by the National Trust warden. Among these birds are a few Little and Arctic Terns and, sometimes, a colony of Sandwich Terns. During the summer some areas are fenced off. In autumn the Point becomes one of the top migration spots in the country and many birders walk the whole way from Cley Beach to the Point and back, examining every bush along the way. Scarce migrants turn up every year, including Wryneck, Bluethroat and Barred Warbler.

Access: from Cley Beach car park walk west to the Point and back. Alternatively, in summer, take a boat from Morston Quay. In Blakeney itself there is a large quayside car park, from which a sea-wall leads out along the eastern shore of the Harbour.

Permits: not required.

BLACKTOFT SANDS, HUMBERSIDE OS 112

Location: this RSPB reserve lies where the Rivers Ouse and Trent meet to form the Humber, upstream from Hull to the north of Scunthorpe.

Habitat: a vast area of intertidal mud and extensive reed beds. Though a noted haunt of Pink-footed Geese and a good variety of duck for many years, it was always a difficult area to watch, with passage waders offering little more than fleeting glimpses in the distance. Then the RSPB arrived and created their Blacktoft Sands Reserve, with artificial lagoons and hides among the reeds, and the area was transformed. This is now a splendid place to watch a wide variety of different species.

Birds: in summer the reed beds are alive with Sedge and Reed Warblers, together with Water Rail and Bearded Tit. At this time the lagoons have several species of ducks and waders, including Little Ringed Plover. It is, however, during migration that Blacktoft really sparkles, with all the usual waders passing through in good numbers. These include Black-tailed Godwit, Ruff, Little Stint and Curlew Sandpiper, along with a scattering of rarities. Exotic wanderers such as Red-necked and Long-tailed Stints, and Semipalmated and Western Sandpipers may prove difficult to identify.

In winter there is usually a good collection of ducks together with the more regular waders, especially at high tide. Marsh Harriers are reasonably regular, as are Short-eared Owl, Marsh and Hen Harrier. Geese sometimes put in an appearance and, particularly early in the season, Bearded Tits are often very active.

Access: leave the M62 at Exit 36 to Goole and take the A161 southwards. After 2–2½ miles turn left to Reedness and on to Ousefleet. The reserve centre will be seen on the left, by a sharp right-hand turn in the road. Several hides overlook the lagoons.

Permits: open six days a week (not Tuesday at time of going to press) with a charge for non-RSPB members.

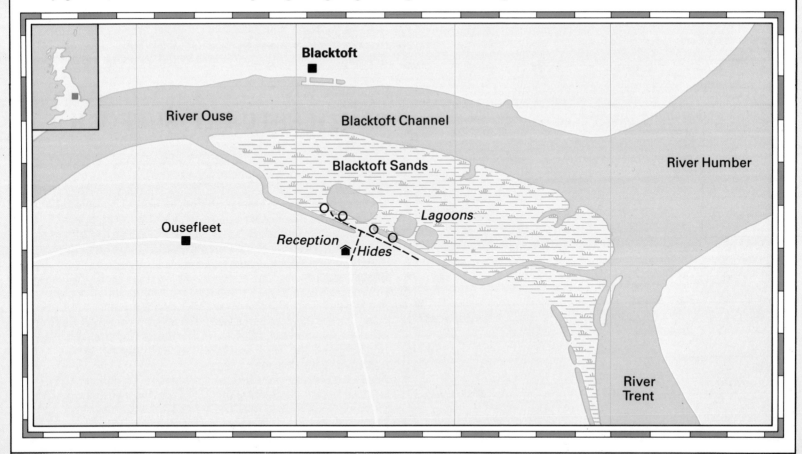

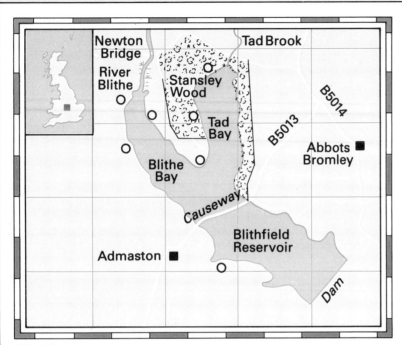

BLITHFIELD RESERVOIR, STAFFORDSHIRE OS 128

Location: 10 miles west of Burton-on-Trent.

Habitats: created in 1952, the natural banks offer varying amounts of muddy edge, depending on weather and season. By early autumn the mud attracts waders. In winter the shallows at the head of the reservoir are reflooded and are sometimes high enough to flood the surrounding grassland, offering fine feeding opportunities for wildfowl. The eastern shore has a conifer plantation and there is a mixed wood at the northern end of the reservoir.

Birds: one of the best reservoirs for birds in the country. The winter collection of ducks is always very impressive, with outstanding numbers of Mallard, Teal and Wigeon. There are also usually several of the scarcer duck species present, including Pintail, Goosander, Ruddy Duck and Goldeneye, together with a regular herd of Bewick's Swans. During passage periods waders and terns are regular and, in autumn, these include Green and Curlew Sandpipers, Little Stint and Black Tern, with Little Gulls regular.

Access: the B5013 northwards to Uttoxeter from Rugeley crosses the reservoir by a causeway that offers good views.

Permits: annual permits are issued by the West Midland Bird Club.

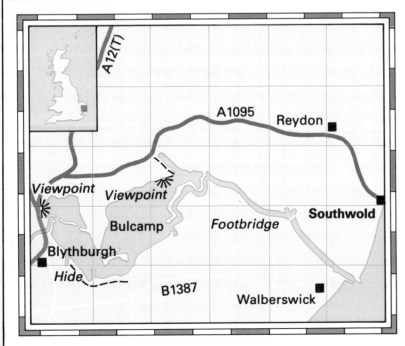

BLYTH ESTUARY, SUFFOLK

OS 156

Location: a partly reclaimed estuary on the Suffolk coast at Blythburgh, on the A12 south of Lowestoft.

Habitats: channelized for much of its lower course, the River Blyth has burst its banks to re-establish this estuary, which thus lies a little way inland rather than at the mouth of the river. It is an extensive area of intertidal mud banks with saltmarsh and reed beds on the southern shore. The surrounding farmland, heath and pine coverts are strictly out of bounds.

Birds: though terns and common waders breed here, spring and autumn passage periods are outstanding, with good numbers of Black-tailed Godwit and Spotted Redshank. Autumn brings Little Stint, Curlew Sandpiper and Greenshank, while in winter there are usually good numbers of Redshank, Bar-tailed Godwits, Marsh and Hen Harriers, and Short-eared Owls regularly quarter the surrounding rough fields.

Access: access is strictly limited. Just north of the village, there is a layby on the left hand side of the A12. Cross the road and view from the bank. Walk back toward The White Hart and take a track about 75m before the pub. A footpath leads to a hide among the reeds.

Permits: not required.

BRADWELL, ESSEX OS 168

Location: a surprisingly lonely area on the southern shore of the Blackwater estuary, 8½ miles north of Burnham-on-Crouch.

Habitats: a huge sea-wall separates a vast area of grazing marshes from the mud banks of the Dengie Flats. Here a group of enthusiasts have established and maintained the Bradwell Bird Observatory.

Birds: though a bird observatory with an inevitable bias toward migration periods, Bradwell is really better during the winter for general birdwatching. Then there are vast flocks of Brent Geese, wildfowl and waders. Grey Plover, Knot, Curlew, Turnstone and Dunlin are all very numerous. Hen Harriers and Short-eared Owls are often present and Merlins regularly winter. Just a short way along the shore to the south, a good variety of breeding waders – Redshank, Ringed Plover and Oystercatcher – can be observed in summer. Common Terns also breeds there.

Access: from Maldon or South Woodham Ferrers, follow signs to Southminster and then to Bradwell. In Bradwell-on-Sea take a road right to a car park by Eastlands Farm and then walk 1 mile to St Peter's-on-the-Wall and the Observatory.

Permits: not required.

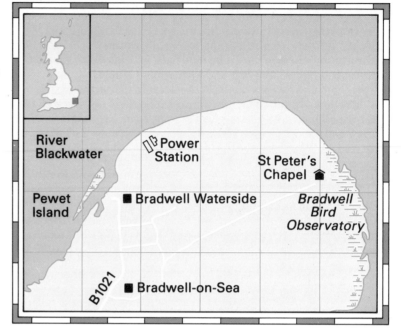

BROWNSEA ISLAND, DORSET

OS 195

Location: the largest of several islands in Poole Harbour, near Bournemouth.

Habitats: large areas of intertidal mud and sand, and heathland. Once a derelict and overgrown privately-owned 'sanctuary', Brownsea has been converted into a first-class bird reserve.

Birds: in summer the lagoon holds a colony of Sandwich Terns and there is a large heronry. Nightjar, Dartford Warbler and feral Golden Pheasant breed on the heaths. Waders seen in spring and autumn, include Little Stint, Curlew Sandpiper, Black-tailed Godwit, Greenshank and Spotted Redshank. Avocets frequently winter here.

In winter there is a good chance of a scarce grebe, a diver or Red-breasted Merganser, while the population of Black-tailed Godwits is one of the most important in the country. Ruff are also frequently present, but all of these birds must be sought from the mainland because Brownsea is closed from September to March.

Access: by regular boat from Sandbanks on Poole Quay.

Permits: on arrival.

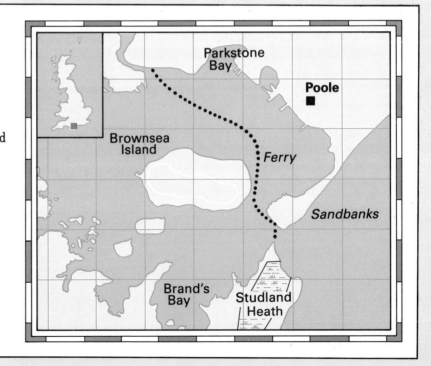

BREYDON WATER, NORFOLK OS 134

Location: this 'inland' estuary lies west of Great Yarmouth, the mouth of several rivers that drain the Norfolk Broads.

Habitats: huge area of intertidal mud flats, with low-lying grazing marshes intersected by dykes and with patches of mud.

Birds: there may be good numbers of waders in the northern part, with roosts easily viewable from the area west of the railway station. The most abundant species are Grey Plover, Knot, Redshank, Curlew and Dunlin. Spring and autumn passage can be productive, with Avocet, Whimbrel, both godwits, Ruff, Spotted Redshank all regular, and rarer visitors, such as Broad-billed Sandpiper, a possibility. Other reasonably regular migrants include Spoonbill and Black Tern, both in spring and autumn.

Many of the more exciting winter birds frequent the marshes south of the estuary where harriers, Rough-legged Buzzard (in some winters), Merlin, Peregrine, Short-eared Owl, both Bewick's and Whooper Swans, Twite, Snow Bunting and a regular, if elusive, flock of Lapland Buntings may be found. This huge area is well worth the effort of exploration and, though there are usually birders present at weekends, the weekday watcher may well walk for miles without seeing another soul.

The RSPB reserve at Berney Marshes is fast becoming one of the outstanding wetland reserves in East Anglia, with some really good breeding populations.

Access: from Great Yarmouth railway station walk along the wall westwards to two hides. Views are perfectly satisfactory without entering. A footpath along the southern shore starts at the Haven Bridge, but many birders prefer to start at Burgh Castle at the head of the estuary.

Permits: available for the hides, but casual observers usually do not bother to enter. The RSPB reserve is best approached by railway at Berney Arms Station.

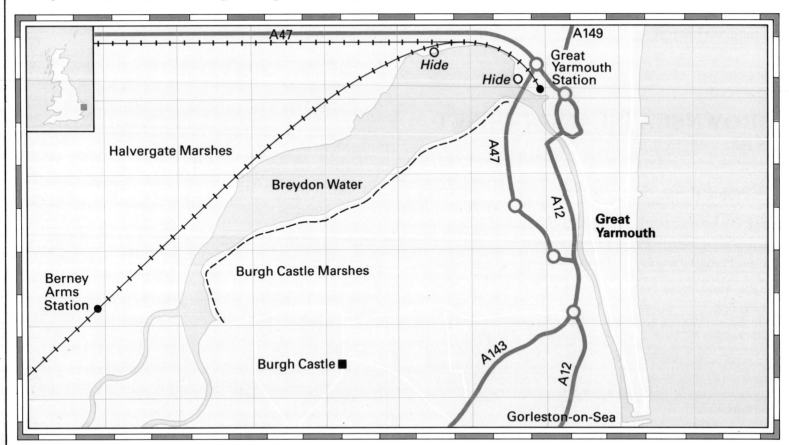

BULLERS OF BUCHAN, GRAMPIAN OS 30

Location: these cliffs lie on the east coast about 23 miles north of Aberdeen and 7 miles south of Peterhead.

Habitats: the area of sea cliffs here is one of the most accessible of seabird colonies, while the little wooded valley behind Cruden Bay is often worth searching for small migrants, especially in autumn.

Birds: though there is nothing rare or unusual here, Bullers of Buchan is a delightful seabird colony, with thousands of birds wheeling and calling at close range. All the usual species are present, including Guillemot, Razorbill and Puffin, Kittiwake, Shag and Fulmar. Many birders rank these cliffs as some of the best for seabirds in mainland Scotland.

Access: stop on the A975 north of Aberdeen just beyond Cruden Bay, where a track leads to Robie's Haven. Check that you have the correct track with the OS map. Another track leads via the wooded valley to Port Errol.

Permits: not required.

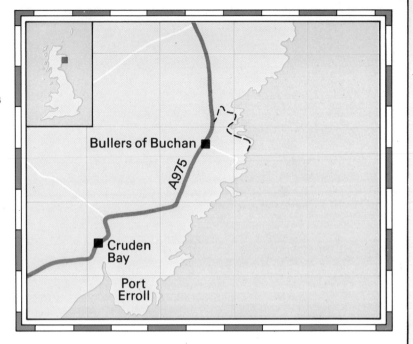

BURRY INLET, WEST GLAMORGAN OS 159

Location: about 7 miles west of Swansea, and partially enclosed by the Gower Peninsula to the south.

Habitats: the inlet is the huge intertidal estuary of the river Loughor. The sand and mud here attract a huge population of birds, but access is made awkward by the presence of large areas of saltmarsh. At the estuary mouth is Whiteford Burrows, a large dune system with marram grass and plantations of conifers.

Birds: primarily a winter birdwatching site, known internationally for huge numbers of Oystercatchers. Knot and Dunlin are plentiful, as are Curlew, Redshank and Turnstone. Other birds include Brent and Eider duck, a few scarcer grebes, both godwits and even the occasional overwintering Greenshank. Viewing is difficult in passage periods though.

Access: good views can be obtained along the B4295 west of Penclawdd, notably at Crofty. Access to Whiteford Burrows is restricted to a marked path that runs from Cwm Ivy (where there is a National Nature Reserve Information Centre) through the pine woods. Opposite Berges Island is a hide that is often good on a rising tide. Continue to Whiteford Point for the high-tide wader roost.

Permits: not necessary, except off the footpaths at the Point.

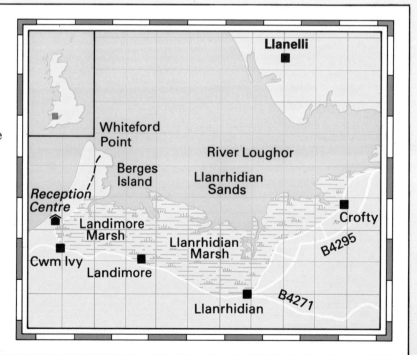

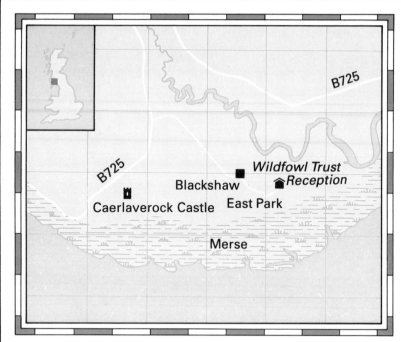

CAERLAVEROCK, DUMFRIES AND GALLOWAY OS 84 & 85

Location: this famous marsh lies on the northern shore of the Solway Firth about 9 miles to the south of Dumfries.

Habitats: the intertidal mud banks of this part of the Solway are backed by extensive areas of saltmarshes, known locally as 'merse'. Sea walls protect an area of farmland divided by well-kept hedges and fences. There are two artificial pools in the grounds of the Wildfowl Trust.

Birds: the merse is the winter home of the entire population of Barnacle Geese that breed on the Arctic island of Spitsbergen. Up to 10,000 can be seen throughout the winter, though in March they split into smaller groups. Also present are even larger numbers of Pink-footed Geese. Like the Greylags they prefer feeding on farmland. There are plenty of ducks and waders in winter here with attendant Peregrine, Merlin and Hen Harrier. Also good during passage periods.

Access: from Dumfries southward on the B725 and park by Caerlaverock Castle. Take a minor road right to the Wildfowl Trust Centre at East Park Farm.

Permits: admission fee at the Wildfowl Trust Centre.

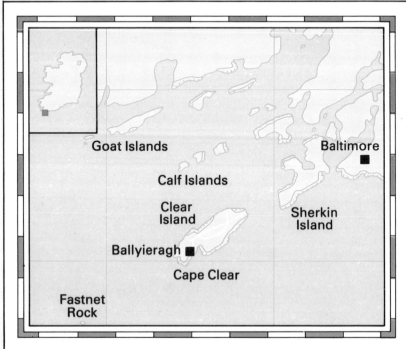

CAPE CLEAR, CO. CORK, IRISH REPUBLIC IOS½ 24

Location: the extreme south-west of Ireland, facing the open Atlantic, 50 miles west of Cork.

Habitats: an inhabited island with a crofting and fishing community. There are moors, cliffs and comparatively little cover. It is the geographical position rather than specific habitats that gives Clear its excellent reputation as a birdwatching site.

Birds: breeding birds include Black Guillemot and Chough, while migration brings a wide variety of scarce and rare species. One of the best seawatch stations around the shores of the British Isles, the current fashion for ocean-going small boat trips in autumn can trace its origins to the pioneering work of the Cape Clear Bird Observatory.

From the southern headlands of Pointanbullig, Blananarragaun and Pointabullaun autumn seawatchers may observe spectacular movements of shearwaters, including Great, Cory's and Sooty. There are vast numbers of Manx Shearwaters, together with petrels, Great Skuas, Gannets and the odd albatross. There are records of Little Shearwater and claims of Wilson's Petrel.

Access: by boat from Baltimore, about 7 miles south-west of Skibbereen.

CAIRNGORMS, HIGHLAND OS 35 & 36

Location: this vast area, covering 180 square miles, is centred on the growing holiday resort of Aviemore.

Habitats: as diverse as it is large, this area offers the visiting birder the chance of a lengthy holiday of exploration, with a host of excellent birds to find. There are grassy fields and even hedgerows along the banks of the River Spey, but these quickly give way to more rocky areas of heath, with deciduous and coniferous trees. There are remnants of the old Caledonian forest of Scots Pine (particularly at Rothiemurchus) as well as modern plantations. At higher altitudes open heather moorland becomes dominant and this gradually becomes more sparse until on the high tops of Cairn Gorm one finds a sort of Scottish tundra with rocks and dwarf vegetation.

Birds: essentially a summer haunt of breeding birds, many in need of protection, so exact directions cannot always be given. There are Golden Eagles and Peregrines here, though the only 'public' site for either is the cliffs above Craigellachie where the falcon is frequently seen. The elusive Honey Buzzard, Goshawk and Greenshank also breed here, along with the more common Black Grouse, Capercaillie, Scottish Crossbill and Crested Tit. Finally, on the high tops, there are Ptarmigan, Snow Bunting and Dotterel. The region has, in recent years, been the home of breeding Temminck's Stint, Wood and Green Sandpipers, as well as Brambling, Lapland Bunting and Shore Lark.

Access: a good map, compass and sensible waterproof clothing are essential. Start at Aviemore and take the road to Loch Morlich for the old Scots Pine forests. Continue up to the ski-lift station and, if the weather is good, take a lift to the top for high-level birds. Further south take the track starting at Feshiebridge along Glen Feshie; this penetrates remote country and for the energetic there is a climb up Carn Ban Mor. For those who prefer wild, unfrequented country an approach from the south via Deeside is charming.

Permits: none required.

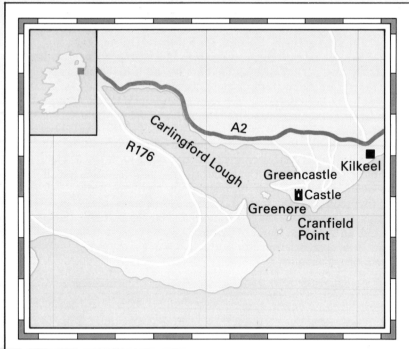

CARLINGFORD LOUGH, CO. DOWN, NORTHERN IRELAND

OSNI 29

Location: this inlet lies on the east coast of Ireland and stretches inland as far as Newry, forming the boundary between Northern Ireland and the Irish Republic.

Habitats: less an estuary than a sunken valley carved by a former glacier. Intertidal areas are thus confined to the narrow inner area toward Newry and a large bay west of Greencastle Point.

Birds: Curlew, Redshank, Dunlin and other waders are numerous, especially in winter. Several of the more widespread species of duck reach good numbers, though the flock of Scaup is fast declining. Brent Geese also winter here. In summer there are sizeable colonies of terns on Green Island, which is an RSPB reserve. These include Common, Arctic, Sandwich and the rare Roseate Tern. Black Guillemot breed at Cranfield Point.

Access: the inner estuary can be seen from the roads that line each side. The eastern one, the A2, leads to the largest area of mud viewable from Greencastle. This is also the best viewpoint for the birds of Green Island, which is out of bounds.

Permits: not required; not available for Green Island.

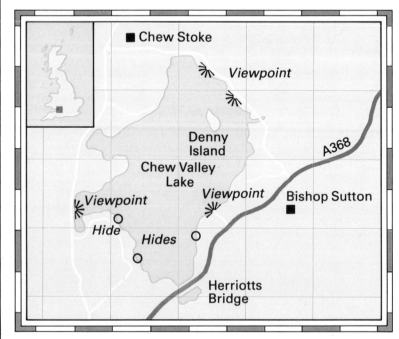

CHEW VALLEY LAKE, AVON

OS 172 & 182

Location: this large artificial lake lies about 5 miles south of Bristol, between the city and the Mendip Hills.

Habitats: the reservoir was flooded in 1953. It is shallow in many places with gently shelving banks. There are reed beds as well as areas of woodland and bushes.

Birds: winter brings an excellent collection of wildfowl that regularly includes Bewick's Swan, together with good flocks of Wigeon, Shoveler, Pochard and Tufted Duck. Ruddy Duck are present throughout the year and Garganey regularly spend the summer here. Less numerous in winter, but nevertheless regular, are Goldeneye, Goosander, Golden Plover and Dunlin. Other waders, including Ruff, Greenshank, Spotted Redshank, Black-tailed Godwit and Little Stint, are regular on passage, especially in autumn. Terns also pass through, Black Terns being regular both in spring and autumn.

Access: the A368 crosses the south-eastern arm of the reservoir near Herriot's Bridge. Public roads allow viewing at many spots. There is a nature reserve at Herriott's Bridge and there are several hides along the southern and western shores.

Permits: not required.

CHICHESTER HARBOUR, WEST SUSSEX OS 197

Location: this huge area lies between Portsmouth and Chichester, alongside Langstone Harbour, which is in Hampshire (*see page* 61).

Habitats: an intertidal basin that, at low water, exposes a huge expanse of mud. The central channels remain full of water, even at low tide, and the surroundings are a mixture of urban, suburban and rural landscapes, but Chichester is far more popular with the yachting fraternity than Langstone where the birds are generally less disturbed.

Birds: wildfowl and waders in autumn and winter are the main attraction. Brent Geese, numbering up to 10,000, can be seen, along with good numbers of ducks, including Pintail and Wigeon. Red-breasted Merganser and Goldeneye are regular along with the occasional scarce grebe, though these species are more often found at Langstone. Waders include good numbers of Knot and Grey Plover, together with both godwits.

Access: leave Havant and the A27 southwards on the A3023 to Langstone Bridge, where good views can be obtained. Continue to Hayling Island, turn left to North Hayling and take the road to the sea-wall at Tye. Continue to South Hayling and to Black Point.

Permits: not required.

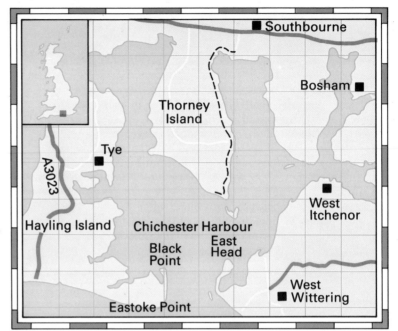

CLIFFE AND HALSTOW, KENT

OS 178

Location: on the southern shore of the Thames estuary to the north of the Medway towns of Chatham, Gillingham and Rochester.

Habitats: from Cliffe to Allhallows lies a huge area of low-lying grazing land, separated from intertidal mud banks by a large sea-wall. Inland, there are bushy hedgerows and woods. Both the clay pits at Cliffe and the mudflats at Yantlett Creek attract birds.

Birds: waders on passage are excellent, with good numbers at Cliffe Pools, including Little Stint, Curlew and Wood Sandpipers, Ruff, Black-tailed Godwit and often a rarity. Black Terns are regular, both in spring and autumn. In winter White-fronted Geese can be seen, along with Bewick's Swans and a good variety of duck on the Thames. The nearby RSPB heronry is worth a visit. Merlin, Hen Harrier and Short-eared Owl all visit during hard weather.

Access: from Cliffe village follow a track westwards to the pools and then turn right out to the coastguard cottages. Several pools can be seen from this footpath as well as from other tracks to the south. St Mary's and Egypt Bay are reached by turning northwards ½ mile east of High Halstow to Decoy Farm and Swigshole. Walk to the sea-wall. Northward Hill RSPB Reserve is famous for its heronry.

Permits: required only for the RSPB reserve.

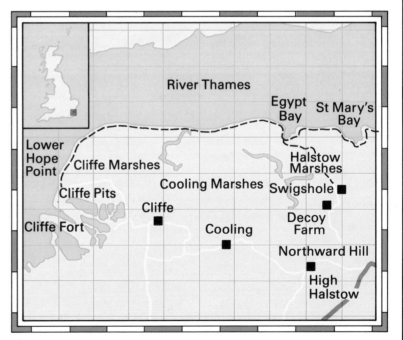

27

CLEY, NORFOLK OS 133

Location: the North Norfolk coast 1 mile to the east of Blakeney.

Habitats: an outstanding and varied wetland on an excellent coast.

Birds: Cley has long been regarded as the best birding spot in Britain. In summer, there are breeding Bittern, Bearded Tit, Avocet, and Sedge and Reed Warblers. But it is the passage periods that bring peak numbers of both birds and birders. In spring, waders include Kentish Plover and Temminck's Stint, Spoonbills are often present, and Black-tailed Godwit, Ruff and Garganey may or may not stay to breed. In autumn Greenshank, Wood Sandpiper, Little Stint, Curlew Sandpiper and Spotted Redshank are more or less continually present, along with minor rarities. All can be seen from the hides opposite the warden's house. Seawatching is also good. A northerly wind may produce Manx Shearwater, Arctic, Great and Pomarine Skuas, Gannet and divers, but several other scarcer seabirds are also seen every year. Small migrants turn up around the village. Barred Warbler is regular every autumn, along with many of the commoner warblers, chats and flycatchers.

In winter, Brent and Greylag Geese are plentiful and there are good flocks of waders and gulls, the latter including a regular Glaucous Gull. Shore Lark and Snow Bunting are also seen.

Access: Cley Marshes are a reserve of the Norfolk Naturalists' Trust and are open daily from April to October except Mondays. There are well-marked paths, hides and a visitor centre. Cley Coastguards is an excellent public spot. A small car park giving access to the East Bank – a great meeting place for birders. From here there are excellent views over the reed beds and, near the shore, over Arnold's Marsh, one of the best wader pools in Britain.

Permits: available at 10.00 a.m. from the Norfolk Naturalists' Trust centre on the A149 east of the village. Essential for autumn visits.

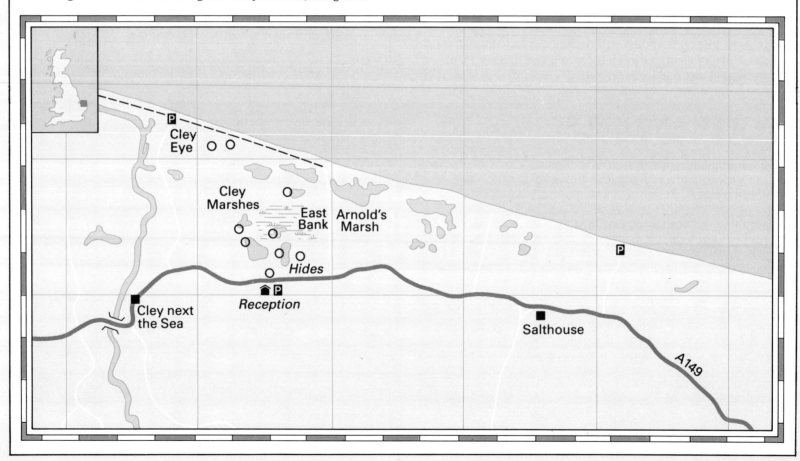

CLO MOR, HIGHLAND OS 9

Location: these fearsome cliffs are more or less the north-western tip of mainland Scotland near Cape Wrath.

Habitats: the cliffs are the highest on the British mainland and boast a major and spectacular seabird colony. Inland, the rolling moors are bleak and hostile, but hold exciting birds in summer.

Birds: the usual collection of cliff-nesting seabirds can be seen, but in fantastic numbers and against a spectacular backdrop. The colonies of Guillemot and Puffin are huge, but there are Razorbills, Black Guillemots and Kittiwakes along with Fulmars and a continuous offshore movement of Gannets that do not, however, breed here. Peregrines do breed, however, and there are Golden Eagle and Ptarmigan, Greenshank and Great Skua here as well.

Access: take the foot ferry across the Kyle of Durness and then the minibus towards Cape Wrath. Get off at a track that leads northwards to Kearvaig and walk to the right along the cliff tops to Clo Mor. It is possible to return to the road 'overland' via Loch Inshore, but this is tough country and should be treated with the respect it merits. Make sure you are equipped with proper weatherproof hiking gear, map, compass and other survival equipment.

Permits: not required.

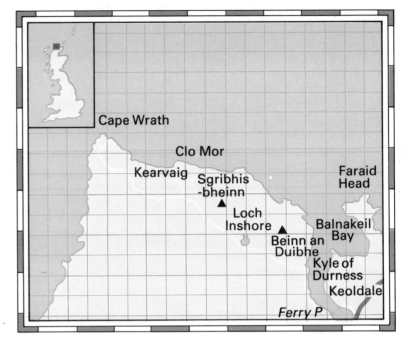

CLUMBER AND THE DUKERIES, NOTTINGHAM OS 120

Location: between M1 and A1 north of Nottingham is a series of large mansions and estates collectively known as the Dukeries.

Habitats: parkland, ornamental lakes, woodland and estate farms.

Birds: the Clumber-Welbeck area is a stronghold of the Honey Buzzard, a fact which remained unpublished until quite recently. Even now birders should restrict their activities to the roads and other areas of public access. May to August is the best time. Otherwise there is a good cross section of woodland birds that includes Sparrowhawk, all three woodpeckers, the commoner warblers, Hawfinch and Redstart. The Hawfinches, as elsewhere, are easiest to see in winter.

Access: from the B6034 south of Worksop turn west towards Norton. The lakes of Welbeck Park are on the right, and there is parking space for a few cars. Here there are good views across the water to the woods beyond for soaring Honey Buzzard. Return to the B6005 and cross it to Carburton and fork right to the chapel in Clumber Park where woodland can be explored.

Permits: parking fee at Clumber.

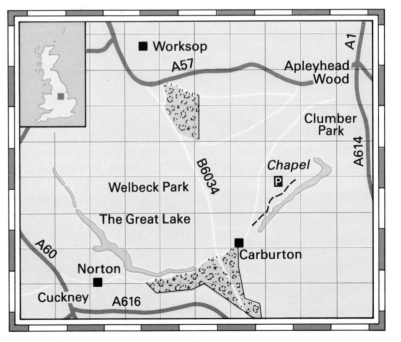

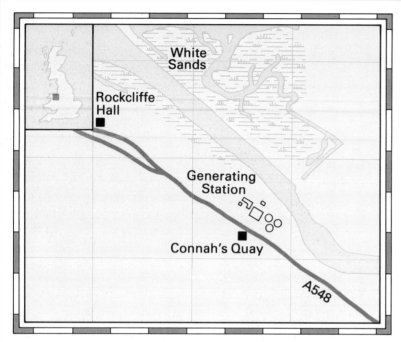

CONNAH'S QUAY, CLWYD OS 117

Location: this area lies at the head of the Dee Estuary about 7 miles to the west of Chester in a predominantly industrial landscape.

Habitats: the Central Electricity Generating Board has declared a large area surrounding its power station a nature reserve. It includes fields, saltmarshes and intertidal mud. A 'scrape' has been created – an area of shallow, brackish water and mud dotted with small islands to attract breeding birds – and there are hides and a reserve centre.

Birds: waders use the pools here as a high-tide roost and are best at the highest tides, but there are always good numbers of these birds on passage and in winter. Spotted Redshank are something of a local speciality, especially in winter, and in autumn Little Stint, Curlew Sandpiper, Ruff and Black-tailed Godwit are regular. Ducks include most of the species found on the estuary, including Pintail, Wigeon, Shoveler, Goldeneye and Red-breasted Merganser, and both Peregrine and Merlin are regular winter visitors.

Access: from the A548 at Connah's Quay Power Station.

Permits: are essential and may be obtained from The Station Manager, Connah's Quay Power Station, Connah's Quay, Deeside; or from the Deeside Naturalist's Society, Melrose, 38 Kelsterton Road, Connah's Quay, Clwyd. There is an open day once a month.

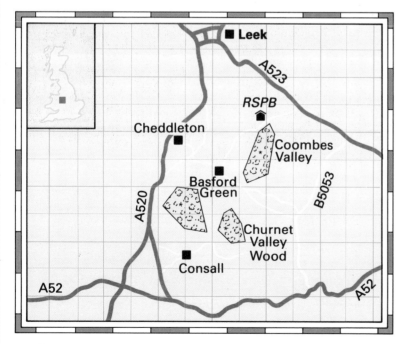

COOMBES VALLEY, STAFFORDSHIRE OS 118

Location: to the south of Leek the RSPB has established three reserves centred on its original Coombes Valley site. They can all be visited in a day: Coombes Valley, Rough Knipe, Booth's Wood. Stoke-on-Trent is about 13 miles to the south-west.

Habitats: this area is deeply dissected by steep-sided valleys with rough, tumbling streams. The valley sides are covered with mixed deciduous woodland, with a surrounding network of grassy fields broken by more extensive areas of woodlands and scrub.

Birds: a typical woodland fauna exists here and a visit to this site offers a chance to enjoy beautiful walks and a day of pleasant, relaxed birding. Birds include all three British species of woodpecker, Pied Flycatcher, Wood Warbler, Tawny and Long-eared Owls, Tree Pipit and Sparrowhawk, plus Dipper, Kingfisher and Grey Wagtail.

Access: leave Leek southwards on the A523. Turn left signposted Apesford and the reserve entrance is on the left after about 1 mile. The two other reserves lie off the A520, turning left to Consall and then following a footpath. Coombes Valley is open every day except Tuesday and there is a nature trail and hides.

Permits: free on arrival.

COPINSAY, ORKNEY OS 6

Location: this small island lies to the east of the Orkney Mainland about 2 miles south-east of Point of Ayre.

Habitats: this is a mainly cliff-bound island, with a green interior and a low-lying rocky shoreline that is neither isolated nor exposed to the prevailing westerly winds.

Birds: Copinsay is an RSPB reserve purchased in memory of James Fisher, the ornithologist and bird publicist/author who had a profound influence on 20th-century British ornithology. Its cliffs hold major seabird colonies, including 15,000 pairs of Guillemot, along with Razorbill, Black Guillemot and Puffin. There are countless Kittiwake and Fulmar, a large colony of Shag and a colony of Arctic Tern.

Access: by boat from Skaill, which lies north of Point of Ayre. Contact Mr S. Foubister (Tel: 085 674252) to make arrangements for a day trip at any time. Best in May and June. Visitors are requested to take great care when approaching the cliff tops.

Permits: not required.

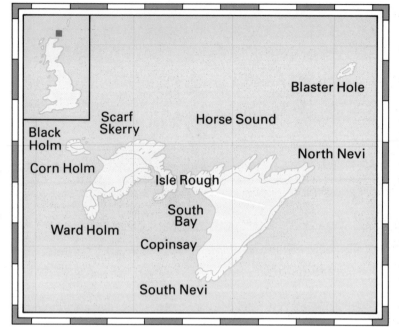

COQUET ISLAND, NORTHUMBERLAND OS 81

Location: this RSPB reserve lies just off the coast of Northumberland, opposite the village of Amble (just north of Hauxley: *see page* 48) and near the mouth of the River Coquet, about 24 miles to the north of Newcastle.

Habitat: this is a relatively low island with a grassy flat top that, while being quite unsuited to cliff-nesting seabirds, does provide a home for large colonies of terns and other birds, similar to those of the Farne Islands (*see page* 40) about 24 miles to the north.

Birds: among the terns that breed here are large colonies of both Common and Arctic, along with more densely packed Sandwich Terns. A few pairs of Roseate Terns still breed each year but it is difficult to pick them out from among the milling masses of the more abundant and widespread species. The top of the island offers ideal conditions for Puffins to excavate their burrows. Several hundred of these attractive little auks breed here, as do a number of Eider.

Access: from the A1068 to Amble. Arrange with the boatman Mr Easton (Tel: 0665 710384 or 712460) to take a trip around the island.

Permits: no landing is allowed, but the birds can be seen well from the boat.

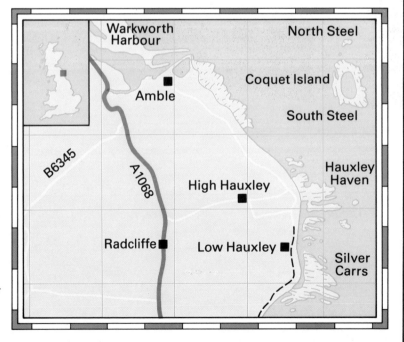

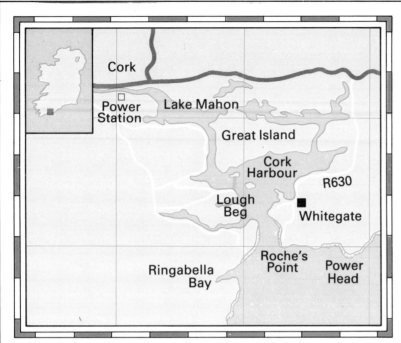

CORK HARBOUR, CO. CORK, IRISH REPUBLIC IOS½ 25

Location: immediately south of Cork on the southern coast.
Habitats: this is a deep inlet with a maze of channels and backwaters similar to those found along the coasts of south Devon and Cornwall. Large intertidal areas exist, but are separated from one another by narrow, steep-sided shorelines.
Birds: this is one of the finest wildfowl and wader sites in Ireland with several species reaching significant numbers. Ducks are often abundant, with the Shelduck flock being, at one time, the largest in the country. There are also Wigeon, Teal, and a regular flock of Pintail. Mostly these are concentrated in the North Channel that extends west to east at the top of the estuary. Here too are many waders, including an autumn roost of Oystercatcher as well as Dunlin, Redshank and an important flock of Black-tailed Godwit. Waders are generally more widespread and less concentrated than ducks. Cork also has the largest gull roost on the southern coastline and unusual species may occasionally be found alongside the commoner ones.
Access: the whole area can be explored via public roads from Cork, starting at Tivoli and Lough Beg in the west.
Permits: not required.

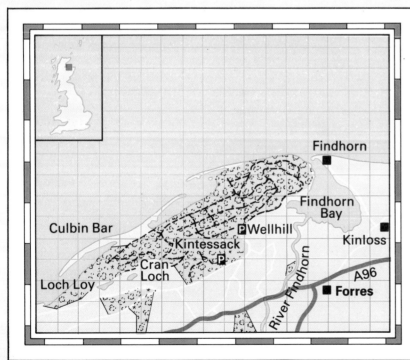

CULBIN BAR AND FINDHORN BAY, GRAMPIAN & HIGHLAND

OS 27
Location: on the Moray Firth, 4 miles north of Forres.
Habitats: an offshore sand bar protects a large dune system that has been planted with conifers. To the east, Findhorn Bay is an almost land-locked intertidal basin.
Birds: Crested Tit and Scottish Crossbill are present, along with Capercaillie, Long-eared Owl and Buzzard. The shoreline supports a few Eider, Ringed Plover and terns. On passage waders are often good, especially at Findhorn Bay, where Greenshank, Spotted Redshank and Whimbrel are regular. The sea in winter is excellent for divers and ducks, and on occasions huge numbers of Scoter, Velvet Scoter and Long-tailed Duck may be observed.
Access: explore a network of tracks through the forest by leaving Forres westward on the A96 and taking a minor road north to Kintessack. Continue to Welhill Gate; park and walk from there. Findhorn Bay is also reached from Forres by following the B9011 east and north to Findhorn and viewing from the road.
Permits: not required.

DORNOCH FIRTH, HIGHLAND

OS 21

Location: on the east coast of Scotland 28 miles north of Inverness.

Habitats: extensive intertidal areas along both shorelines, mainly in large bays, but fortunately the best birds are concentrated on the sea at the north, and on the small Skibo Inlet.

Birds: waders and wildfowl are the main attraction, with a significant population of seaducks occurring regularly at the mouth of the firth northwards to Embo. These include Long-tailed Duck, Eider and both British species of scoter, along with Merganser and Goldeneye, and reasonably regular King Eider and Surf Scoter. Winter waders include the more common species, along with regular Purple Sandpiper. Hen Harrier, Peregrine and Short-eared Owl are sometimes present at this season. Passage waders are not outstanding, but Osprey is regular in summer and autumn and Arctic Tern sometimes abundant; they breed at Loch Fleet (*see page 66*) a little way to the north.

Access: the surrounding roads offer good views, particularly at Tain and the Skibo Inlet, which is reached via the A9, turning southwards at Clashmore to Meikle Ferry. Embo lies north of Dornoch, east of the A9. Loch Eye should not be missed in winter.

Permits: none required.

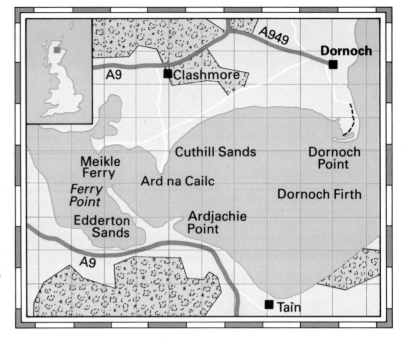

DRAYCOTE WATER, WARWICKSHIRE   OS 151

Location: this large reservoir lies about 4 miles south of Rugby off the M45.

Habitats: covering 700 acres Draycote offers waterbirds a refuge in what is otherwise a rather barren area. It has part natural and part concrete-lined banks, with a shallow area in the north. It is widely used for water sports, but still attracts birds.

Birds: this is essentially a winter site, with ducks the main attraction. There are decent numbers of Wigeon and Shoveler, and good-sized flocks of the more common diving ducks. It is, however, the possibility of seeing the less usual species, such as Scoter, Scaup, Smew and Goosander, that makes this reservoir attractive to local birders. Spring and autumn passage bring terns, including Black Terns, and there are a few waders in autumn.

Access: for the non-regular visitor there is access from the A45 or the A426 via a public footpath that runs along the northern shoreline between Thurlaston and Toft. This passes a hide. Regulars can obtain a permit that enables them to drive.

Permits: available from Kites Hardwick garage nearby and from Severn-Trent Water, Avon House, Demountford Way, Cannon Park, Coventry CV4 7EJ.

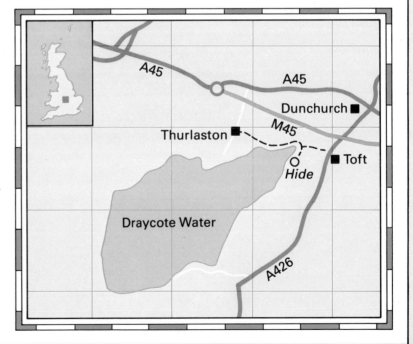

DUNGENESS, KENT OS 189

Location: the peninsula extends into the English Channel, 3 miles south-east of Lydd.

Habitats: low-lying shingle that has been excavated for gravel forming extensive freshwater lakes. The point attracts hosts of migrants. There is a well-run bird observatory and a large RSPB reserve.

Birds: in winter the gravel pits are a haunt of ducks, divers, waders and gulls. Smew, Goldeneye and Goosander are frequently present, as are divers (mostly Red-throated, but sometimes Black-throated and Great Northern) and Black-necked Grebes.

During passage periods waders and terns are usually good, with Little Gulls in autumn. Gulls and terns frequent 'The Patch', the warm-water outlets of the nuclear power station. Small birds include all the usual warblers, chats and flycatchers together with a few major rarities. Seabird passage regularly produces skuas, shearwaters, Gannet, terns and auks, with Pomarine Skua in the first half of May. In summer, there are good breeding colonies of Common and Sandwich Terns, with a few Mediterranean Gulls. Black Redstarts breed on the power station and a few pairs of Wheatear breed at specially created nest sites.

Access: several roads lead southwards from the A259 to Dungeness. The road between Lydd and Lydd-on-Sea passes the best gravel pits and the RSPB reserve lies to the west of this at Boulderwall Farm. It is open daily except Tuesday throughout the year and has four hides overlooking the main water. Dungeness proper is reached by following signs over a private road that starts near 'The Pilot' pub.

The bird observatory is situated at the end of a small terrace of houses and is reached by taking a left at the old lighthouse. It offers accommodation and information, and holds regular open days. The power station must be approached via the old lighthouse, *not* the access road near the pits. 'The Patch' can be reached on foot.

Permits: only required for the RSPB reserve.

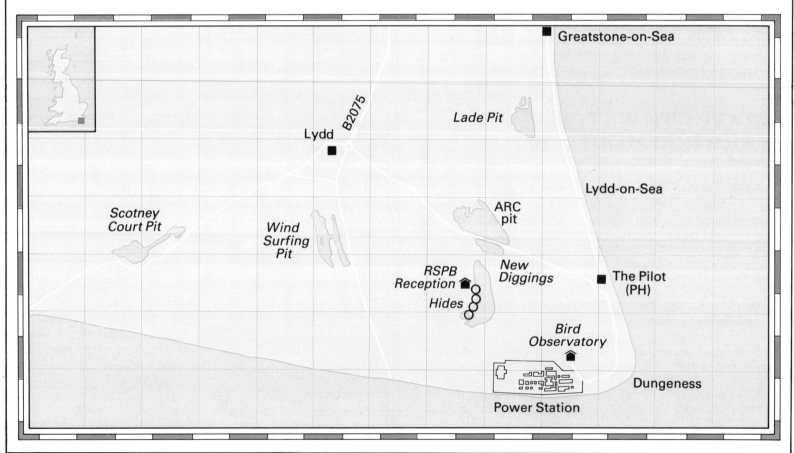

DUNNET HEAD, HIGHLAND OS 12

Location: the most northerly point of mainland Scotland.

Habitats: this is a rocky promontory extending northwards into the Pentland Firth, with extensive areas of cliffs in the north and east. The top is rolling rather than rugged, with areas of moorland broken by many lochs. To the south is the sandy Dunnet Bay, with St John's Loch to the west.

Birds: a fine collection of breeding seabirds, including Guillemot, Razorbill, Black Guillemot, Puffin and Kittiwake. There are usually Gannets and Great Skuas offshore and the doves are probably the genuine wild Rock Dove. The sandy bay to the south has Arctic Tern and Great Northern Diver in summer and is a regular haunt of divers and seaducks in winter. Other ducks, together with Whooper Swan, can be found at this time on St John's Loch.

Access: leave the A836 at Dunnet on the B855 to Dunnet Head, where there is a car park a short distance from the lighthouse. Walk north and east for the cliffs, but be careful. The lochs on the Head can be seen from the road or via paths. The A836 east of Dunnet passes St John's Loch, while to the west there is a parking area at the north-eastern corner of Dunnet Bay.

Permits: not required.

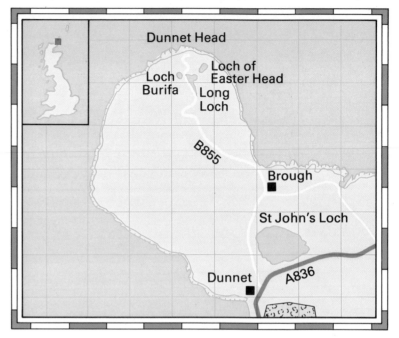

DYFI ESTUARY, DYFED & GWYNEDD OS 135

Location: below Machynlleth and Aberdyfi (formerly called Aberdovey).

Habitats: a large intertidal area with good areas of mud. The northern shoreline is steep, but to the south are large areas of saltmarsh backed by grazing marshes. Cors Fochno (Borth Bog), with extensive sand dunes all but closes the river mouth.

Birds: in winter a small flock of Greenland White-fronted Geese can often be seen from the northern shore along the A493 at the head of the estuary. There are also good flocks of Wigeon, Red-breasted Merganser and Goldeneye. Birds of prey include Hen Harrier and Merlin. Divers, mainly Red-throated, may sometimes be seen at the estuary mouth, but are always present offshore. There are some waders but gulls may be more interesting during passages.

Access: near the mouth at Ynyslas is a National Nature Reserve information centre with good views over estuary and sea. There is further access on the south shore by following the footpath along the bank of the Afon Leri where it crosses the B4353 just over ½ mile east of Ynyslas. The A493 along the northern shore will produce geese and ducks, but the views are too distant for much else.

Permits: not required.

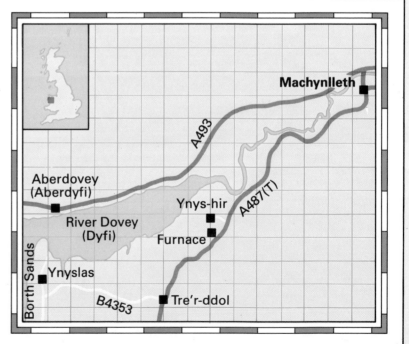

35

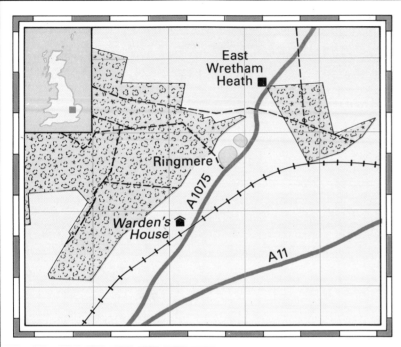

EAST WRETHAM HEATH, NORFOLK OS 144

Location: this area of Breckland lies north of Thetford along the A1075.

Habitat: originally a stony wasteland of infertile soils grazed by sheep, Breckland has been broken up by the planting of Scots pine windbrakes and more recently by extensive conifer plantations and conversion to arable farmland. Here and there, mainly in nature reserves, areas similar to the original landscape can be found.

Birds: this Norfolk Naturalists' Trust Reserve holds a cross section of the birds for which Breckland is best known. There is not, however, a single area left where all of the specialities can be seen, so dashing around is usually a necessary ingredient of a day in the Brecks. Here there is a good cross-section of heath and woodland specialities. Breckland is best known for Stone-curlew, Crossbill, Woodlark and the all-but-gone Red-backed Shrike.

Access: from Thetford northwards on the A11 and take the A1075. Stop at the first house on the left after the railway where the warden will issue permits from 10.00 a.m. (except Tuesdays). The reserve lies some 2 miles north on the left and is well signposted.

Permits: as above for a small charge.

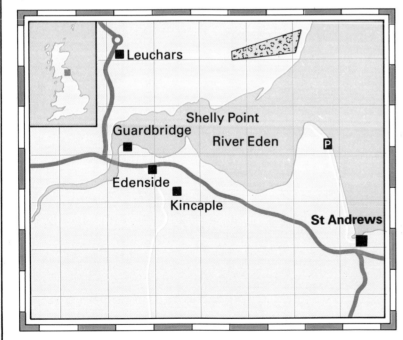

EDEN ESTUARY, FIFE OS 59

Location: this site lies on the east coast of Scotland immediately north of the famous Royal & Ancient golf course at St Andrews.

Habitats: this is, by Scottish standards, a small estuary that enables the visitor to see most of the birds that frequent the intertidal banks of mud. There are extensive areas of dunes at the mouth and a rocky shoreline at St Andrews.

Birds: the Eden is one of the very best of Scottish estuaries for waders and, in autumn in particular, there are really good numbers of several species, including Greenshank as well as Black-tailed and Bar-tailed Godwits. In winter, too, there are good numbers of waders, with Grey Plover and Black-tailed Godwit being notable for Scotland. At this season there are also good concentrations of seaducks, divers and grebes at the estuary mouth.

Access: there is a road from St Andrews northwards along the coast to the estuary mouth at Out Head, from where there are excellent views of the sea and estuary. At the head of the estuary there are good views from the bridge where the A91 crosses the river at Guardbridge.

Permits: though a large area of the estuary is a local nature reserve, permits are not required to view from the locations described above.

ELMLEY MARSHES, KENT OS 178

Location: on the southern shore of the Isle of Sheppey in north Kent, 4 miles north-east of Sittingbourne.

Habitats: the Sheppey shore of the Swale is a maze of rough grazing land, broken here and there by large 'fleets' – old backwaters that have been reclaimed from the estuary. The RSPB has established its Elmley Reserve here and created a large floodwater that now acts as a major high tide roost for wildfowl and waders, as well as a fine stop-over site for migrant waders.

Birds: Elmley is often regarded as predominantly a winter spot, with White-fronted Goose, thousands of ducks and even more waders, with regular Hen Harrier, Peregrine, Merlin and Rough-legged Buzzard. But the passage periods are also excellent for waders, including Little Stint, Curlew, Sandpiper, Ruff, Black-tailed Godwit and Spotted Redshank. In summer there are visiting Montagu's and Marsh Harriers, Avocet, and breeding Little Tern and Ringed Plover.

Access: cross Kingsferry Bridge on to the Isle of Sheppey and watch out for a track on the right after about one mile. Thereafter follow signs to the RSPB car park, the flood and hides.

Permits: available daily on arrival, except Tuesday.

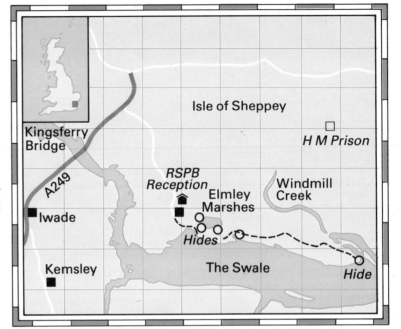

EXE ESTUARY, DEVON OS 192

Location: this fine estuary lies between Exeter and Exmouth on the south Devon coast. Birdwatching is better on the west side.

Habitats: intertidal mud and sand with a reed bed near Exminster. At the mouth is Dawlish Warren, a dune system with interesting slacks (damp hollows between the dunes).

Birds: 600 Black-tailed Godwit, 2000 Brent and 4500 Wigeon winter here, along with Ruff, Greenshank, Grey Plover and thousands of the more common waders. A few Avocets, a Peregrine and a collection of water birds that includes Slavonian Grebe and divers can also be found. During passage periods there is a wider variety of waders, with Whimbrel in spring and Greenshank in autumn. Dawlish Warren may hold interesting small birds and there are terns at the estuary mouth. Fields and hedgerows nearby may hold Cirl Bunting in summer.

Access: approach the head of the estuary from Exminster by parking at the Swans Nest pub and walking the footpath to the Topsham foot ferry. Walk southwards from here to Turf. Also on the west bank there is a tunnel under the railway at Powderham and a track leads northwards from the church. There is free access to the estuary mouth at Dawlish Warren (where there is a hide).

Permits: not required.

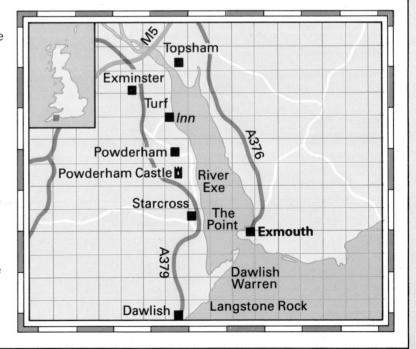

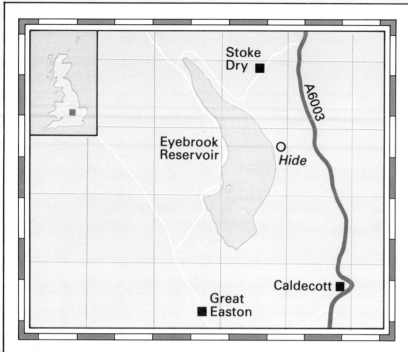

EYEBROOK RESERVOIR, LEICESTERSHIRE OS 141

Location: between Leicester and Peterborough, 4 miles north of Corby.

Habitats: some reservoirs are vast, daunting and give only poor chances of observation. Eyebrook is a complete contrast. An attractive place, it is large enough to hold birds but easily viewed over its entire area. It has mainly shallow, natural banks, with a fine marsh at the northern inlet end. The eastern shore has been planted with conifers.

Birds: in winter Eyebrook is an important wildfowl site, with regular herds of Bewick's Swan and flocks of Greylag Geese. Ducks include Wigeon, Pintail, Goosander and Goldeneye, and there are sometimes a few Smew. Grebes and divers are often present in the new year, though Black-necked Grebes are more frequent in autumn. At this time the western shore and marsh are excellent for waders, including Little Stint, Curlew Sandpiper and Greenshank. Autumn also brings Black and other terns. Ruddy Duck can be seen throughout the year.

Access: from the A6003 or B664. A road runs around the western and northern parts of the reservoir.

Permits: unnecessary for non-regular visitors.

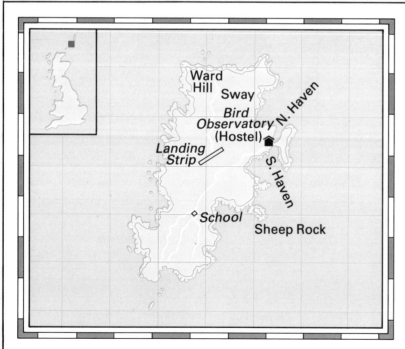

FAIR ISLE, SHETLAND OS 4

Location: roughly half way between Shetland and Orkney.

Habitats: Fair Isle attracts storm-driven waifs from a huge area. On arrival, they find shelter where they can; among the crofters' vegetable patches, along dry-stone walls and in the few areas of scrub. Otherwise Fair Isle is open moorland, with some towering, precipitous sea-cliffs.

Birds: there are thriving colonies of seabirds, including Guillemot, Razorbill, Black Guillemot and Puffin, Kittiwake and Fulmar, plus good numbers of Great and Arctic Skuas, Common and Arctic Terns, Storm Petrel and a gannetry. During spring and autumn Fair Isle becomes really outstanding, attracting many birds that have wandered north of their migration routes. It is also visited by extremely rare Siberian birds, particularly in autumn. Rarities include Lanceolated and Arctic Warblers, Pechora and Olive-backed Pipits, Yellow-breasted Bunting and even Siberian Rubythroat.

Access: there are regular flights by Loganair from Shetland that connect with mainland services. There is also a regular mail boat from Shetland, though the crossing can be rough. Full-board accommodation can be booked at the Bird Observatory, Fair Isle, Shetland, ZE2 9JU.

Permits: none required.

FAIRBURN INGS, NORTH YORKSHIRE OS 105

Location: Fairburn lies on the A1, just north-east of Castleford.

Habitats: the 'Ings' are a series of shallow lagoons, created by mining subsidence, that have matured to produce a number of reed-fringed waters, with some areas of mud and much shallow water. They now form an RSPB reserve with access paths and hides.

Birds: winter wildfowl are a primary attraction. There is a good herd of Whooper Swan, and ducks include Teal, Shoveler, Pochard and Tufted Duck in good numbers, plus regular Goldeneye and Goosander. A gull roost produces the occasional semi-rarity. During passage (particularly after easterly winds during spring) terns may be interesting, with Black Tern regular. In summer the breeding scene is dominated by a large colony of Black-headed Gulls.

Access: leave the A1 at Fairburn and turn westwards toward Allerton. The reserve centre is well marked after one mile and is open at weekends, with access to a board walk and hides. A footpath from the village (off Cut Lane) leads to public hides that are open at all times and good views can also be obtained along the roadsides.

Permits: only needed at weekends: available on arrival at the information centre at Newton, about 1½ miles west of Fairburn (opening hours 10.00 a.m.–5.00 p.m.). Otherwise unnecessary.

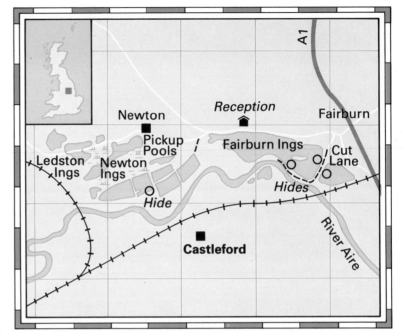

FARAID HEAD, HIGHLAND OS 9

Location: this headland is situated on the north coast of Scotland 3 miles north of Durness and about 9 miles east of Cape Wrath. It is a superb alternative to the better known Clo Mor (*see page* 29) to the west.

Habitats: magnificent cliffs that, though lower and holding fewer birds than those at Clo Mor, are of decidedly easier access and quite magnificent in their own right. The headland is otherwise a windswept moor broken only by a few tracks.

Birds: the usual cliff-dwelling species are present in good numbers, with Fulmar, Kittiwake, Guillemot, Razorbill, Black Guillemot and Puffin all on view. The latter have honeycombed the tops of the eastern cliffs. Gannets are regular offshore, sometimes accompanied by Great Skuas. The bay to the west, as well as the Kyle of Durness itself, is a regular haunt of divers, often including Great Northern, which remain well into summer.

Access: leave Durness on the road to Balnakeil, inspecting the lochs along the way. Continue on tracks to Faraid Head and explore the whole coastline.

Permits: none required.

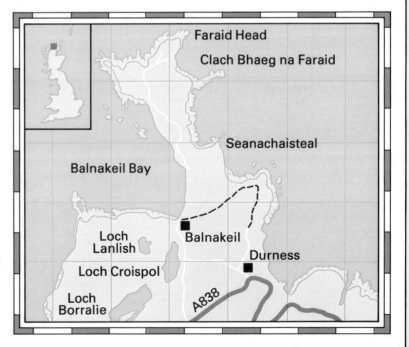

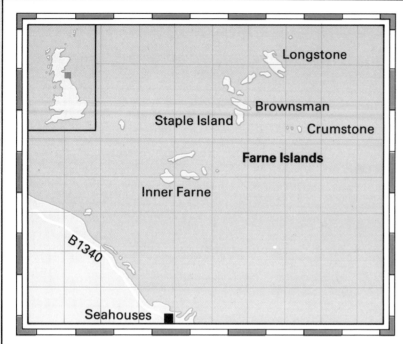

FARNE ISLANDS, NORTHUMBERLAND OS 75

Location: these scattered islands lie 1½ miles off the Northumberland coast near Bamburgh.

Habitats: though they are all rocky, the larger inner islands are lower and flatter, while the outer areas are cliff-girt with deep clefts and gullies. There are also some magnificent isolated stacks.

Birds: the Farnes have long been famous for their connections with the 7th-century Benedictine hermit St Cuthbert, who established Britain's oldest bird sanctuary. They are one of the most visited seabird colonies in the country with thousands of visitors every year. The birds seem quite unconcerned. All the usual auks breed, including vast numbers of Puffin, along with huge numbers of terns that are mainly Arctic and Sandwich, but also Common and a few Roseate. Eider too are numerous and, as elsewhere, remarkably tame, and there are also Shag, Fulmar and Kittiwake.

Access: there are daily boat trips from nearby Seahouses to Staple Island in the mornings and Inner Farne in the afternoons. The latter is best. It is a good idea to book in advance. Contact the National Trust Information Centre, 16 Main Street, Seahouses, Northumberland (Tel: 0665 720424).

Permits: a landing fee is payable on arrival.

FETLAR, SHETLAND OS 1

Location: south of Unst (*see page* 102) and to the east of Yell.

Habitats: in contrast with the rest of Shetland, Fetlar is a 'green' island, with lushy grassy fields covering much of the southern half. The north has more typically Shetland landscape, with open moors and hills rising gradually to the top of quite extensive cliffs.

Birds: this island has for long been the jewel in the Shetland crown. Snowy Owls bred here in the mid-1960s, but do not breed today for lack of a male. Even so, other specialities, Whimbrel and Red-necked Phalarope, are still present and the cliffs hold vast numbers of auks, Shag, Fulmar and Kittiwake. A boat trip to view the screaming hordes of seabirds on the cliffs is an unforgettable experience, and should be arranged if at all possible – Mid-Yell is the place to try.

Access: the inter-island ferry service, developed as Shetland entered the 'oil-age', makes travel within the islands both simple and cheap. Fetlar can thus be reached via Yell and Unst. There are also regular air services by Loganair. Crofters take paying guests. Explore eastwards to the Loch of Funzie for Whimbrel and Red-necked Phalarope and on Vord Hill for the Snowy Owls.

Permits: available for the Snowy Owls from the RSPB warden at Bealance, Fetlar, Shetland ZE2 9DJ.

FIFE NESS, FIFE OS 59

Location: 10 miles south-east of St Andrews, the headland extends eastwards at the mouth of the Firth of Forth on its northern shore.

Habitats: a low-lying, rocky shore is broken by sandy bays and backed by a golf course and agricultural land. The lack of cover makes it easy to find small migrants.

Birds: this site is best in spring and autumn, when it is visited by a good range of passage migrants, including all the regular chats, flycatchers and warblers. Among them is a scattering of rarities and semi-rarities that regularly includes Wryneck and Bluethroat – both most likely to be visitors from Scandinavia. With a good easterly or north-easterly wind, seawatching can be excellent, with regular Manx and Sooty Shearwaters in autumn, as well as Little Gull, plus Arctic and Great Skuas (and the occasional Pomarine Skua). Common, Arctic and Sandwich Terns, and sometimes Little Terns, too, can be seen on passage in spring and autumn. Divers, auks and seaducks are regularly seen in winter.

Access: from the A917 at Crail. Take the road to the airfield and continue to Fife Ness. Park at the car park by the golf club. All of the small areas of cover can be explored on foot, but do not trespass on private property.

Permits: none required save for parking fees.

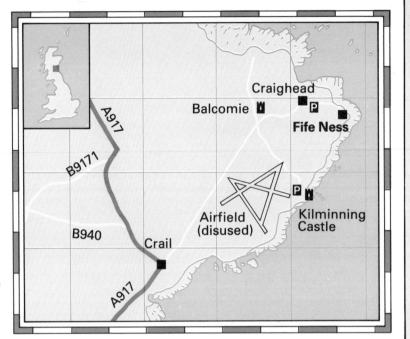

FINGRINGHOE WICK, ESSEX OS 168

Location: this reserve lies on the western shore of the Colne estuary about 5 miles south of Colchester.

Habitats: the open shoreline of the Colne estuary offers a considerable area of mud at low tide. The Essex Naturalists' Trust have created a reserve inside the sea-walls based on an area of disused gravel pits which, together with the surrounding reeds, fields and a small area of woodland, has become one of the finest sites for estuary birds along this coast.

Birds: in winter the area is widely used for feeding and roosting by wildfowl and waders, with many of the more common species present in quite respectable numbers. Red-throated Diver and Slavonian Grebe are also regular visitors. Fingringhoe also attracts Hen Harriers, Short-eared Owl, Merlin and sometimes even a Peregrine. During passage periods there is a greater variety of waders, with Little Stint and Curlew Sandpiper often present in autumn. In summer there are breeding Shelduck, Redshank and Ringed Plover.

Access: leave Colchester southwards on the B1025 toward Mersea and turn left after 2½ miles, following signs to South Green. The car park, nature trails, hides and nature centre lie off this road.

Permits: available on arrival. The reserve is closed on Mondays and reserved for members-only on Sundays.

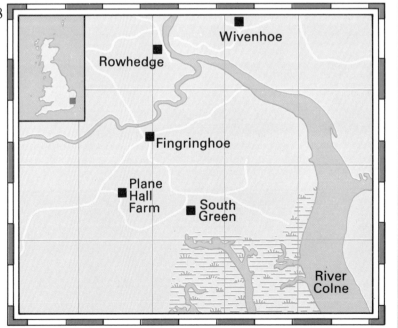

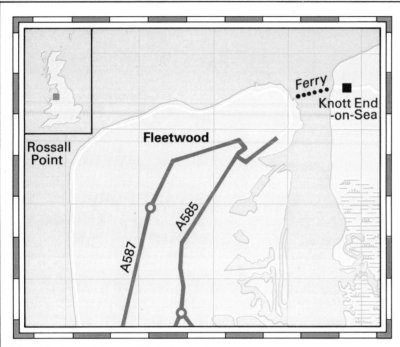

FLEETWOOD, LANCASHIRE OS 96

Location: the town of Fleetwood lies immediately north of Blackpool at the mouth of Morecambe Bay, but the area described here extends eastward for about 10 miles along the southern shore of this great intertidal area as far as Cockerham.

Habitats: Morecambe Bay is one of Europe's most important intertidal zones for both waders and wildfowl, with several species forming flocks of international significance. There are large mussel beds and saltmarshes and huge flats of sand and mud. This means that unless a visit is made at the correct state of the tide, the sea and the birds can be miles away.

Birds: huge flocks of Knot, Dunlin, Oystercatcher and Redshank are the dominant birds throughout the winter, but there are also good numbers of Bar-tailed Godwit, Curlew and Turnstone, together with smaller numbers of Purple Sandpiper. Although passage brings more waders, including outstanding numbers of Sanderling, these are generally more 'open-shore' birds than the commoner species.

Access: from Fleetwood head west to Rossall Point for rocky-shore waders and the chance of a Glaucous Gull. To the east Knott End is another good spot, as is Pilling (*see page* 84).

Permits: not required.

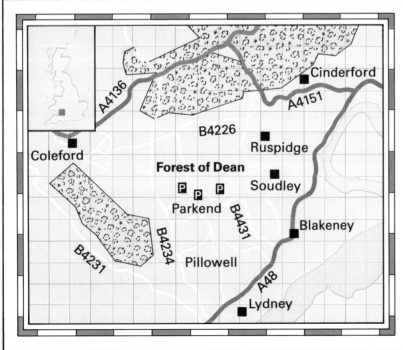

FOREST OF DEAN, GLOUCESTERSHIRE OS 162

Location: within 25 miles of Gloucester and Newport, this old-established forest lies between the east bank of the River Wye and the north bank of the Severn.

Habitats: the woodlands here are extensive and old. Though there are new plantations, there are also areas of mature mixed hardwoods that include oak, together with beech, rowan and birch. There are more open areas too, and several forest streams that tumble over rocky beds.

Birds: the bird community consists of relatively commonplace species that can be seen throughout lowland Britain, though there is a distinct westerly bias. There is, for example, a large population of Pied Flycatchers, mainly as a result of an intensive programme of erecting nest boxes. Here too are Wood Warblers, Buzzards and Dippers, as well as Tree Pipits and the three British woodpeckers. The RSPB's Nagshead Reserve is near the centre of the forest.

Access: leave the A48 northward on the B4431. Beyond Parkend watch for a track on the right to the RSPB car park. There are well marked trails and hides. Otherwise there are plentiful roads from which to explore the forest.

Permits: not required.

FOULA, SHETLAND OS 4

Location: among the most isolated of all inhabited islands in Britain, Foula lies to the west of the main island of Shetland, Mainland, near the meeting of the Atlantic Ocean and North Sea.

Habitats: the 4 square miles of this small island consist essentially of a mountain surrounded by an often fierce sea, which has cut huge cliffs from almost the whole of the coastline. At over 350m, some are among the highest to be found in Britain and are teeming with birds. Yet Foula remains largely unvisited by birdwatchers, though it has regular transport services and a welcoming local population.

Birds: all of the usual cliff-breeding seabirds can be found, including large numbers of Fulmar, Kittiwake, Guillemot and Puffin. There are Razorbill, Black Guillemot and Shag too, as well as a small colony of Gannet, a sizeable colony of Manx Shearwater and both Storm and Leach's Petrels. The Great Skua has a major breeding stronghold here. Despite its isolated position, there has been little investigation of migration here, even though rare birds have been found. What an opportunity awaits.

Access: there are flights from Shetland once a week during the summer and twice weekly sailings throughout the year. Be prepared for the ferry to be cancelled or delayed.

Permits: none required.

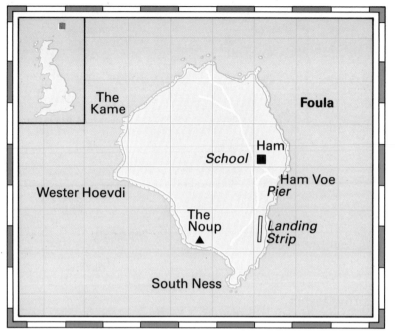

FOWLSHEUGH, GRAMPIAN OS 45

Location: the cliffs here lie on the east coast, next to the village of Crawton, about 16 miles south of Aberdeen and 4 miles south of Stonehaven.

Habitats: though nowhere near as formidable as some of the island seabird cliffs, these are among the best in mainland Britain. Only 60m high, they are readily accessible – though, as always at such sites, great care should be taken near the cliff-edge.

Birds: the most abundant species are Guillemot and Kittiwake, with about 30,000 pairs of each breeding regularly. With a good breeding colony of 5000 pairs of scarcer Razorbill, this a particularly important site nationally for all three species. As a bonus, there are smaller numbers of Puffin, Fulmar, Shag and Herring Gull. All these species combine to produce that hurly-burly, non-stop noise of a truly great seabird site. Eider are also regularly present on the sea itself.

Access: about 3 miles beyond Stonehaven turn left to Crawton and park at the small cliff-top car park. Walk northward along the cliff top path for views at many places. Though 1½ miles of the cliffs are an RSPB reserve, there is no warden.

Permits: not required.

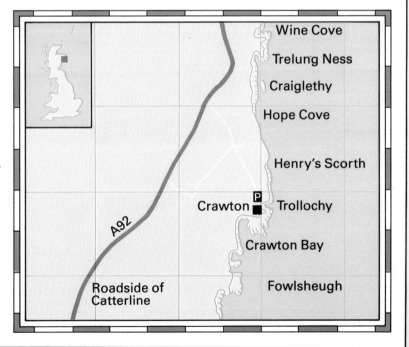

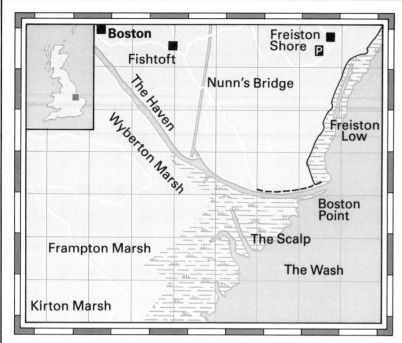

FRAMPTON MARSH, LINCOLNSHIRE OS 131

Location: 3 miles south of Boston at the western point of The Wash.

Habitats: three rivers have their estuaries at this corner of The Wash and all have been artificially embanked and straightened to ease the passage of flood waters. Where they meet there is a maze of saltmarshes and, behind the sea-wall, a system of dykes between the fields. This is a lonely place, usually ignored by birders, but it is what most of our coastal marshes were like before reclamation.

Birds: all the waders that frequent The Wash, one of Europe's top wetland sites, can be seen here – sometimes in spectacular numbers at passage seasons and in winter. Arrive an hour before one of the highest tides for the impressive spectacle of vast numbers of Knot, Dunlin, Curlew, Bar-tailed Godwit, Grey Plover and other waders. There are also wintering Hen Harrier, Merlin and Short-eared Owl, ducks and possibly geese too.

Access: leave Boston southwards on the A16 and turn left on to a maze of roads through Wyberton to Frampton Marsh. Continue to the sea-wall and the mouth of the River Witham. The area can also be approached from the north bank of the river via Fishtoft: walk to the sea-wall and walk 1¼ miles to the wader roost at Boston Point.

Permits: none required.

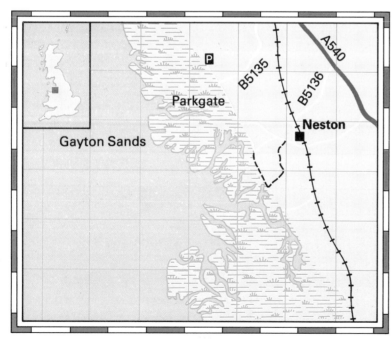

GAYTON SANDS, CHESHIRE OS 117

Location: this intertidal area lies on the north-east shore of the Dee Estuary at Parkgate, about 6 miles from Birkenhead.

Habitat: the huge sand flats here are backed by a large area of saltmarsh that was purchased by the RSPB and now constitutes its Gayton Sands reserve. There is also a reed bed.

Birds: this is predominantly a site for wintering wildfowl and waders. These include 30,000 each of Knot and Dunlin, plus lesser numbers of Bar-tailed Godwit, Grey Plover, and a nationally important flock of 1000 Black-tailed Godwit. Pintail are often the most common of the ducks, along with Wigeon and Shelduck, and there are regular Peregrine, Merlin and Hen Harrier. Often difficult to see are the flocks of small birds among the saltings, but careful watching may produce Water Pipit, Brambling and Twite. Just occasionally, a party of Pink-footed Geese or Bewick's Swans will put in an appearance.

Access: leave the main A540 between Hoylake and Chester on to the B5135 to Parkgate, where there is parking at the Old Baths car park, near the Boathouse Restaurant. Walk north along the public footpath or south to a reed bed at Neston that may hold Water Rail and Jack Snipe in winter, Grasshopper Warbler in summer.

Permits: not required.

GELTSDALE, CUMBRIA OS 86

Location: immediately south of the A69 from Carlisle to Newcastle-upon-Tyne. Its north-western boundary lies about 4 miles south of Brampton.

Habitat: open moorland, with large areas of heather and rough grass but also grassy fields and valley floors. Woodland along the valley sides, and tumbling rivers.

Birds: the heather moors hold breeding Red Grouse, Curlew and Golden Plover. Pied Flycatcher, Wood Warbler and Redstart breed in the woodlands, and Common Sandpiper, Dipper and Grey Wagtail on the streams. There are breeding Buzzard, Sparrowhawk, Hen Harrier, Merlin and Peregrine, as well as Goosander and Short-eared Owl. In winter, Whooper Swan may be seen on the tarn.

Access: the RSPB has established a reserve here consisting of 12,000 acres of moorland, with 300 acres of woods. Leave Brampton eastwards on the A69 and fork right on to the A689 to Tindale. A road southward leads to a disused railway, where there is parking for Tindale Tarn. Alternatively, take the A69 westwards from Brampton and turn left to Low Geltbridge. Park and walk south-eastwards through woods along the bank of the river. The third approach is to leave Brampton southward on the B6413 to Castle Carrock and turn left to Jockey Shield, where there is a track.

Permits: none required, but keep to rights of way on the moors.

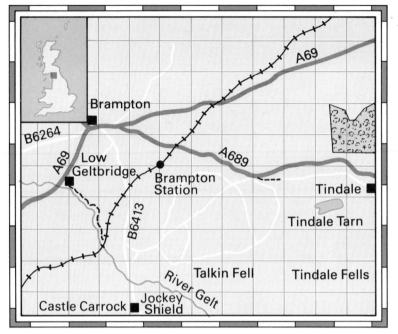

GIBRALTAR POINT, LINCOLNSHIRE OS 122

Location: 3 miles south of Skegness on The Wash.

Habitats: the coastline is backed by dunes, with 'slacks' (damp hollows) between. There is a good growth of scrub, broken by areas of fresh water and marsh – a perfect combination of habitats for small migrants. There is also a golf course, a 'scrape' (an artificial area of brackish water with small islands) and an area of saltmarsh.

Birds: the area is a National Nature Reserve and the site of Gibraltar Point Field Station, a bird observatory and a visitor centre. During passage periods there are all the regular chats and warblers with, in autumn, a fair chance of a 'fall' of large numbers of migrants, including rarities. Even in winter large numbers of waders can be seen at a nearby roost, also divers, Brent Geese and a variety of raptors that regularly includes Peregrine. Migration in spring and autumn can be very dramatic.

Access: follow the minor road south along the coast from Skegness to the Point, where parking is available at two sites. There is a hide at The Mere and the visitor centre is open daily in the summer and at weekends throughout the year.

Permits: none required. Contact Gibraltar Point Field Station, Skegness, Lincolnshire, PE24 4SU, for accommodation.

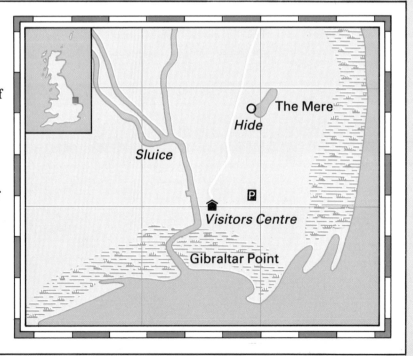

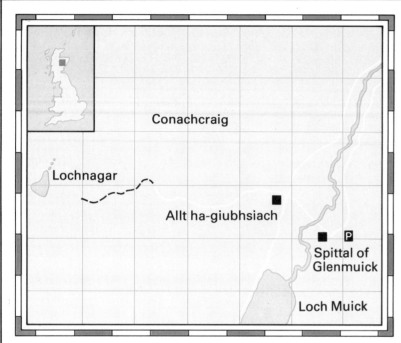

GLEN MUICK AND THE EAST GRAMPIANS, DEE OS 44

Location: the River Dee rises in the Grampian Mountains. The area described here includes the Dee Valley east and west of Ballater, as well as Glen Muick to the south and lies about 40 miles west of Aberdeen, where the Dee reaches the sea.

Habitats: mountains, valleys, old woods and new plantations, lakes, ponds, marshes and streams – all are to be found in this remarkable area, that has almost all the Scottish specialities usually associated with Speyside.

Birds: though there are geese here in winter, this is primarily a superb summer spot for the best of Scottish birds. Golden Eagle cruise over the higher hillsides and there are Ptarmigan and Dotterel on the tops, Hen Harriers on the lower slopes, and Goshawk and Sparrowhawk in the woods. These also hold Black Grouse and Capercaillie, along with Scottish Crossbill, Redstart and Wood Warbler. In fact, the only Scottish woodland speciality that is missing is the Crested Tit.

Access: take the A93 westward from Aberdeen and explore the minor roads to the north and south between Aboyne and Braemar. One of the best leaves Ballater southwards to Glen Muick.

Permits: not required, but keep to public rights of way.

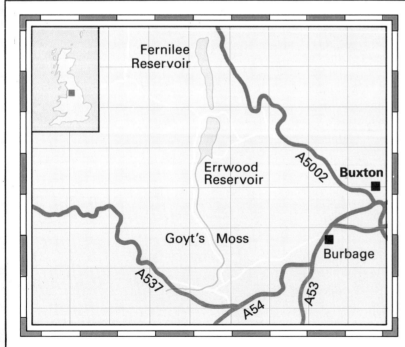

GOYT VALLEY, DERBYSHIRE

OS 118

Location: the north-western corner of Derbyshire, close to its borders with Greater Manchester, Cheshire and Staffordshire.

Habitats: this is one of those beauty spots that attracts people from all directions. At certain times, particularly summer weekends, it may be chock-a-block with visitors, making birding all but impossible. The valley is beautiful and the Goyt here is a stream tumbling over a rocky bed before entering a string of reservoirs, whose banks are clothed by magnificent woods. High above are open sheep moors.

Birds: a community of typical upland breeding birds of a variety of habitats makes this very much a spring and summer place. The high tops, easily accessible by road, hold Red Grouse, Curlew and Golden Plover. Along the stream live Dipper, Grey Wagtail and Common Sandpiper, while the woods contain Redstart, Tree Pipit and Wood Warbler. Also there are Great and Lesser Spotted Woodpeckers, Ring Ousel, Whinchat and, on the reservoirs, Great Crested and Little Grebes.

Access: by minor roads from the A537, A54 or A5002. There is a car park at Errwood Reservoir. This is a partially traffic-free zone.

Permits: none required.

GRAFHAM WATER, CAMBRIDGESHIRE   OS 153

Location: this lowland reservoir lies just 1¼ miles west of the A1 about 5 miles south-west of Huntingdon.

Habitats: most of the banks of this huge reservoir are natural and gently shelving. For years it was England's largest reservoir (this title now rests with Rutland Water, *see page* 88) and is in great demand for various leisure pursuits, but there are protected areas.

Birds: in winter there are good numbers of the commoner ducks, including Wigeon, Teal and Shoveler, along with smaller numbers of Goosander and Goldeneye. Bewick's Swan is regular and there may be really impressive numbers of Great Crested and Little Grebes. During passage periods Black and Common Terns are regular and, chiefly in autumn, waders include a scattering of the usual 'freshwater' species, such as Common, Green and Wood Sandpiper.

Access: leave the A1 westwards on the B661 to the dam. There are roads to the north and the south which lead to car parks with views over the water. Just beyond West Perry, in the south, the car park gives access to a waterside footpath that leads to a hide.

Permits: the Bedfordshire and Huntingdonshire Wildlife Trust reserve at the western end has no access and even the hide is open only on winter Sundays, for a small charge.

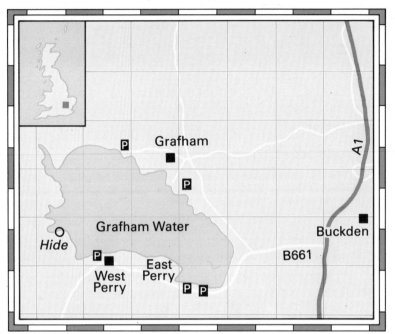

GWENFFRWD AND DINAS, DYFED   OS 146 or 147

Location: these RSPB reserves lie to the north-west of the A483 about 8 miles north of Llandovery.

Habitats: though much of the reserves consists of open moorland and rough grass, the main centre of interest lies in the lovely old oakwoods and the rippling streams that cut through them.

Birds: the Red Kite, still persecuted and still endangered, finds a stronghold hereabouts and a good view of one of these lovely birds is one of the primary objects of a visit. They can be seen soaring gracefully over the woods, though most larger raptors seen here are Buzzards. The woods are alive with Pied Flycatcher, Wood Warbler, Redstart, woodpeckers, Woodcock and Tree Pipit. The streams have Dipper, Grey Wagtail and Common Sandpiper, and there are Merlin, Red Grouse and possible Peregrine, too.

Access: leave Llandovery on minor roads to Rhandirmwyn. The Dinas reserve is found off the road to Llyn Brianne dam. There is a summer information centre by the car park and the start of a nature trail here. For the Gwenffrwd reserve and its two nature trails report to the Dinas centre and check details with the warden. Access is restricted by the lack of parking space.

Permits: see access; no Friday access.

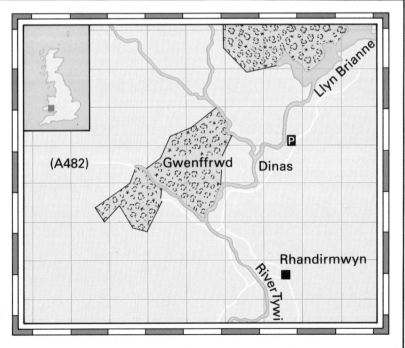

47

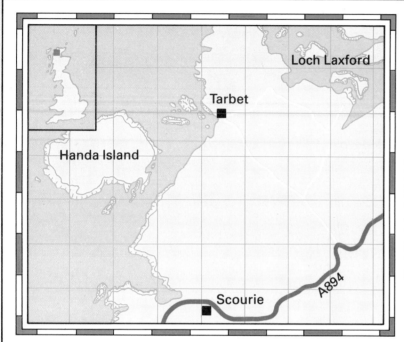

HANDA, HIGHLAND OS 9

Location: just a mile's ferry crossing from the north-west coast of Scotland – and about 17 miles south of Cape Wrath.

Habitats: Handa is a large island consisting mainly of rough, steep grazing land and heather, but with impressive cliffs in the north and sandy bays and beaches in the south and east. Its position and its cliffs make Handa one of the best seabird colonies in Britain.

Birds: altogether there are some 100,000 pairs of breeding seabirds here; Guillemot alone number nearly 30,000 pairs. They include Razorbill, Puffin, Kittiwake, Fulmar and Shag, plus strong populations of Great and Arctic Skuas. Peregrine and Buzzard are regular visitors. On the boat crossing watch for Red-throated and Black-throated Divers, plus Great Northern Diver in early summer.

Access: there are regular boats from Tarbet, which is reached from the A894 via a minor road north-west, about 3 miles north-east of Scourie. The boats depart from about 10.00 a.m. daily except Sunday throughout summer. Handa is open between 1 April and 10 September. There is a warden, and visitors are requested to keep to the marked paths.

Permits: see access above.

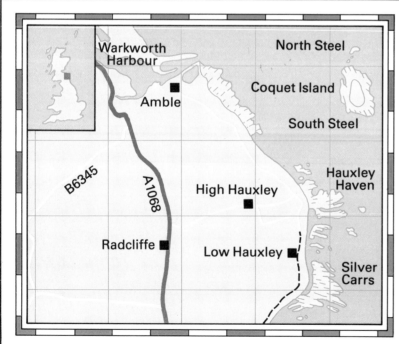

HAUXLEY, NORTHUMBERLAND OS 81

Location: Hauxley is situated on a bulge in the rugged stretch of coastline about 25 miles to the north of the Tyneside conurbation.

Habitats: a long sandy foreshore is broken by a rocky area that juts into the sea, forming a headland that regularly attracts birds.

Birds: the main attractions at Hauxley are the migrants, the foreshore waders and the seabirds. The latter include all the species that regularly breed on nearby Coquet Island (*see page* 31) and among which Common, Arctic and Sandwich Tern are often numerous. Careful watching may produce one or two of the rare Roseate Tern. It is, however, in late summer and autumn that the area really begins to shine. The terns then feed and rest along the shoreline and skuas regularly appear among them. These are mostly Arctic, but Great and Pomarine Skua are sometimes present as well. Manx Shearwater, too, are regular and Sooty, Cory's and Great Shearwaters are seen annually. Small migrants may be good in autumn too; an easterly element in the wind helps. Among the warblers, chats and flycatchers there are always some semi-rarities.

Access: south of Amble, off the A1068. Continue to Low Hauxley where the road south to Bondicare is a public footpath.

Permits: none required, but do not trespass on private land.

HAVERGATE ISLAND, SUFFOLK OS 169

Location: in the estuary of the River Alde about 2½ miles south of Orford; Ipswich lies 16 miles to the west.

Habitats: after widening out below Snape and forming a minor estuary, the River Alde is diverted southwards by the huge sweep of Orfordness, eventually reaching the sea at Shingle Street. Along this narrow part it divides in two, with Havergate forming the island between. Wartime flooding enabled Avocets to recolonize Britain in 1947 here and at nearby Minsmere (*see page* 77).

Birds: the Avocet still has a major colony here and Common and Sandwich Terns, too. Short-eared Owl also breed, as do a few waders. In autumn the exposed mud attracts many waders, including Spotted Redshank, Little Stint, Curlew Sandpiper and Greenshank, yet rarities are seldom found – presumably because access to birders is restricted outside the breeding season.

Access: by boat several days each week during the summer, less frequently from September through the winter.

Permits: there is a charge for the boat trip – RSPB members pay less than half price. Details of arrangements for the current season and reservations by post only from The Warden, 30 Mundays Lane, Orford, Woodbridge, IP12 2LX.

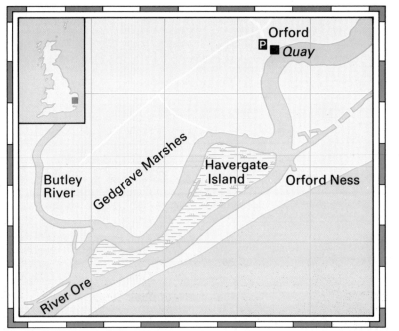

HAYLE ESTUARY, CORNWALL OS 203

Location: the Hayle is the nearest estuary to Land's End – and the nearest in England to North America. The town of Hayle all but embraces it and the resort of St Ives, with its outstanding seawatching site (*see page* 90), is about 3 miles to the north-west.

Habitats: this is a small estuary, with mud banks at low tide, a small saltmarsh and a detached tidal lagoon called Carnsew Pool.

Birds: the peak season is autumn, when waders include Greenshank, Spotted Redshank, Common Sandpiper, Little Stint, Curlew Sandpiper and the chance of an American rarity or two. Dowitchers are among the most likely of these, but a variety of rare waders, including Pectoral and White-rumped Sandpipers, have turned up here. Terns and gulls include a scattering of semi-rarities, though winter is usually better for the gulls. At this time divers and the scarcer grebes are regular and there are always a few ducks.

Access: the Hayle as well as Copperhouse Creek can be seen well from the B3301, from which there is also access to Carnsew Pool. The RSPB have a public hide on the south of the estuary near the Old Quay House Inn, which has a large car park that can be used by birders.

Permits: not required.

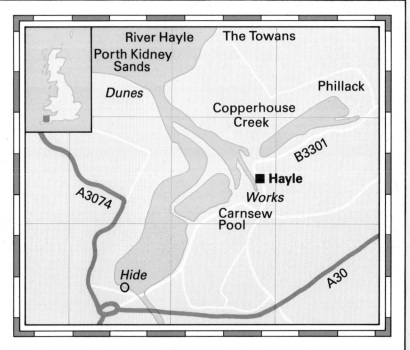

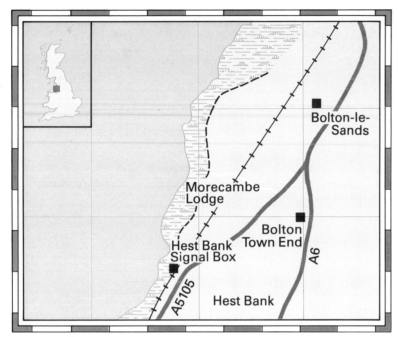

HEST BANK, LANCASHIRE   OS 97

Location: this area lies on the shores of the huge Morecambe Bay, at the southern end of the RSPB reserve, just to the north of Morecambe itself (*see page 76*).

Habitats: Morecambe Bay is vast intertidal complex and one of the most important wetlands in Europe. Hest Bank is one of the best sites on the shores of this great area.

Birds: this is a spot that, if visited at the right time, can produce an unforgettable bird spectacle. If visited casually it can, on the contrary, produce no more than a few common waders. The secret is timing. Choose a winter spring tide during the daylight hours and arrive at Hest Bank an hour or so before high tide. Then watch for waders pouring in by the thousand. Numbers of wintering waders in Morecambe Bay can be staggering, with totals of 80,000 Knot, 50,000 Dunlin, 45,000 Oystercatcher, 8000 Bar-tailed Godwit and 7000 Redshank. Hest Bank is one of the prime wader roosts. Passage brings large numbers of Sanderling and Ringed Plover and there may be other species such as Greenshank present.

Access: leave Morecambe northwards on the A5105 to Hest Bank and cross the railway at the level crossing, to reach a large car park. Walk northwards toward the wader roost.

Permits: none required.

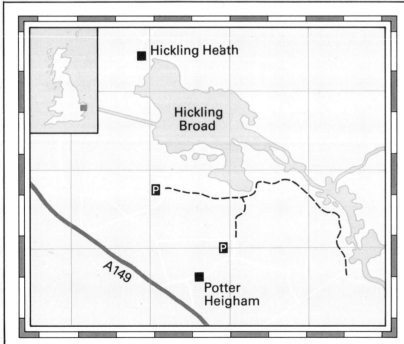

HICKLING BROAD, NORFOLK

OS 134

Location: to the north-east of the more famous 'boating' broads. Great Yarmouth lies some 11 miles to the south-east.

Habitats: this is a large open water surrounded by vast reed beds. It is a National Nature Reserve and partly a reserve of the Norfolk Naturalists' Trust, with a series of shallow lagoons that attract many passage waders.

Birds: all the Broadland specialities can be found here in summer, including Bittern and Bearded Tit, Sedge, Reed, Grasshopper and Savi's Warbler, and visiting Marsh Harrier. There are Common Terns nesting on specially sited rafts and Black Terns are regular in both spring and autumn. Waders include Green and Wood Sandpipers, Greenshank, Little Stint, Curlew Sandpiper and Spotted Redshank.

Access: by permit to a nature trail and series of hides in the north-east of the broad via the Norfolk Naturalists' Trust. Much of the southern part can be seen via a footpath along the shore starting from Decoy Lane, or via another from Potter Heigham church.

Permits: the Norfolk Naturalists' Trust Warden has an office along Stubb Lane, which is next to the Greyhound Inn. Permits are issued in half-day sessions, except on Tuesdays, and fees are modest.

HILBRE, MERSEYSIDE OS 108

Location: three separate islands off the Wirral peninsula at the mouth of the River Dee, about 8 miles west of Birkenhead.

Habitats: these are three low, flat rocky islands – Hilbre, Little Hilbre and Little Eye. Though there is a bird observatory on Hilbre Island, as well as good visible migration through the late autumn and rewarding seawatching after gales, these islands are famous chiefly as a major roost for waders on the Dee estuary.

Birds: though wader numbers are smaller than they were, due to disturbance, this is still a spectacular spot for these birds. Dunlin, Knot, Redshank, Bar-tailed Godwit and Grey Plover dominate, but there are also good numbers of Oystercatcher, Purple Sandpiper and Turnstone. At other times the islands hold little of interest, though autumn gales often drive Leach's Petrel close to the islands.

Access: the islands can be reached on foot at low tide, but it is essential to start at least three hours before high water from West Kirby on the mainland. The nearby Red Rocks are another wader roost, which can be reached with considerably less walking.

Permits: no access without a free permit from Wirral Borough Council Department of Leisure, Town Hall, Brighton Street, Wallasey, Merseyside L44 8ED. Or telephone the ranger's office: 051 6484371.

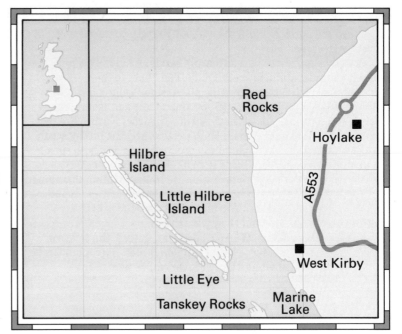

HOBBISTER, ORKNEY OS 6

Location: this large RSPB reserve (1875 acres) lies in the south of Orkney Mainland, about 3 miles to the south-west of Kirkwall. Its southern boundary lies on the shores of Scapa Flow.

Habitats: an area of open moorland dominated by heather, with bogs and marshes and a corner of the Loch of Kirbister. It also includes a substantial length of shoreline, part of which comprises low cliffs.

Birds: this is one of several Orkney breeding strongholds of the Hen Harrier, and there is a good chance of seeing one from the road. Short-eared Owl and Merlin also breed, as do Red-throated Diver, Curlew and Snipe. There is a good breeding population of Red Grouse on the moor. The cliffs hold Fulmar and Black Guillemot. In winter divers, grebes and seaducks are regular. Hobbister is a pleasant area of open countryside and shore with a good chance of seeing several exciting birds.

Access: there is a track that loops across the southern half of the reserve from the A964 near Waulkmill Bay, starting at a minor road or nearby track. This is the only access.

Permits: not required for access described above.

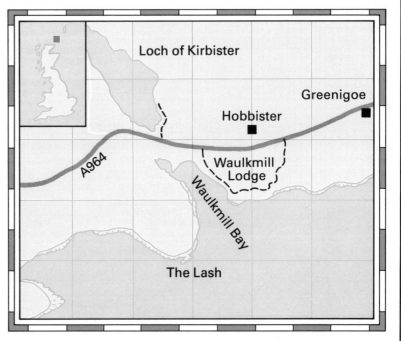

HOLKHAM AND WELLS, NORFOLK OS 132

Location: the north Norfolk coast about 10 miles to the west of Blakeney (*see page* 18).

Habitats: the foreshore here is mainly sandy. A muddy deep channel extends inland to Wells Quay. The dunes to the west have been stabilized with extensive pine plantations. Inland lies Holkham Hall, a large park with specimen trees and several lakes. Much of the seaward side of the A149 is a National Nature Reserve.

Birds: the grounds of Holkham Hall, particularly the birchy scrub on the landward side, are splendidly productive during both spring and autumn passage, with birds such as Pied Flycatcher, Wryneck and Barred Warbler turning up annually. In the autumn, this same area regularly produces an impressive number of rarities, including Yellow-browed and Pallas's Warblers, and sometimes extreme rarities such as Radde's and Dusky Warblers.

In winter, Brent Geese, Wigeon, seaducks, grebes, the common waders, Red-breasted Merganser, Common Scoter, Slavonian Grebe, Knot, Bar-tailed Godwit and Grey Plover can be seen at the shoreline and harbour mouth. Winter also sees geese flock to the fields between the pines and Holkham Hall. Egyptian Goose are invariably present here, as are feral Greylags. Search for Hawfinch on the hornbeam trees just inside the Park.

Access: explore the pines from the Wells end, taking the road northwards along the western side of the quay to a car park at the far end. Walk up the sea-wall to the right and view the channel mouth. From the western side of the car park walk westwards, along the northern side of the boating lake (check for terns in season) and explore the scrub on the landward side of the pines. Turn north opposite Holkham Hall along Lady Anne's Drive to the pines. Walk over the boardwalk to the sea and also east and west behind the pines. Holkham Park can be visited via a small gate to the left of the main gate. Further west, the A149 gives excellent views over the goose flocks, but parking on the road is banned.

Permits: not required for the access detailed above.

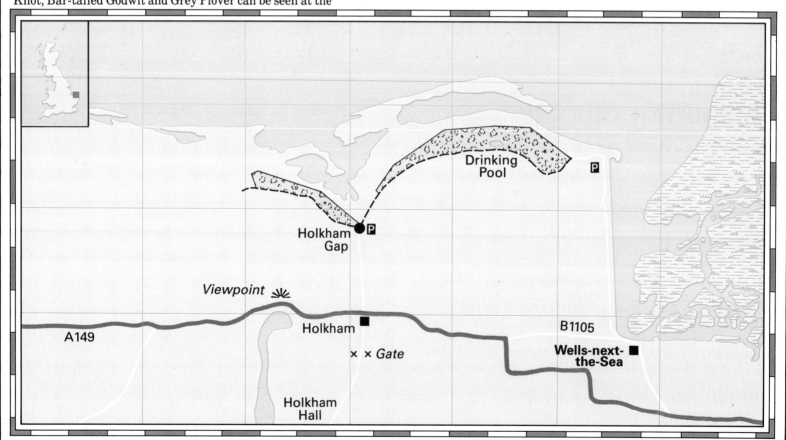

HOLBEACH, LINCOLNSHIRE

OS 122 & 131

Location: these marshes lie at the western corner of The Wash between the outlets of the River Welland and the River Nene.

Habitats: this is a huge area of reclaimed fen that lies below sea level, protected by a sea-wall and drained by dykes. Beyond the sea-wall a vast area of saltmarshes extends to the mud banks of The Wash.

Birds: Holbeach has long been famous as one of the major wader resorts of The Wash. Spring tides are virtually essential for success here – the higher the better. At such times a proportion of the huge wader flocks of this major wetland are forced off the saltmarshes and over the sea-wall at Flushing Creek Wall. Knot, Dunlin, Oystercatcher and Redshank are the most numerous species, but there are also good numbers of Bar-tailed Godwit and Curlew. The area also attracts a good selection of wintering raptors, including Merlin and Hen Harrier.

Access: leave the A17 at Chapelgate northwards on the B1359 and turn left on to a minor road, signposted Holbeach St Matthew. Continue through the village to the sea-wall. Walk out to Flushing Creek Wall at the mouth of the River Welland.

Permits: not required.

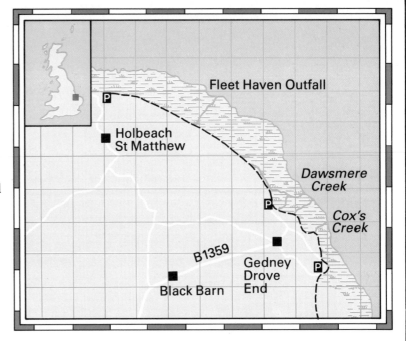

HOLME, NORFOLK   OS 132

Location: where the north Norfolk coast turns into The Wash. The best area lies between Holme-next-the-Sea and Thornham Harbour.

Habitats: the shoreline here is wide and sandy, and is backed by extensive dunes. A large pool, called Broad Water, is surrounded by reeds, while to the west is an area of 'scrapes' (artificial areas of shallow, brackish water with low-lying islets for attracting birds). Thornham Harbour has large mud banks and saltmarshes.

Birds: the Norfolk Ornithologists' Association has a private bird observatory here, while the Norfolk Naturalists' Trust's reserve covers the larger part of the area. In summer the latter holds Avocet, Little Tern, Bearded Tit and both Reed and Sedge Warbler. In winter there are divers, ducks and grebes offshore, and Brent Goose on the fields. Hen Harrier, Snow Bunting and Shore Lark are regular. During spring and autumn passage periods the 'scrapes' hold waders, while the scrub and pines sometimes produce scarce migrant warblers, chats and flycatchers, including Barred and Yellow-browed Warblers and Red-breasted Flycatcher.

Access: leave the A149 northward to Holme along Beach Road and turn right along a track (a small toll is payable in summer).

Permits: are available every day except Tuesday for the NNT reserve and every day for the NOA area. These are available on site.

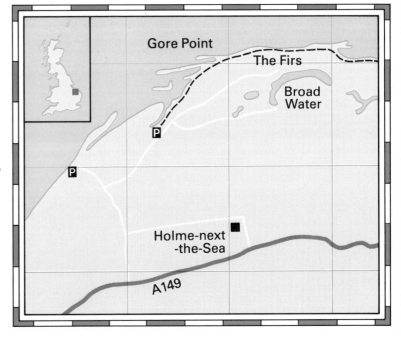

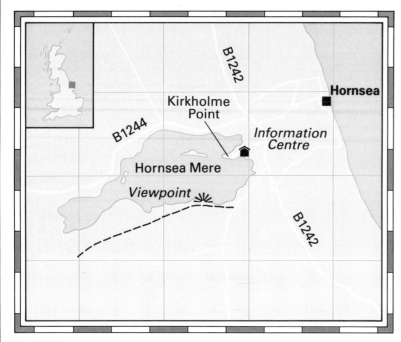

HORNSEA MERE, HUMBERSIDE OS 107

Location: just west of the B1242 and the small coastal town of Hornsea. Hull is about 12 miles to the south-west.

Habitats: this is a large freshwater lake surrounded by extensive reed beds just a short distance from the North Sea coast. There are areas of woodland and much surrounding farmland.

Birds: Hornsea is an RSPB reserve that is most interesting in winter and during spring and autumn passage periods. Ducks include hundreds of Teal, Wigeon, Gadwall, Pochard and Goldeneye, the latter forming a notable flock for a freshwater site. Divers and grebes are often present during hard weather. If the water level is low enough to expose the muddy shoreline, waders can be interesting in autumn, though they are never as regular as the Little Gull that is present all season. Black and other terns are regularly present during spring and autumn passage seasons.

Access: the RSPB have an information centre at Kirkholme Point open during summer weekends, and cars may be parked here. Simply follow signs to 'The Mere' from Hornsea town centre. There is also an excellent public footpath along the southern shore that starts in Hull Road.

Permits: not required.

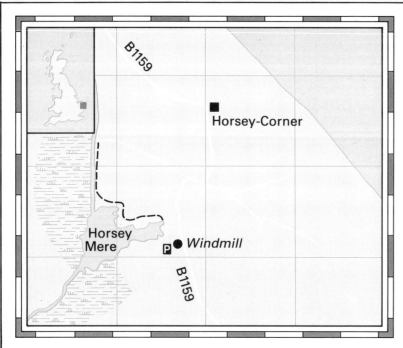

HORSEY MERE, NORFOLK OS 134

Location: less than a mile from the coast, and about 10 miles to the north of Great Yarmouth. As a birdwatching site, it is often overshadowed by the neighbouring Hickling Broad (*see page* 50).

Habitats: Horsey is a medium-sized broad surrounded by extensive reed beds and is a nature reserve belonging to the National Trust.

Birds: for many years, Horsey was a stronghold of the Broadland specialities, but several of these sadly no longer breed there, though Bearded Tit and Water Rail still hold on. The Marsh Harrier is now only a visitor and the status of the Bittern is precarious to say the least. Nevertheless, the reeds are full of warblers and there are often good numbers of waders and terns during spring and autumn passage periods. In winter Hen Harrier, Short-eared Owl and a good population of ducks visit the area and Bewick's Swan are sometimes present in small numbers.

Access: viewing the mere is difficult as access is restricted, and most birders give it no more than a quick once-over. A more active conservation policy, including strategically sited hides, might well produce more birds. At present, the mere can be viewed only from the track that leads from the windmill, where there is a car park.

Permits: not required for access detailed above; not available otherwise.

HOY, ORKNEY OS 7

Location: Hoy is one of the southern Orkney islands, separated from the mainland of Scotland by the Pentland Firth and from Mainland Orkney by the narrow Hoy Sound.

Habitats: this is the bleakest of the Orkneys with huge areas of moorland with heather, rough grass, bogs and lochs. In the west are some of the most spectacular of seabird cliffs. The RSPB reserve of North Hoy contains all of these habitats, culminating in the fearsome 335m St John's Head cliffs, and the 140m Old Man of Hoy, Britain's highest sea stack.

Birds: seabirds in summer include many Guillemot, Razorbill, Shag and Kittiwake. The cliffs also hold nesting Peregrine, and there is a Manx Shearwater colony. Off the north-west coast are colonies of Great and Arctic Skuas, while inland there are Golden Plover, Dunlin and Curlew. The lochs have the largest population of Red-throated Diver in Orkney and there are Hen Harrier and Merlin on the hills inland.

Access: Hoy can be reached by passenger ferry from Stromness to Moress and a car ferry from Houton to Lyness. Take the B9047 and turn westward to Rackwick. Here there are paths leading to the Old Man and inland between Ward Hill and the Cuilags. Take care on the cliff-tops, as these are crumbling in places.

Permits: none required.

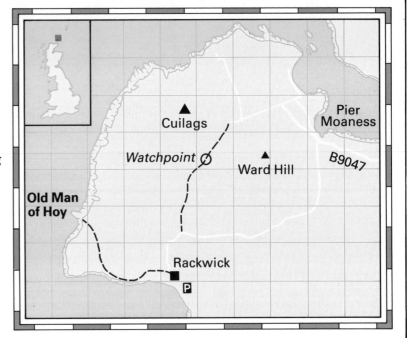

HUNSTANTON, NORFOLK OS 132

Location: the Victorian resort of Hunstanton lies at the north-east corner of The Wash, between the major bird sites of Holme (*see page* 53), and Snettisham (*see page* 95).

Habitats: the prime attractions are the sea and shoreline. As the tide rises, it pushes wildfowl and waders towards the promenade. Here they can be watched from a few strategically-sited shelters. To the north of the town, the sandy cliffs offer another viewpoint.

Birds: wildfowl and waders here are predominantly winter birds and, in summer, there are only a few Fulmars along the cliffs. Brent Geese are regular in small numbers and Bar-tailed Godwit, Curlew, Grey Plover, Redshank and Turnstone are invariably present. All of these birds are best watched on a rising tide, while at high water there may be quite impressive flocks flighting along the coast to roost. At this time, seaducks move inshore, including good numbers of Scoter, along with Velvet Scoter, Long-tailed Duck, Eider and Goldeneye. Red-throated Diver are also present.

Access: from the centre of town and turn north-east along a road with open grass on the left and the cliffs beyond. There are several shelters to choose from. Continue to the higher sandy cliffs with Fulmar, but less winter shelter.

Permits: none necessary.

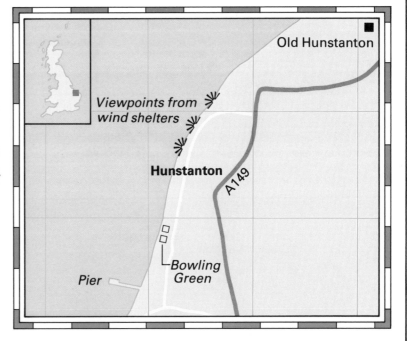

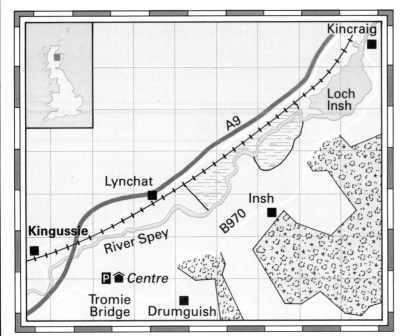

INSH MARSHES, HIGHLAND OS 35

Location: these marshes lie between Kingussie and the Cairngorm Mountains, immediately south of the main A9 road.

Habitats: this is an RSPB reserve covering the low-lying floodlands along the River Spey. Additionally there is the large Loch Insh to the north and Glen Tromie to the south. The valley itself is a mixture of rough grass with open pools in a setting of birch and willow scrub. In winter the whole area is frequently flooded.

Birds: most birdwatchers visit Insh Marshes in summer, when a variety of ducks breed, including Wigeon, Teal and Shoveler, as well as Goldeneye, which use nest-boxes. Greylag Geese also breed at this site. Tree Pipit, Redstart, Great Spotted Woodpecker breed in the woods, together with the occasional pair of Pied Flycatcher. The streams have nesting Dipper and Grey Wagtail, while Redshank, Curlew and Grasshopper Warbler breed on the marshes themselves. The Osprey is a regular visitor throughout the summer. In winter there is a regular herd of Whooper Swan, plus Greylag and Pink-footed Geese, and a variety of ducks.

Access: leave Kingussie on the B970 toward Insh and after 1¼ miles the RSPB reserve centre is on the left before Tromie Bridge.

Permits: the reserve is open every day except Tuesday.

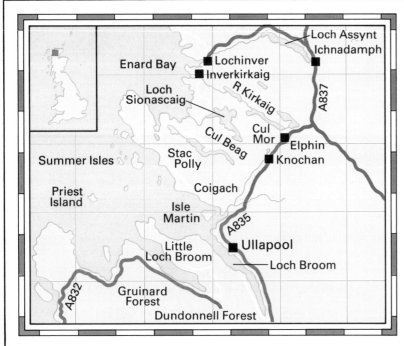

INVERPOLLY, HIGHLAND OS 15

Location: wild country in the north-west of Scotland, one of the remotest parts of Britain. Ullapool is the nearest town of any size.

Habitats: this is a dramatic landscape of rugged mountains, vast moors, innumerable lochs, wild sea coasts and delightful islands, much of it protected in a huge National Nature Reserve, covering 26,827 acres. Offshore are the Summer Isles, with breeding seabirds.

Birds: all of the open-country, non-woodland Scottish bird specialities occur here. Divers, Red-breasted Merganser, Goosander, Wigeon, Golden Eagle, Peregrine, Merlin, Ptarmigan, Red Grouse, Dunlin, Greenshank, Redwing and Twite all breed. The cliffs and islands have Black Guillemot, Eider, Greylag Goose, Arctic Tern and even Storm Petrels. There is a chance of finding breeding Scottish Crossbill in the woods and Snow Bunting on the higher slopes. A good deal of walking and serious preparation are essential: make sure you are equipped with a compass, map, torch, food, water and warm, weatherproof clothing.

Access: leave Ullapool northwards on the A835 and after about 14 miles, stop at the Knockan Information Centre, open from May to mid-September. Otherwise explore off the minor roads with the OS map. Boats from Ullapool regularly visit the Summer Isles.

Permits: only needed from 15 July to 21 October.

ISLAY, STRATHCLYDE   OS 60

Location: this is one of the larger Inner Hebrides, lying some 14 miles west of the Kintyre and about 70 miles west of Glasgow.

Habitats: there are areas of farmland and grazing, of loch and moor; there are streams and bogs, and cliffs and dune beaches.

Birds: up to 20,000 Barnacle Geese winter here, mainly in the Loch Gruinart area where the RSPB has a reserve. These birds come from Greenland and they are often accompanied by several thousand Greenland Whitefronts. To the south Loch Indaal is a good place for wintering seabirds, with Great Northern Diver, Slavonian Grebe, Scaup, Goldeneye, Red-breasted Merganser, Common Scoter and Eider. Resident birds that may be seen include Chough, Golden Eagle and Peregrine, plus the chance of a wandering White-tailed Eagle from the island of Rhum, about 70 miles to the north, where this magnificent raptor was re-introduced between 1975 and 1985. In summer there are divers, terns and auks.

Access: the B8017 and the road northwards to Ardnave along the western side of Loch Gruinart are both excellent for geese. Loch Indaal is easily explored from the A847 which, in the east, leads to the cliffs of The Oa, and the A846 north of Bowmore. There are ferries from Kennacraig in Kintyre and flights from Glasgow.

Permits: none required.

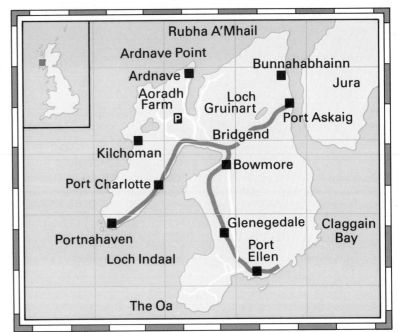

ISLE OF MAY, FIFE   OS 59

Location: 'the May', as it is affectionately called, lies at the mouth of the Firth of Forth, with Anstruther, about five miles to the north-west, the nearest port on the mainland.

Habitats: this is a rather bleak island, so migrants tend to find their way to the observatory garden. There are also fine sea-cliffs.

Birds: breeding seabirds include Guillemot, Razorbill, Puffin, Kittiwake, Shag and Fulmar, together with Arctic and Common Tern. But the real objective of a visit is for migrants. The Isle of May has been known as a major migrant watch point since 1907 and a bird observatory was established in 1934. The regular chats, warblers and flycatchers are best in autumn with easterly winds and sometimes occur in dramatic 'falls' of large numbers. With them are Bluethroat and Wryneck and sometimes Barred and Icterine Warblers with a chance of extreme rarities. Almost any bird can turn up here. Seabirds are often visible offshore in autumn.

Access: the observatory operates on a self-catering basis and the 1 hour crossing from Anstruther can be arranged when booking. Contact Mrs R. Cowper, 9 Oxgangs Road, Edinburgh EH10 7BG. Day trips can be arranged in Anstruther.

Permits: none required. The island is a National Nature Reserve.

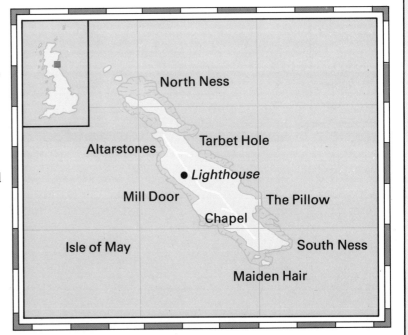

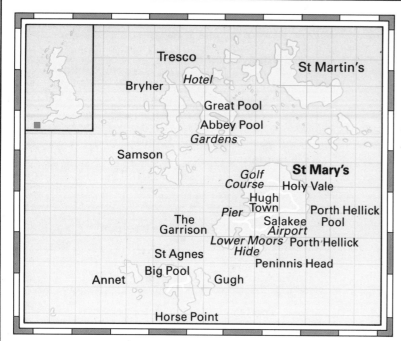

ISLES OF SCILLY OS 203

Location: over 150 islands off the coast of Land's End in Cornwall, with nothing between them and America but the Atlantic Ocean.

Habitats: only five of the islands are inhabited. The rest are mostly rocky with areas of rough grass. These are low-lying islands with few significant cliffs. Much of the landscape on the larger islands is agricultural, with early vegetables and flowers.

Birds: Scilly does have breeding seabirds, including Razorbill, Puffin, Manx Shearwater and Storm Petrel, but a boat trip around Annet is usually as close as anyone gets to them. Tresco has both Common and Roseate Tern, the latter as rare as ever. Spring passage can be good and regularly produces a rarity that has overshot its destination, including Hoopoe, Golden Oriole and Woodchat Shrike but it is October that is the prime time for Scilly birdwatching. Over 375 species have been recorded on the islands, including the rarest of rare birds and many 'firsts' for Britain.

Access: most visitors stay on St Mary's, the main centre. There are regular helicopter flights from Penzance, but early booking is essential. There are also flights by plane from Plymouth and Exeter and daily sailings by boat from Penzance. The boat is good for seabirds, but the 2½ hour crossing may be very rough.

Permits: none required, but do not trespass on private land.

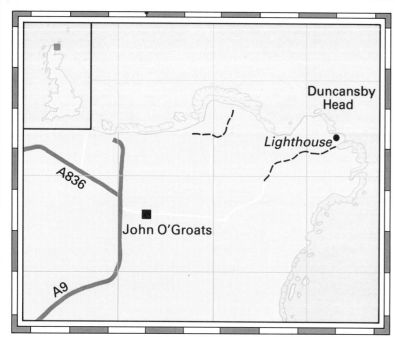

JOHN O'GROATS, HIGHLAND OS 12

Location: the north-eastern-most point of Scotland, more or less the furthest point on the mainland from Land's End. The nearest town is Wick, about 17 miles to the south.

Habitats: John O'Groats is a scattering of tourist shops just a short distance from Duncansby Head, which is the real centre of birding interest. Here the cliffs fall directly to the sea, offering a home to large colonies of seabirds. These cliffs extend southwards along the east coast to Brough Head.

Birds: the cliff-dwelling seabirds are abundant along this stretch of coastline, and include Guillemot, Razorbill, Puffin, Black Guillemot, Fulmar and Kittiwake. There are Shags here too, as well as Great and Arctic Skuas nesting a short distance inland. Though they do not breed, Gannets are abundant throughout the summer and reasonably pure Rock Doves can also be found.

Access: from John O'Groats take the minor road to the lighthouse at Duncansby Head, where you can enjoy good views of the highest cliffs. Return southwards on the A9 and stop where the cliffs are closest. Walk to the edge to view the low cliffs teeming with birds. Brough Head is a good place to stop.

Permits: none required.

KENFIG, MID-GLAMORGAN OS 170

Location: between Cardiff and Swansea, three miles north of Porthcawl and strategically situated near the South Wales coast.

Habitats: this 70-acre freshwater dune-slack lake lies among over 1000 acres of open dunes and is surrounded by extensive marshy areas with reed and scrub. The coastline itself is mainly sandy, with intertidal areas and a rocky outcrop at Sker Point.

Birds: in summer there are warblers among the lakeside vegetation, including Reed and Grasshopper Warbler, both of which breed. Spring and autumn passage periods bring terns, including regular Black Tern, and a good variety of ducks and waders, including substantial flocks of Whimbrel. In winter the shoreline holds Grey Plover, Purple Sandpiper and Turnstone and, at high tide, some of these birds move to Kenfig to roost, bathe or continue feeding. There are usually plenty of gulls here, but rarities are seldom found. Water Rail, Hen Harrier and Ruff are also reasonably regular at this time.

Access: leave the M4 at Exit 37 or 38 and join the B4283, from where a road leaves southward across the motorway to Kenfig. South of the village there is a reserve centre of the Mid-Glamorgan County Council with paths around the pools, where there is a hide.

Permits: not required, but check at the centre that the hide is open.

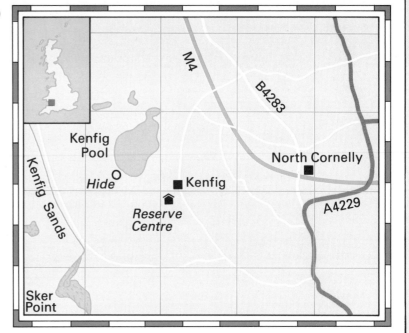

KYLE OF TONGUE, HIGHLAND

OS 10

Location: this sea inlet is situated on the north coast of Sutherland, between John O'Groats and Cape Wrath.

Habitats: the Kyle is a long tidal inlet that is remarkably shallow, with large areas of mud exposed at low tide. Offshore there are several substantial islands that hold seabirds, while inland lies one of the remotest moorland and mountain areas in Britain.

Birds: there are Britain's most northerly Rooks here and a good seabird population, especially on Roan Island with its Black Guillemot, Great Skua and Storm Petrel, along with Peregrine. The inland lochs attract breeding Red-throated and Black-throated Diver, Dunlin and Greenshank, with the occasional Wood Sandpiper and even Red-necked Phalarope. Golden Eagle, Merlin, Ptarmigan and Ring Ousel breed on the moors.

Access: the coastal A838 gives good views of the Kyle of Tongue and the A836 leads past Loch Loyal and Ben Loyal. Otherwise it is a matter of exploring all the roads and tracks and not being afraid of cross-country trekking. Roan can be reached by boat from Tongue.

Permits: this is grouse-shooting and deer-stalking country, with restrictions during late summer and autumn. Look out for notices giving details of deer-stalking.

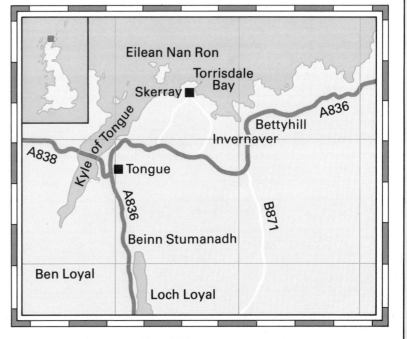

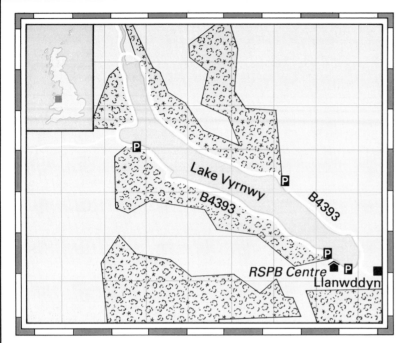

LAKE VYRNWY, POWYS OS 125

Location: this large reservoir lies in the Berwyn Hills of northern Powys, a remote area of mid-Wales. Welshpool lies about 18 miles to the south-east, Machynlleth about 25 miles to the south-west.

Habitats: the reservoir is surrounded by typical Welsh hill country, with extensive heather moors broken by conifer plantations, but also features delightful wooded valleys and rippling streams. The lake has shallow margins in several areas and there are considerable areas of scrub.

Birds: in this lovely range of hills it is possible to find a typical cross-section of Welsh woodland and mountain breeding birds. The oaks have Wood Warbler, Pied Flycatcher and Redstart; the streams hold Grey Wagtail, Dipper and Common Sandpiper; the lake boasts Goosander and Kingfisher. Overhead there are Buzzard and Sparrowhawk, while the conifers, when young, are home to Hen Harrier, and, when mature, to Crossbill. Providing the heather moors can be protected, the Vyrnwy area will remain the best place to go birding in this part of Wales.

Access: the B4393 from Llanfyllin goes right round the reservoir. There is an RSPB centre at the dam, a hide in the north-west and plenty of good woodland walks.

Permits: not required.

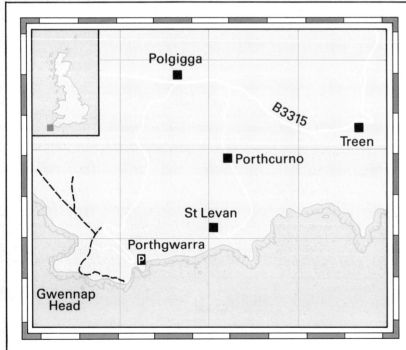

LAND'S END, CORNWALL OS 203

Location: famous as the extreme south-western tip of England, surrounded by the Atlantic Ocean.

Habitats: surrounded by dramatic granite sea cliffs, the Land's End peninsula is an area of moorland, heath and small fields, broken here and there by deep valleys.

Birds: the area is good for migrants in both spring and autumn, and October sees a scattering of rare birds. Every year there is an American species or two, along with eastern rarities such as Red-breasted Flycatcher and southern ones like Woodchat Shrike. Scarce waders, such as Dotterel, are regular on St Just Airfield and this is also a good spot for Buff-breasted Sandpiper.

Access: from Penzance take the B3315 to Treen and later a minor road at Polgigga to Porthgwarra. Walk up the Porthgwarra valley west to the coastguard cottages and on a choice of paths around Gwennap Head. Check the village gardens in Porthgwarra and the dense bushes in the valley for birds. Continue on the B3315 to Land's End, turn right on the A30, then left on the B3306 to St Just Airfield. Turn left to Nanquidno and scan the short grass for waders. To the west of the airfield the Nanquidno valley, with its dense cover, also produces migrants, including American rarities.

Permits: none required.

LANDGUARD POINT, SUFFOLK

OS 169

Location: the southernmost tip of the Suffolk coast, at the mouth of the joint estuary of the Rivers Stour and Orwell, it lies between Harwich and the docks of Felixstowe.

Habitats: this is a shingle spit extending southwards across the estuary mouth, with large areas of low cover surrounded by sprawling docks. There are disused pits, wartime defences, and a small pool. It was not until the 1980s that Landguard became a notable birdwatching site. In 1983 a bird observatory was established and scarce migrants have been recorded ever since. There is also a reserve here, managed by the Suffolk Trust for Nature Conservation. The main emphasis is on small migrants in spring and autumn, with birds arriving and departing during day and night, particularly in autumn. Pied Flycatcher, Bluethroat and Wryneck are all regular, along with the more widespread warblers and chats. The docks and old fort provide nesting sites for Black Redstart, while Ringed Plover and Little Tern breed on the shingle.

Access: leave Felixstowe southwards on a minor road to Landguard nature reserve.

Permits: these are not required for the nature reserve and not available for the observatory. There is no accommodation.

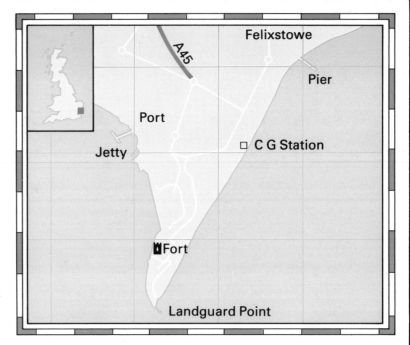

LANGSTONE HARBOUR AND FARLINGTON MARSHES, HAMPSHIRE OS 196 & 197

Location: the large tidal inlet of Langstone Harbour is east of Portsmouth. Farlington Marshes extend into it.

Habitats: the areas of mud exposed at low tide offer shorebirds good feeding opportunities and there are low-lying islands that offer safe roosts to waders. Farlington is an area of rough grazing land intersected by dykes and a few low-lying freshwater marshes.

Birds: winter brings up to 10,000 Brent Geese. Wigeon, Teal and Pintail are also numerous and waders include good flocks of Knot, Black-tailed Godwit, Grey Plover and especially Dunlin, and a few wintering Greenshank, Spotted Redshank and Ruff. Goldeneye and Red-breasted Merganser feed in the deep channels and Black-necked Grebe frequent the Langstone Bridge area. On spring and autumn passage there is a wider variety of waders. Gulls have included the rarest species found in Britain.

Access: leave the A27 at its junction with the A2030 and take a track off the roundabout leading eastward to the marshes. A footpath leads around the peninsula.

Permits: though partly an RSPB reserve, no permits are required.

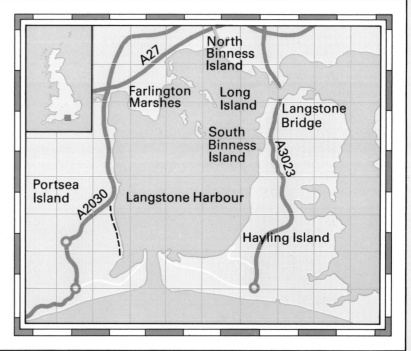

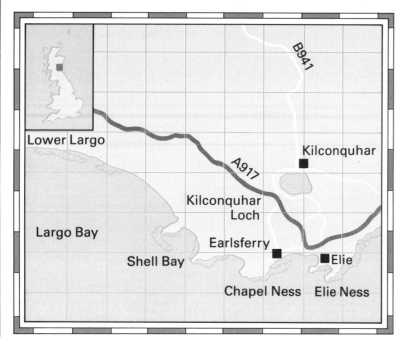

LARGO BAY AND KILCONQUHAR LOCH, FIFE OS 59

Location: on the northern shore of the Firth of Forth, east of Leven.
Habitats: the sea itself is the major attraction here. Loch Kilconquhar has a roost of Greylag Geese – and much more besides.
Birds: though grebes and ducks breed on the loch, this is mainly a winter site, when seaducks are particularly good. Scoter, Goldeneye and Scaup are dominant, but Long-tailed Duck is regular in good numbers, often approaching quite close inshore. Both Red-throated and Black-throated Divers are regular, the former being by far the most numerous, and Slavonian Grebe can usually be seen. The rocky shorelines hold Purple Sandpiper, as well as the more widespread Turnstone, Dunlin, Grey Plover and Redshank. Spring and autumn passage periods bring in good numbers of terns, including a few Roseate Terns, while Little Gull is something of a local speciality, with several hundred sometimes appearing at Loch Kilconquhar.
Access: Leven is worth a look as is Lower Largo to the east. Elie Ness and Earlsferry are probably the best seawatching spots. For Kilconquhar Loch leave the A917 on to the B941 to the village and view from the north by the church.
Permits: none necessary.

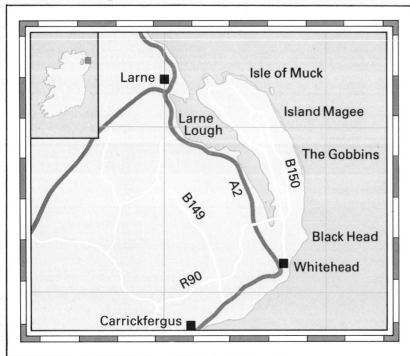

LARNE LOUGH, CO. ANTRIM, NORTHERN IRELAND OSNI 9

Location: this is an inlet of the sea less than 30 miles to the north-east of Belfast that almost cuts off Island Magee from the mainland. Larne itself is a ferry terminal.
Habitats: there are extensive mud banks that offer good feeding opportunities to wildfowl and waders, but comparatively small areas of saltmarsh. Sadly, the estuary is being used as a dump by industry.
Birds: there is a small flock of Brent Geese here through the winter, along with up to 2000 Wigeon, and smaller numbers of Teal and Shelducks. Goldeneye (sometimes 50 or more) can be regularly seen on the channels. The tiny (¼-acre) RSPB reserve of Swan Island, on the inner part of the lough, is a major high-tide wader roost and shelters large numbers of ducks, and has small breeding colonies of Roseate and Sandwich Terns, as well as breeding Red-breasted Mergansers.
Access: the main A2 from Larne to Belfast passes along the western shoreline, though the railway line between it and the lough prevents complete exploration of the site. The B90 crosses the head of the estuary and offers access at several sites along the eastern shoreline.
Permits: there is no access to Swan Island; no permit is required for the rest of the area.

LAVAN SANDS, GWYNEDD OS 115

Location: on the North Wales coast, to the east of Anglesey.

Habitats: the massive intertidal sands are broken only by the Ogwen estuary. The Conwy estuary, about 10 miles to the north-east, is an excellent site, while 5 miles to the north of the Conwy are the dramatic limestone sea-cliffs of Great Ormes Head.

Birds: the Ogwen estuary has Wigeon, Shelduck, Goldeneye and Red-breasted Merganser. Waders are found here too, though the largest roost is usually just to the west of Llanfairfechan. This is also a good area for the scarcer winter grebes, and for wintering Firecrest, Chiffchaff and even Water Pipit. Winter also brings Red-throated Diver, a few Great Northern Divers, and small flocks of Twite on the saltmarshes, while at Great Orme there are Purple Sandpiper. There is a hide overlooking the estuary on one side and a small pool in a wood on the other; Kingfisher and Water Rail are often seen here in winter. Spring and autumn passage brings a greater variety of waders, especially to the 6000-acre Traeth Lavan Local Nature Reserve.

Access: from the A55 at Tal-y-bont a minor road leads north to the reserve and hide. The other sites are reachable from the A55.

Permits: none required at present, but check with the reserve on arrival for access to Traeth Lavan.

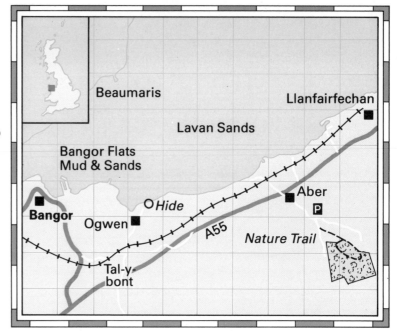

LEIGHTON MOSS, LANCASHIRE OS 97

Location: this RSPB reserve lies in a limestone valley in north-western Lancashire, near the head of Morecambe Bay.

Habitats: this is now one of the largest reed beds in the country. There is plenty of scrub and open water, surrounded by hilly woods.

Birds: this is now the main breeding stronghold of the Bittern in Britain. Bearded Tit, too, breed, along with Reed, Sedge and Grasshopper Warblers. Several duck species (including Shoveler and sometimes Gadwall and Garganey), also breed, as do Buzzard and Sparrowhawk. Spring and autumn passage brings regular Garganey, Marsh Harrier and Black Tern. Passage waders include Greenshank, Green Sandpiper and Spotted Redshank. In winter there are many ducks, Greylag Goose, Water Rail, as well as resident Bittern.

Access: from the A6 or M6 at junction 35 (via Carnforth) or 36 (via Milnthorpe). The reserve entrance is on the left near Silverdale railway station. There is public access across the middle of the reserve, and a public hide, as well as four RSPB-only hides. The reserve is open daily, except Tuesday; the car park and reserve centre lies to the south of the public track.

Permits: a fee is payable by non-RSPB members.

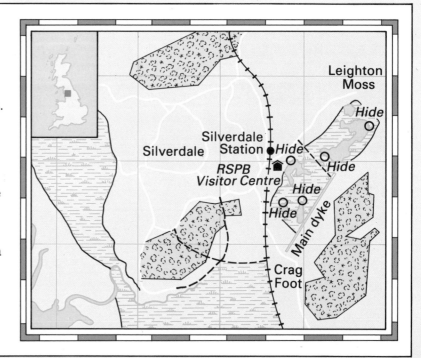

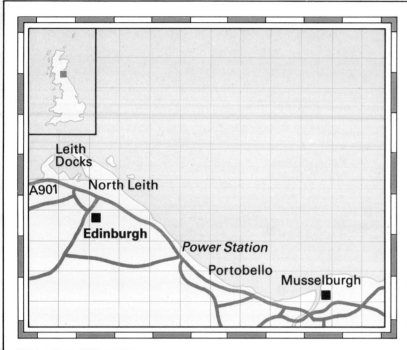

LEITH AND MUSSELBURGH, EAST LOTHIAN OS 66

Location: this bay extends from the dockland of Leith eastwards along the southern shore of the Firth of Forth.

Habitats: the rich feeding grounds of the Forth have attracted both wildfowl and waders to this area for many years. For a long time this attraction was enhanced by a sewage outfall, but sadly that has now gone. One result is that, instead of boasting one of the largest flocks of Scaup in the country (with a peak of 30,000 or more in 1968–9), the bay now rarely holds more than a handful of these seaducks.

Birds: Merganser, Long-tailed Duck, Common and Velvet Scoter, Goldeneye and Eider are all present here in good numbers. Red-throated Diver is regular too, along with Slavonian Grebe. Waders tend to be the regular Redshank, Turnstone and Dunlin, but during spring and autumn the Goose Green Ash Lagoon may hold a wider variety of species. There may also be gulls.

Access: the A1 runs parallel with the shores of the Firth of Forth east of Edinburgh and there is a promenade giving excellent views to the west. It is worth exploring the whole of this shoreline, stopping to view the birds from the many vantage points. The Goose Green Ash Lagoon lies at Musselburgh, just off the A1.

Permits: none required.

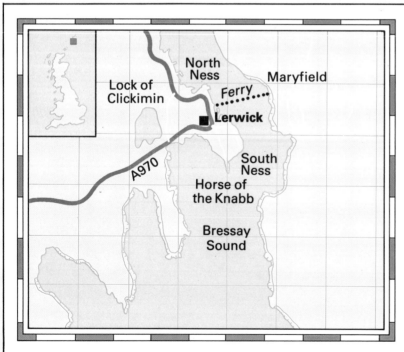

LERWICK, SHETLAND OS 4

Location: the capital of Shetland, Lerwick lies on the eastern side of Mainland, the biggest island, and is sheltered by the island of Bressay, to the east.

Habitats: the main attraction of Lerwick to birders is its busy harbour, where scavenging seabirds regularly gather in large numbers. There are also gardens offering cover to migrants, but no convenient spot from which these birds can be easily watched.

Birds: in summer, there are always gulls and Black Guillemot, but the real time for a visit is mid-winter, especially after gales. Then the local gulls are regularly joined by both Glaucous and Iceland Gulls and, just occasionally, by one of the really rare species, such as Ivory Gull. These same storms may force some of the birds that winter elsewhere in Shetland to seek shelter: these include Long-tailed Duck, Eider and Slavonian Grebe. Great Northern Diver occurs every winter and each one should be checked carefully in case it is a rare White-billed Diver.

Access: there are regular connections to Lerwick from Aberdeen by air and ferry. A good place to start exploring the area is the sewage outfall immediately south of Loch of Clickimin. Respect the islanders' privacy when looking into gardens.

Permits: not required.

LINDISFARNE, NORTHUMBERLAND OS 75

Location: this island, also known as Holy Island, is joined to the north Northumberland coast at low tide by a causeway. It lies about 9 miles south of Berwick-upon-Tweed and the Scottish border. The Lindisfarne National Nature Reserve is mainly intertidal and includes Budle Bay. The area described here includes the mainland from Goswick in the north to Bamburgh in the south. The A1 provides both a boundary and convenient access.

Habitats: predominantly an intertidal area of mud and sand, sheltered from the open sea by a coastline of large dunes. The largest area of dunes lies at the northern end of Holy Island. The causeway to the mainland is covered by the tide for several hours each day. This is no place to run out of petrol, though people do every year. The largest area of sand is Fenham Flats, but in Budle Bay to the south large areas of mud and sand are exposed at low tide. About 9 miles to the south the castle at Bamburgh stands atop cliffs that are frequented by seabirds.

Birds: the number of birds here in winter can be quite staggering, with Dunlin the dominant wader and Wigeon the commonest duck. The latter have reached 40,000 on occasion. Of the waders there are 14,000 Dunlin, 10,000 Knot, 4500 Bar-tailed Godwit, 1000 Redshank and lesser numbers of Sanderling, Turnstone and Grey Plover. As well as Wigeon, wildfowl include about 600 Scoter, 200 Long-tailed Duck, 600 Shelduck and virtually the whole British wintering population of the Pale-bellied sub-species of Brent Goose, which breeds on the island of Spitsbergen (Svalbard) in the Arctic Ocean and which is rapidly declining. There is also a 400-strong herd of Whooper Swan. Red-throated Diver are regular and Black-throated Diver are often present, too. Slavonian is the most common grebe, but Red-necked Grebe is also regular.

Spring and autumn passage periods bring a wider variety of waders, including Spotted Redshank, both Black-tailed and Bar-tailed Godwits and, in autumn, Little Stint. Terns, too, are regular (mainly Common, Arctic and Sandwich), and are often accompanied by Arctic Skua. Small migrants are often good, but rarities are few and even species such as Bluethroat and Wryneck that turn up regularly at other east-coast sites are scarce.

Access: there are several easy access points that make exploration straightforward. They are, from north to south, Goswick; Beal for the causeway to Holy Island, which is certainly worth exploring as far as Castle Point; Fenham; Ross to Ross Links and Ross Back Sands; via Budle to Budle Point; and from Bamburgh northwards. Take careful note of the tide times and instructions prominently displayed at the causeway before attempting to cross to Holy Island.

Permits: permits are not necessary, but keep strictly to the public rights of way as outlined above.

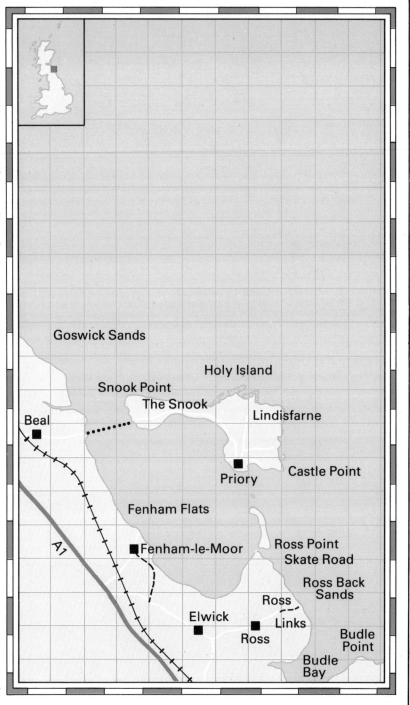

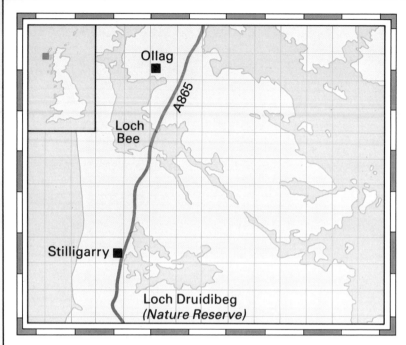

LOCH DRUIDIBEG, OUTER HEBRIDES OS 22

Location: this National Nature Reserve is situated in the northern part of the island of South Uist.

Habitats: Druidibeg is a shallow freshwater loch with grassy margins and fields; there are damp areas and some taller vegetation. To the west the land rolls gently toward the shellsand beaches, while to the east the coast is more rugged and hostile.

Birds: the flock of about 150 Greylag Geese is the largest native population in Britain. The birds breed here and spend the winter grazing the surrounding grasslands. Some are also found on Loch Bee to the north. Though mainly winter visitors, Whooper Swans sometimes stay for the summer, though there has been no proof of breeding for over 40 years. The area holds Corncrake in summer.

Access: the main A865 passes the western shore of Druidibeg and there are minor roads running eastward to facilitate exploration, especially the B890. South Uist can be reached by British Airways flights to Benbecula; alternatively, there are Caledonian MacBrayne ferries from Oban to Lochboisdale (voyage 6–9 hours), or from Uig, on Skye, to Lochmaddy, North Uist (voyage 2 hours).

Permits: none required outside the breeding season; keep to the public roads at other times.

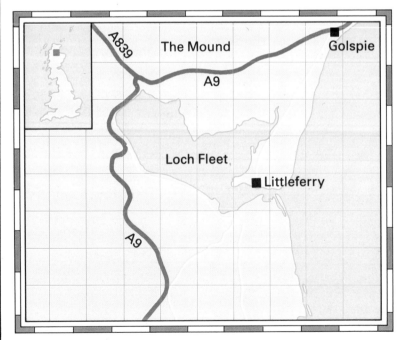

LOCH FLEET, HIGHLAND OS 21

Location: five miles north of the Dornoch Firth and 3 miles to the south-west of Golspie on the east coast of northern Scotland.

Habitats: the loch is almost totally enclosed by land and has only a narrow opening to the sea, at Littleferry. Its intertidal banks offer feeding opportunities to waders and wildfowl, while the attempted draining of the upper part of the estuary with 'The Mound' in 1815 simply created a freshwater marsh that has become a dense 'fen'. Near the coast the dunes extend northwards to Golspie.

Birds: winter is probably the best season here, with good numbers of the more common waders and plentiful wildfowl. The latter include Whooper Swan and Greylag Goose, along with good numbers of seaducks, including Long-tailed Duck and Eider. The area seems to have an attraction for long-stay rarities, including King Eider and Surf Scoter. Breeding birds include Scottish Crossbill, Arctic Tern and Eider. Ospreys visit in summer.

Access: the main A9 runs along The Mound and gives views over the fen and upper estuary. The best birds are often near the mouth, or just outside, and can be viewed by taking the road southward near Golspie to Littleferry then walking along the shore back toward the town. Embo, to the south, should not be ignored.

Permits: not required for access along rights of way.

LOCH GARTEN, HIGHLAND OS 36

Loch: this famous Scottish loch lies about 3½ miles east of the A9 at the point at which the road leaves the Spey valley, about 25 miles south-east of Inverness.

Habitats: the loch actually lies within Abernethy Forest which is treated separately (*see page* 9) because of its appeal to a different kind of birdwatcher. Loch Garten is surrounded by old Scots pine forest with open areas of heather and juniper.

Birds: this reserve celebrates the return of the Osprey to breed in Britain and is an important PR exercise for the RSPB. The number of visitors is extraordinary and the staff ensure that the observation post and the powerful fixed binoculars are used to maximum effect. Most visitors see the birds, buy a souvenir and are soon on their way to the next tourist site. Birders may walk the paths in their search for Scottish Crossbill, Crested Tit, Redstart and Siskin, but would be well advised to follow a different approach for the scarcer species.

Access: leave the B970 on a minor road 1 mile north east of Boat of Garten and follow signs marked 'To the Ospreys'. There is ample parking and information, an RSPB shop, the observation post and helpful staff.

Permits: none required and nothing to pay.

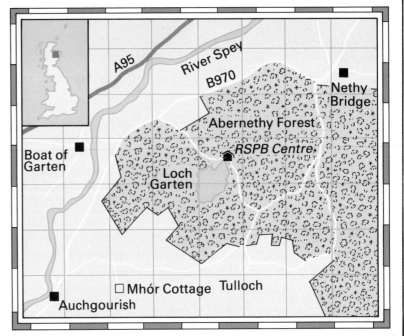

LOCH KEN, DUMFRIES AND GALLOWAY OS 77, 83 & 84

Location: inland of the north shore of the Solway, extending from just west of Castle Douglas to New Galloway.

Habitats: the damming of the River Dee has created a long and narrow loch with natural grassy banks and marshes. There is an RSPB reserve (the Ken–Dee Marshes Reserve).

Birds: for many years, this has been one of the finest sites for wintering geese in Britain. Greylag and Greenland Whitefront are the major species, but the decidedly scarce Bean Goose also occurs, mainly after Christmas, and there are also Pink-footed Goose as well as Whooper Swan. Ducks include Wigeon, Teal, Shoveler, Pintail, Goldeneye, Goosander and Merganser. Raptors are regular, including Buzzard, Merlin and Hen Harrier.

Access: starting at Castle Douglas, view Carlingwark Loch to the west before continuing on the A75 to Threave Wildfowl Refuge. Take the track to the right to Kelton Lodge where there are free hides. Explore Loch Ken from the A713 on the east and A762 on the west. The RSPB reserve may be visited only escorted and by previous appointment, but all the birds can be seen from the roads.

Permits: only necessary for escorted visits to RSPB reserve: contact The Warden, Midtown, Laurieston, near Castle Douglas, DG7 2PP.

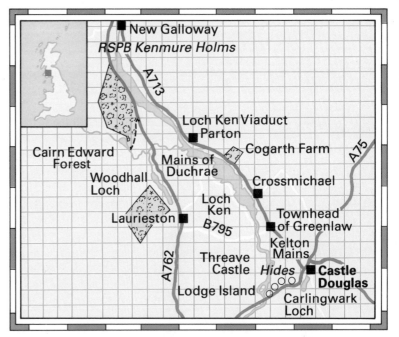

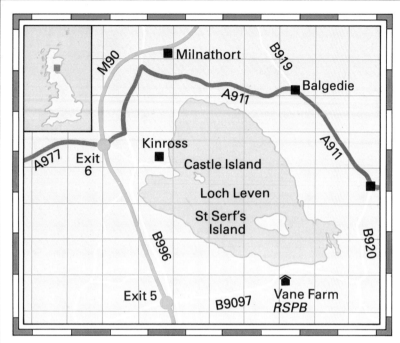

LOCH LEVEN, TAYSIDE OS 58

Location: between the Firths of Forth and Tay.

Habitats: Loch Leven is one of the richest lowland lakes in the country and is surrounded by agricultural land. It has several islands, marshy banks, and a 'scrape' at the RSPB's Vane Farm Reserve.

Birds: Loch Leven has long been famous as the most important breeding site for ducks (with over 1000 pairs) in Britain and one of the major arrival points for wintering geese. In autumn over 12,000 Pink-footed Geese use the water as a roost, with large numbers remaining all winter, with many Greylag Geese. Wintering ducks include very good numbers of Goosander and Goldeneye, as well as huge numbers of the more common species. Peregrine is frequently to be seen. The geese are best seen at dusk and dawn.

Access: though there is access at Kirkgate Park, Burleigh Sands and from roads at other points, the RSPB reserve at Vane Farm is usually the best entry point at all seasons. Leave the M90 at Exit 5 and take the B9097 eastwards along the southern shore. There is an excellent visitor centre that is open daily except during January to March, when opening is restricted to weekends, and good hides.

Permits: available from the RSPB reserve centre. Non-members pay a small charge.

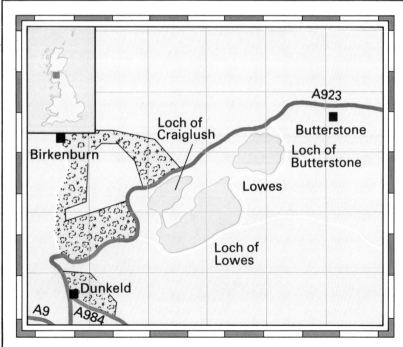

LOCH OF LOWES, TAYSIDE OS 53

Location: this Scottish Wildlife Trust reserve lies immediately east of Dunkeld only a short distance from the A9 trunk road.

Habitats: this is a shallow loch with a good growth of emergent vegetation that offers food and shelter to a good range of birds. It is surrounded by mature woodlands that provide protection from casual disturbance.

Birds: Ospreys breed every year and this is only the second (after Loch Garten) eyrie of these birds to be widely publicized and open to visiting, despite the continued increase in numbers of these charismatic raptors. Other breeders include Great Crested Grebe and both Sedge and Grasshopper Warblers. Despite rumours, this is not a regular site for breeding Slavonian Grebe. The woodlands hold all the species one would expect in this region and there are Black Grouse and Capercaillie nearby. In winter the loch acts as a major roost for Greylag Geese.

Access: leave the A9 at Dunkeld on the A923 and turn right after 1½ miles. There is a visitor centre here that is open daily from April to September, and the hide is open throughout the year.

Permits: not required, but you will help ensure the birds will continue to bring enjoyment by joining the Scottish Wildlife Trust: donations are also gratefully received.

LOCH OF SPIGGIE, SHETLAND

OS 4

Location: this lowland loch lies in the southern part of Shetland's chief island, Mainland, to the west of the main Lerwick–Sumburgh road and only about ¼ mile from the Bay of Scousburgh.

Habitats: Spiggie is a shallow freshwater loch that is rich and fertile. It is surrounded by grassland, with dunes to the north and a marsh to the south that separates it from the neighbouring Loch of Brow. Part of the latter, as well as the whole of Loch of Spiggie, is included in an RSPB reserve.

Birds: breeding birds include Shelduck and Curlew, and it is regularly used by a variety of seabirds for bathing and resting. These include Great and Arctic Skuas and Arctic Terns. In spring there is a regular gathering of Long-tailed Duck that indulge in courtship displays prior to nesting elsewhere. In winter Whooper Swan are regular visitors and there are usually also Greylag Geese and a variety of duck present. During passage periods various waders, often including Red-necked Phalarope, appear.

Access: though there is a summer warden, there are no visiting arrangements. Much can be seen from the surrounding roads. Leave the A970 westwards on the B9122 and view to the south.

Permits: not available.

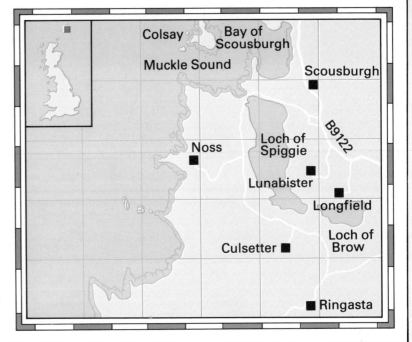

LOCH OF STRATHBEG, GRAMPIAN OS 30

Location: the largest dune lake in Britain. It lies between Peterhead and Fraserburgh in the north-east of Scotland.

Habitats: this is a shallow 'dune-slack' lake that varies greatly in size according to the water-level. It is surrounded by farmland and grassy marshes, with some reedy areas, and is separated from the sea by a large dune system. Much of the area is an RSPB reserve.

Birds: the main interest is in winter, when Strathbeg is a major gathering place for huge flocks of migrating geese. Nearly 40,000 geese, mainly Pinkfeet and Greylags, regularly use the area, and there are good numbers of Whooper Swan, Goldeneye and Goosander. The sea holds all three regular British species of diver, and Hen Harrier are also regular. More irregular visitors include Marsh Harrier and Merlin.

Access: leave Peterhead northwards on the A952 and turn right before Crimond to the Starnafin reserve headquarters. Access is across MoD property. The south side of the loch can be seen from the minor road to the south which leads to Rattray Head.

Permits: no access without a permit: write in advance to The Warden, RSPB, The Lythe, Crimonmogate, Lonmay, Fraserburgh, AB4 4UB. There is a charge to non-RSPB members.

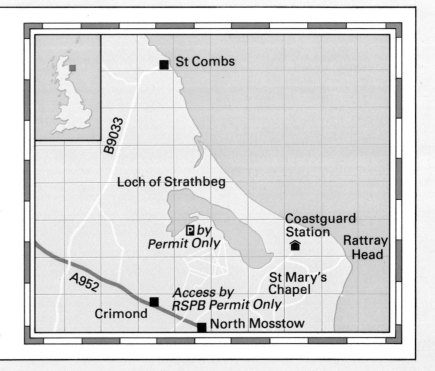

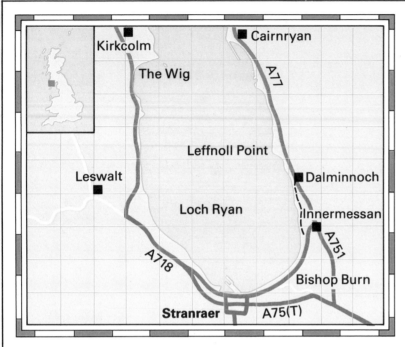

LOCH RYAN, DUMFRIES AND GALLOWAY   OS 76 & 82

Location: at the western end of Galloway, enclosed by the northern arm of the hammerhead-shaped western tip of Galloway, with Luce Bay about 6 miles to the south.

Habitats: this is a large sea loch that is well sheltered by the surrounding hills. There are small intertidal areas of mud.

Birds: this is a favourite site for a good variety of wintering seabirds. Though Red-throated Diver is most common, both Black-throated and Great Northern also occur regularly. Grebes usually include both Slavonian and Black-necked, and seaducks include Wigeon, Scaup, Common Scoter, Red-breasted Merganser, Goldeneye and Eider. The occasional King Eider turns up among the Common Eider; indeed, Loch Ryan is one of the best spots in Britain for this handsome northern vagrant. Most of these birds concentrate on the southern shore off Stranraer, where there is a muddy foreshore that attracts waders. To the south-east lie the twin waters of Black Loch and White Loch, separated by Castle Kennedy. Here Greylag Geese are regular.

Access: the A77 and A718 provide many excellent vantage points, in particular, check east of Stranraer, Cairnryan and The Wig.

Permits: not required.

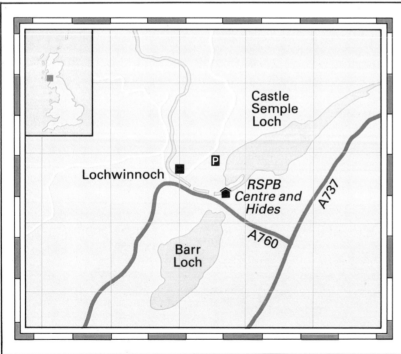

LOCHWINNOCH, STRATHCLYDE   OS 70

Location: this is an RSPB reserve that consists of the south-western shore of Castle Semple Loch, Aird Meadow, a large area of sedge marsh that extends southward almost to the A760 and some way beyond it. Only about 18 miles south-west of Glasgow, it serves an important function as an educational centre encouraging inner-city children to become involved in conservation.

Habitats: as well as the Barr Loch, there is willow and alder scrub, deciduous woodland and the sedge marsh of Aird Meadow.

Birds: breeding birds include Great Crested Grebe, which here finds its Scottish stronghold, plus several duck species, including Shoveler and Teal. There is a Black-headed Gull colony and both Grasshopper and Sedge Warblers breed among the reeds. In winter both Whooper Swan and Greylag Goose use the area, along with many ducks, including up to 1000 or more each of Tufted Duck and Pochard.

Access: leave the A737 on the A760 to Lochwinnoch Station. The reserve centre is beyond this on the right. There is a shop, a fine visitor centre, with a tower hide, and a nature trail that leads to other hides. A small admission charge is made to non-members. The reserve is open throughout the year.

Permits: available on arrival.

THE LODGE, BEDFORDSHIRE OS 153

Location: the headquarters of the RSPB, The Lodge lies just 1 mile east of the town of Sandy, on the A1 between Stevenage and St Neots.

Habitats: chiefly parkland surrounding a Victorian country mansion which houses the RSPB staff: the whole area has been improved to offer a variety of different habitats. There are areas of sandy heath, bracken slopes, birch scrub, mature wood and with old Scots pine, an artificial lake, three ponds and formal gardens surrounding the lodge itself.

Birds: no less than 130 species have been recorded, which is not surprising in view of the presence of so many pairs of expert eyes. They include 50 breeding species, among which Redstart, Lesser Whitethroat, Tree Pipit and all three British woodpeckers are notable. There is a shop and exhibition centre, a nature trail and a hide. The Lodge itself is not open to visitors.

Access: leave the A1 at Sandy eastwards on the B1042. Pass through the town and watch out for The Lodge on the right after 1 mile. The reserve is open daily.

Permits: not required, though only RSPB members and their guests may visit on Sundays.

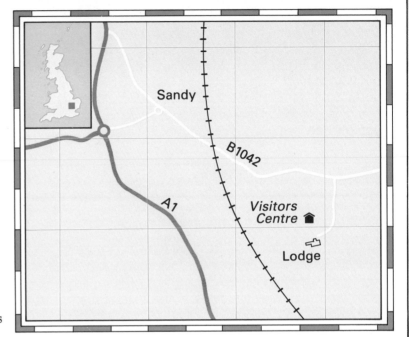

THE LOONS, ORKNEY OS 6

Location: this RSPB reserve lies in the north-western part of Mainland, the chief island of Orkney, directly west of Twatt, which is on the A986.

Habitats: The Loons is a substantial marsh lying in a basin of Old Red Sandstone and covered with an extensive growth of sedges and reeds. To the south it borders the western shore of the Loch of Isbister.

Birds: the marsh has a good breeding population of ducks that includes Shoveler, Wigeon, Pintail and Red-breasted Merganser, along with a mixed colony of gulls and terns that includes Arctic Tern and Common Gull. Though rare, Corncrake may still breed here. Winter brings many wildfowl, among which a small flock of Greenland Whitefronted Geese is notable. The marsh is, of course, a regular haunt of Hen Harrier.

Access: leave Twatt and the A986 just north of its junction with the A967, turning left on to a minor road. The reserve can be viewed from the south side of this minor road at several points. Just before reaching the B9056 there is a hide on the south side of the road giving good views.

Permits: not available; the only access is to the hide, which is open throughout the year.

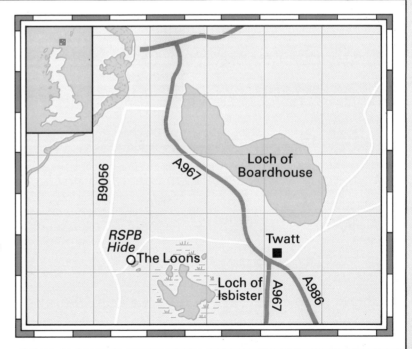

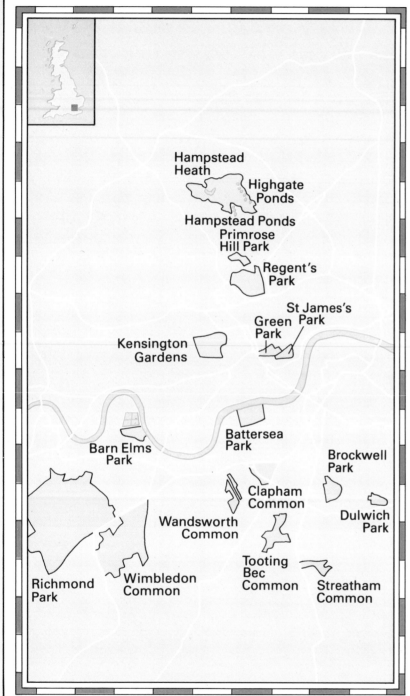

Hampstead
Heath

Highgate
Ponds

Hampstead Ponds

Primrose
Hill Park

Regent's
Park

St James's
Green Park
Park

Kensington
Gardens

Barn Elms
Park

Battersea
Park

Brockwell
Park

Clapham
Common

Dulwich
Park

Wandsworth
Common

Tooting
Bec
Common

Streatham
Common

Richmond
Park

Wimbledon
Common

LONDON OS 176 & 177

Location: the capital, with an area of over 600 sq miles (Greater London), has grown up around the River Thames, some 40 miles from its estuary and the North Sea.

Habitats: though a gigantic urban sprawl, London is surprisingly green when viewed from the air. There are numerous open areas of grassland and parkland, many with ornamental lakes, and in the suburbs the combined area of gardens is larger than that of the buildings. The total area of parks, gardens, squares and playing fields exceeds 20,000 acres, including 6000 acres of Royal Parks.

There has been a tradition of watching birds in London for many years, with attention concentrated on the Royal Parks and the reservoirs. The reservoirs at Barn Elms are treated separately (*see page* 14). More recently the parks and commons of the suburbs have been treated to more intensive study and shown to be mini-Fair Isles set in a sea of concrete. Because breeding birds are so few, it is much easier to count common migrants here than in open countryside.

Birds: ducks and feral geese breed on many ponds and there are Blackbird, Song Thrush and Blue Tit in most open areas, including back gardens. Black Redstart still breed on central redevelopment sites and the River Thames holds good populations of wintering ducks. The tiny reservoirs at Stoke Newington are always worth a winter watch. Since before the First War, diurnal migrants have been watched, particularly in October, from rooftops throughout the capital. In the north, Hampstead Heath has long been a favoured bird haunt, while in the south Wimbledon Common is one of the best sites. Watching for migrant warblers, chats and flycatchers can be rewarding at any substantial open space with trees or bushes and will produce daily Willow Warbler, Chiffchaff, Whitethroat, Lesser Whitethroat, Blackcap and other small migrants in season. Pied Flycatcher is regular and rarities have included Pallas's Warbler.

Access: the best area for migrants is the nearest open space that can be explored adequately in a morning. Over the years the following places have produced good birds: Hyde Park, Kensington Gardens, St James's Park, Regent's Park, Green Park and the string of southern commons that includes Clapham, Tooting, Wandsworth and Streatham. Breeding birds are better at Hampstead Heath and Wimbledon Common which retain more undergrowth, while any rooftop in October will produce birds soon after dawn. If your nearest open space is not listed, do not be put off. A few early morning walks during passage periods will soon show which areas are most productive, though try copses and bushy areas first. Be warned, however: the habit of watching daily can become almost an obsession, although it may produce the occasional real surprise.

Permits: none required.

LOUGH FOYLE, CO. LONDONDERRY, NORTHERN IRELAND OSNI 4 & 7

Location: this large open bay lies at the mouth of the River Foyle beginning about 5 miles downstream from Londonderry.

Habitats: Lough Foyle is a substantial sea lough with mud flats along the southern and eastern shores. The water is shallow and large areas of mud are exposed at low tide.

Birds: this is a major gathering place for migrating waders and wildfowl, with up to 29,000 Wigeon being particularly noteworthy in autumn. Winter numbers are generally much smaller. Brent Goose too is regular and both Whooper and Bewick's Swans form sizeable winter flocks. Several species of wader occur including Oystercatcher, Curlew, Redshank and Bar-tailed Godwit. Migrants include Little Stint, Curlew Sandpiper, Spotted Redshank and Greenshank.

Access: there is a National Nature Reserve (NNR) at the mouth of the River Roe, while the RSPB reserve extends from Longfield Point eastwards almost to the NNR. There is free access to viewpoints at Longfield, Faughanvale and Ballykelly, found by taking minor roads north off the A2. Magilligan Point also has waders.

Permits: none required.

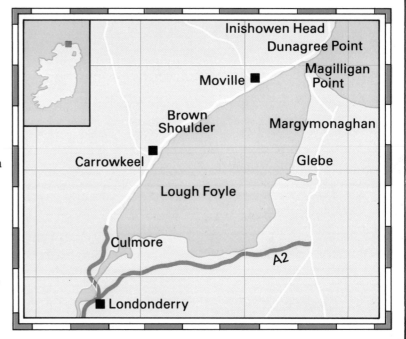

LOUGH NEAGH, CO. ANTRIM, NORTHERN IRELAND OSNI 14, 19 & 20

Location: the eastern shores of this huge lake lie some 15 miles west of Belfast.

Habitats: this is the largest area of freshwater in Britain and Ireland. Some of the newly created dry land has been turned over to agriculture, but much has been allowed to go wild, forming reed beds and swampy fens. To the north is Lough Beg, a similar but smaller water that is even richer in underwater life.

Birds: Lough Neagh is one of the major wildfowl sites in Europe, with massive winter populations of Tufted Duck and Pochard. Total numbers of both these species have, on occasion, exceeded 30,000 birds. More than 2000 each of Teal, Wigeon and Scaup have been recorded, while Goldeneye numbers have exceeded 5000 several times. All three British swans and Greylag Geese are regular.

Access: start at Shanes Castle, an RSPB reserve and estate open to the public. Find the Randalstown Road just west of Antrim. In the south-east corner Oxford Island reserve is reached by leaving M1 at Exit 10 and following signs. There are three hides.

Permits: contact The Warden, Shanes Castle, RSPB Reserve, 67 Greenview Avenue, Antrim.

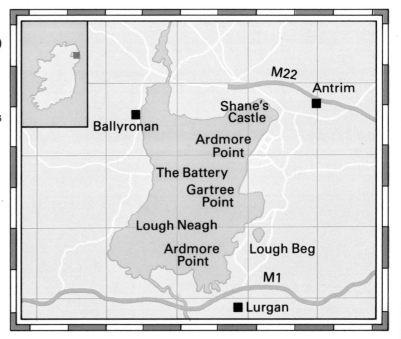

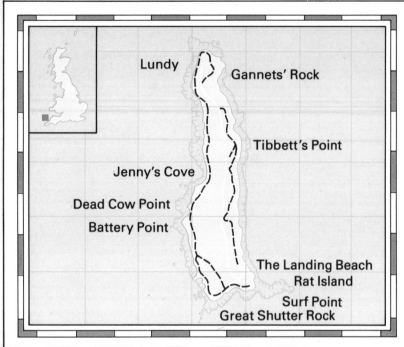

LUNDY, DEVON OS 180

Location: this island lies in the Bristol Channel 11 miles off the north coast of Devon and is reached via Ilfracombe.

Habitats: Lundy is about 3½ miles long, with 100-metre cliffs along its western shoreline. Most of the interior is windswept and virtually devoid of cover, though there are a few sheltered valleys in the east. It is position rather than habitat that makes the island so attractive to birds. Lundy was declared Britain's first Statutory Marine Nature Reserve in 1986.

Birds: though the island's name, given it by Viking raiders, is Old Norse for 'Isle of Puffins', these birds are now down to less than a hundred pairs. Two other species of auks, Guillemot and Razorbill, are more numerous, as are Kittiwake and Fulmar. Gannet are frequently seen offshore and Manx Shearwater and Storm Petrel both breed. During summer and autumn passage periods, all sorts of small birds turn up including a good selection of rarities.

Access: there is a regular boat service from Ilfracombe. Day trips from Ilfracombe allow too little time for exploration. Contact the Island Administrator (Tel: 0271 870870) for details. Accommodation may be booked through The Landmark Trust, Shottesbrooke, Maidenhead, Berks SL6 3SW (Tel: 062 882 5925).

Permits: none required.

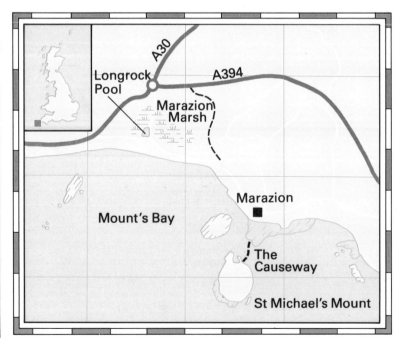

MARAZION MARSH, CORNWALL OS 203

Location: this coastal marsh lies about 3 miles east of Penzance between Longrock and Marazion overlooking Mount's Bay.

Habitats: Marazion Marsh is a largely overgrown swamp, broken here and there by pools of open water. By autumn these usually have muddy margins that attract waders. These also occur along the shoreline, along with gulls.

Birds: the position of Marazion, only 11 miles east of Land's End, makes it an inevitable port of call for various transatlantic vagrants. In particular, it regularly boasts an American wader or two in autumn. At this season it is also one of the best places in the country, along with Slapton Ley (*see page* 94), for Aquatic Warbler. Spring sees a regular influx of southern birds rarities that have 'overshot' their normal summer range in southern Europe, with Hoopoe and Little Egret the most likely. Many rarities have been found here, including now almost regular Ring-billed Gull from North America.

Access: leave Penzance eastward on the A30 and turn right in Longrock along the coast road, from which the marsh can be seen. At the eastern end is a car park from where a footpath leads northwards across the marsh to the railway and beyond.

Permits: none required.

MARTIN MERE, LANCASHIRE OS 108

Location: between the Mersey and Ribble estuaries, some 7½ miles east of the Lancashire coast and about 5 miles east of Southport.

Habitats: at one time a large lake, Martin Mere was drained and converted for agricultural use before being purchased by the Wildfowl Trust in 1969 and, partially at least, reconverted back to open water. There is now a series of pools housing the Trust's collection of captive wildfowl and flamingoes, plus some larger lagoons intended for wild birds.

Birds: Martin Mere is a major arrival point for Pink-footed Goose migrating to Britain. There are both Whooper and Bewick's Swans, tens of thousands of ducks, including one of the country's largest flocks of Pintail, and an impressive selection of raptors. The latter include Peregrine and Hen Harrier. Waders may be good on passage and Ruff and Black-tailed Godwit have bred here. Although it is often a busy place, with thousands of children paying educational visits each year, this is a stunningly good birding spot, and is generously provided with 9 hides.

Access: the Trust is signposted at Mere Brow from the A565, and Burscough Bridge from the A59. It is open daily.

Permits: entrance fee to non-members.

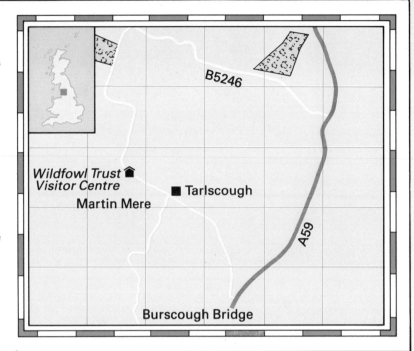

MARWICK HEAD, ORKNEY OS 6

Location: this headland lies on the north-western coast of Mainland, the chief island of Orkney, and is easily located by the memorial to Lord Kitchener who perished offshore in 1916, when the cruiser on which he was travelling was sunk by a German mine.

Habitats: the cliffs here rise to almost 90m and are decidedly crumbly, with some huge landslides. They are backed by grassy fields sloping away to a gentle valley.

Birds: despite their comparatively low height, these cliffs contain one of Britain's most spectacular seabird breeding colonies, and the RSPB recognized this by establishing a reserve here. There are birds everywhere, in the air, crammed together on cliff ledges, and swimming or diving in the sea. Huge numbers of Guillemots, estimated at 35,000, are everywhere, with over 10,000 pairs of Kittiwakes. There are also Razorbills and Puffins, Fulmars and Shags, and sometimes a Peregrine. Both Great and Arctic Skuas are regular visitors and Ravens utter their deep, resonant croaks.

Access: take the B9056 and turn westward on a minor road that leads to Marwick. Watch out for the Kitchener Memorial and walk the track to the cliff-tops. Take great care not to disturb the birds. Take care, also, not to approach the cliff-tops too closely.

Permits: not required.

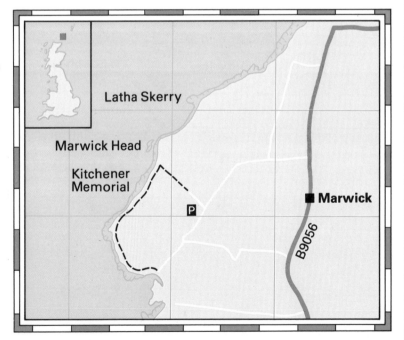

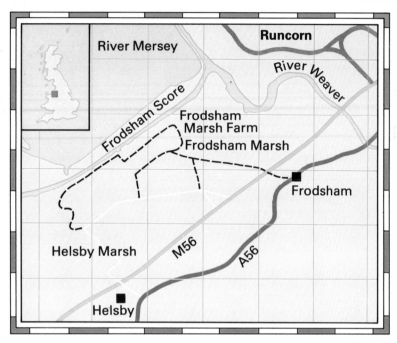

MERSEY ESTUARY, CHESHIRE OS 117

Location: the Mersey extends inland from Liverpool and is one of the most heavily industrialized estuaries in the whole country.

Habitats: access is decidedly awkward and the best places revel in names such as 'the sludge lagoon' and 'the ICI tank'.

Birds: despite its industrialization, the Mersey is of considerable importance for wintering waders and wildfowl, with a population of over 35,000 Dunlin and four-figure totals for Shelduck, Wigeon, Teal and Pintail. Numbers of the latter usually exceed those at any other site in Britain and are among the greatest in north-west Europe. Despite the pollution, the birds are protected from both shooting and disturbance. The best areas are near the head of the estuary, at Hale on the northern shore and at Frodsham on the south. In particular, the sludge lagoons at the latter (search for the current 'wet' lagoon) and the ICI tank are good for waders at all times of the year.

Access: leave the M56 at Exit 12 and follow the A56 to Frodsham. Take Ship Street back across the motorway and follow a gravel track northwards. Continue on foot northwards to Weaver Bend via the ICI Tank. Return via the sludge lagoon.

Permits: though much of the area is private, birders are usually tolerated.

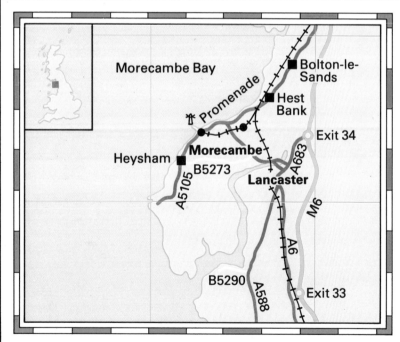

MORECAMBE, LANCASHIRE OS 96

Location: this seaside resort lies at the heart of Morecambe Bay about 20 miles to the north of Blackpool.

Habitats: the huge intertidal area of Morecambe Bay (with about 120 square miles of mud and sand at low tide) extends to north and south and is acknowledged as one of the major wetland areas of Europe. Morecambe promenade offers the easiest access to what can otherwise be a daunting area because of its vast size.

Birds: the birds of Morecambe Bay are abundant and of international importance. Up to 80,000 Knot – more than a quarter of the total population wintering in Britain – can be found here, and both Oystercatcher and Dunlin exceed 40,000 birds. Bar-tailed Godwit, Curlew, Redshank and Turnstone are all abundant and Ringed Plover and Sanderling are numerous on passage, when numbers of Knot may rise to 100,000. In winter there are many seaducks, including Goldeneye, Red-breasted Merganser, Scaup and Long-tailed Duck, and usually also a few divers present. The best time is on a rising tide.

Access: easily reached via the M6; leave the motorway at Exit 34 and follow the signs to Lancaster and Morecambe. When you reach the town, find the promenade.

Permits: not required.

MINSMERE, SUFFOLK OS 156

Location: this famous RSPB reserve is situated on the Suffolk coast between Southwold and Aldeburgh.

Habitats: Minsmere's fame results from the variety of habitats that can be found in its relatively small area of 1470 acres and the wealth of birds that these attract. Basically, it is a low-lying area separated from the sea by a high beach and a protective seawall. One of the most important habitats is the famous 'scrape' (an artificial area of shallow brackish water, mud and low islets), which has been imitated at many other sites. The major part of the reserve is dominated by reed beds. There are open waters here and there, belts of woodland, dry heathland, some farmland and meadow and even a couple of sand pits.

Birds: when the Avocet returned to breed in Britain after the Second World War, it chose Minsmere. The RSPB promptly created a reserve to protect them and the birds equally promptly moved away down the coast to Havergate. The birds returned to breed at Minsmere however, and today they are one of the prime attractions in summer. There are Common and Little Terns here, too, while the reed beds hold Bearded Tit, Bittern and Marsh Harrier. Both Savi's and Cetti's Warblers established breeding colonies at Minsmere, but their present status is precarious. A more recent arrival is Ruddy Duck. The woods hold a fine cross section of woodland birds, and the heaths still have breeding Nightjar, though Woodlark, Stone-curlew and Red-backed Shrike have all disappeared.

Passage can be excellent, with good numbers of waders passing through in both spring and and autumn. Species regularly include Kentish Plover and Temminck's Stint in spring and Little Stint, Curlew Sandpiper, Ruff, Greenshank and Spotted Redshank in autumn. Black Tern, Little Gull, Spoonbill and even Purple Heron are present every year. In winter there are swans and geese, also Hen Harrier and sometimes Rough-legged Buzzard. Snow Bunting and Twite frequent the shoreline and there are usually some seaducks and divers offshore.

Access: the public hide along the shore is open every day of the year. It is reached by taking the Dunwich road eastward from the B1125 at Westleton. Minsmere is signposted before reaching Dunwich. The track at the end is owned by the National Trust and a fee is payable in summer. Park at the cliff end and walk southwards. The reserve proper is reached via Westleton or Eastbridge on minor roads best found with the aid of an OS map. Both routes pass through Scott's Hall Farm to the RSPB reserve centre. Minsmere is closed on Tuesdays and is usually overcrowded during peak weekends and bank holidays.

Permits: not required to view 'The Scrape' from the shore hides; otherwise they are available from the reserve centre on arrival, but are limited, so arrive promptly at 9 a.m.

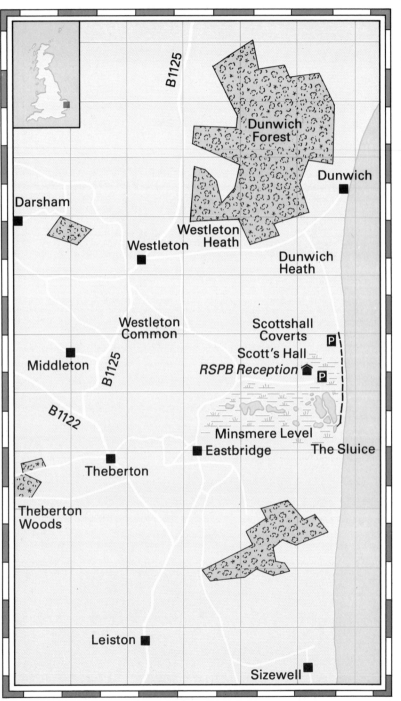

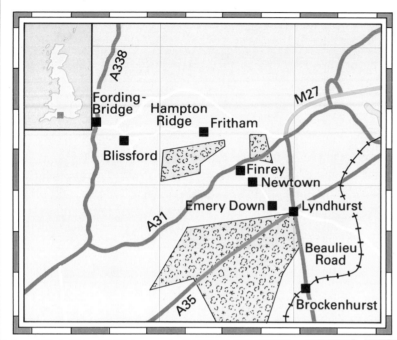

NEW FOREST, HAMPSHIRE

OS 195 & 196

Location: between Southampton and Bournemouth with its centre around the small town of Lyndhurst.

Habitats: much of the New Forest is open heathland and rough grazing, broken by extensive 'inclosures' of deciduous woodland and substantial belts of conifers. Despite its name, it includes one of the biggest areas of open land in southern Britain.

Birds: 'The Forest', as it is generally known, has long provided sites for rare breeding birds that were widely known, but never publicized. Even today it is impossible to give precise locations for birds such as Dartford Warbler, Woodlark, Hobby, Goshawk and Honey Buzzard, though all can be found by a combination of hard work and good fortune. There are breeding Nightjar, Buzzard, Firecrest, Siskin, Wood Warbler and a fine range of other species.

Access: most of The Forest is of open access and can be explored on minor roads, tracks and footpaths with the aid of the OS maps cited above, or OS Outdoor Leisure Map 22. The classic site is Beaulieu Road on the B3056, but Acres Down, Hampton Ridge and Rhinefield are also worth finding and exploring.

Permits: none required, but take care to respect private property and park only in public car parks.

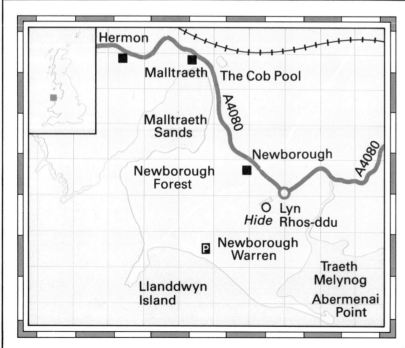

NEWBOROUGH WARREN, GWYNEDD OS 114

Location: in the south-western corner of the island of Anglesey.

Habitats: these include the extensive dune system of the Warren proper, the estuary of the River Cefni with the extensive Malltraeth Sands, and a low-lying marshy interior, partly reclaimed by a huge embankment called the Cob. Half of the Warren area is managed by the Nature Conservancy Council as a National Nature Reserve.

Birds: the breeding season brings a number of common birds to the area. In winter, there are many waders, together with Wigeon, the occasional Pink-footed and White-fronted Goose, and feral Canada and Greylag Geese. Raptors regularly include Hen Harrier, Merlin and Peregrine. Spring and autumn migration periods see regular Greenshank, Spotted Redshank and Little Stint.

Access: Malltraeth Sands, Malltraeth Pool and the damp fields beyond can all be viewed from The Cob or the A4080. The Warren can be explored from a track leading from Newborough Village south-westward. There are marked tracks that can be walked.

Permits: none required for public rights of way. Permits are necessary to visit areas away from designated routes in the National Nature Reserve. Contact the warden at 'Serai', Malltraeth, Bodorgan, Anglesey, Gwynedd LL62 5AS.

NORTH BULL, DUBLIN, IRISH REPUBLIC IOS½ 16

Location: this island lies in the northern part of Dublin Bay at the mouth of the River Liffey, surrounded by the suburbs of Dublin.

Habitats: though the best known of Irish wetlands, North Bull is really only a part of the much larger area that is the estuary of the Liffey. The island is a low ridge of dunes and saltmarsh surrounded by intertidal mud flats. Sadly, it is under continual threat from local authorities in search of dumps for rubbish as well as civic improvement works.

Birds: this is a major haunt of wildfowl and waders, with 1000 Brent and 2500 Wigeon along with lesser numbers of Teal and Pintail. Several species of wader top the 1000 mark, with Knot and Dunlin both exceeding 6000 in winter. Bar-tailed Godwit are also of international importance here, and only Dundalk Bay has larger numbers of waders on the Irish east coast. North Bull is the major wader resort for Dublin Bay, while most of the area's wildfowl can be found on the creek that separates the island from the mainland.

Access: the island is joined to the mainland by a causeway that offers excellent views over the creek and gives access to easy birding over the area.

Permits: not required.

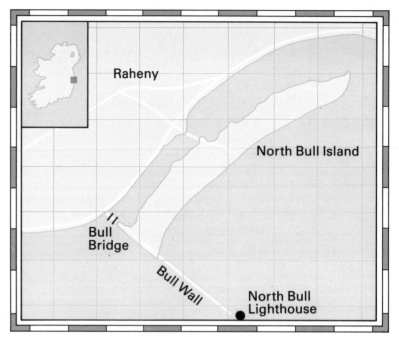

NOSS, SHETLAND OS 4

Location: this small uninhabited island lies about 12 miles east of Lerwick (*see page* 64) and just east of the isle of Bressay.

Habitats: Noss is managed by the Nature Conservancy Council as a National Nature Reserve with an area of almost 1000 acres. Its highest point, the Noup, rises to almost 180m, and it has some fearsome sea-cliffs, but is otherwise rather green and lush compared with most of Shetland.

Birds: Noss boasts one of Britain's most accessible gannetries, with nearly 7000 pairs of Gannets in summer. These numbers are, however, dwarfed by the 65,000 Guillemots, along with good numbers of Razorbill, Puffin, Kittiwake and Fulmar. Both Great and Arctic Skua breed here, too, among a grand total of twelve breeding seabirds.

Access: leave Lerwick on the regular car ferry to Bressay and continue by road across the island to Noss Sound. The nature reserve wardens will then ferry you across to Noss for a small fee. The island may be visited from mid-May to August except Monday and Thursday, but check with the Shetland Tourist Organisation, Market Cross, Lerwick (Tel: 0595 3434) in case these arrangements are changed.

Permits: none required, but keep to the clifftop paths while visiting the reserve.

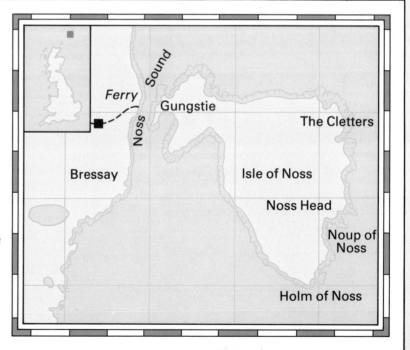

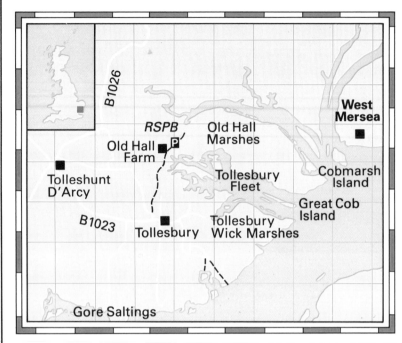

OLD HALL MARSHES, ESSEX OS 168

Location: this RSPB reserve lies on the Essex coast at the mouth of the Blackwater Estuary between Maldon and Colchester.

Habitats: this is a low-lying area of grazing marshes intersected by drainage dykes and broken here and there by a maze of old backwaters, 'fleets' (shallow creeks) and marshy reed beds.

Birds: during the summer, Common Terns breed on the islands and other breeding species include Shelduck, Pochard, Water Rail, Redshank, Yellow Wagtail and Bearded Tit. During spring and autumn passage periods waders include Black-tailed and Bar-tailed Godwits, Curlew Sandpiper, Little Stint and the occasional rarity. Avocet and Marsh Harrier are also regular. The peak season is winter, with up to 4000 Brent Geese, thousands of Wigeon, Teal and Shoveler on the marshes and Goldeneye, Red-breasted Merganser and Eider on the surrounding creeks. Slavonian Grebe find a winter stronghold here and there are usually a few Hen Harrier and Merlin to be seen.

Access: take the B1023 to Tolleshunt D'Arcy. Turn right on a minor road at the village and after 1¼ miles watch out for the track to Old Hall Farm on the left. Park and continue on foot around the sea-wall, but please do not walk or stand on it.

Permits: from The Warden, 1 Old Hall Lane, Tollesbury on arrival.

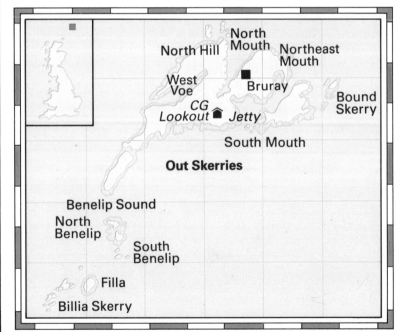

OUT SKERRIES, SHETLAND OS 2

Location: this group of small islands lies about 22 miles east of Mainland, the chief island of Shetland, and about 10 miles north-east of the island of Whalsay.

Habitats: the fact that there is a small crofting community that can offer accommodation, combined with their small size and geographical position at the easternmost point of Shetland makes the Skerries ideal for watching migrant birds.

Birds: migrants and rarities are the species that birders with a sense of independence come to Skerries to search for. In the number of rarities that are recorded each year, the islands are second only to Fair Isle (*see page* 38). Yet, even during the peak autumn period, there are seldom more than a handful of enthusiasts present, whereas Fair Isle can be booked up years ahead. Work on the assumption that anything that turns up at that more famous location can turn up here . . . but then have the satisfaction of finding it for yourself.

Access: there is a regular ferry from Lerwick to Out Skerries twice a week (journey time 3 hours) and flights once a week from Tingwall Airstrip near Lerwick in summer. Contact the Shetland Tourist Organisation, Market Cross, Lerwick.

Permits: none required.

OUSE WASHES, CAMBRIDGESHIRE & NORFOLK OS 143

Location: extending from Earith, Cambridgeshire, in the south to Denver, Norfolk, in the north.

Habitats: the Washes are a great strip of grassland, just over ½ mile wide and over 20 miles long, enclosed between high embankments, intentionally created to act as a reservoir for excess winter floodwater when the Fens were drained during the seventeenth century. Much of the area is now owned by conservation bodies which have improved the habitat with excavations, feeding programmes and suchlike schemes.

Birds: in winter, ducks, especially Wigeon, dominate the scene, with over 35,000 of this species alone. Teal, Shoveler, Pochard and Pintail are also present in good numbers, along with over 2000 Bewick's Swans and 200 Whooper Swans. The Washes have long been the major British haunt of Bewick's Swan, but the creation of a Wildfowl Trust refuge at Welney, plus an intensive feeding programme, has enabled the birds to become habituated to humans in close up. Winter also brings Hen Harrier, Merlin and Short-eared Owl.

By spring the wildfowl are on their way and their place is taken by a fine collection of breeding birds. Black-tailed Godwit and Ruff both returned here to breed after periods of absence from the country. Black Tern sometimes breeds and Little Gull has done so. During spring and autumn passage periods there are even more of these birds and they are joined by many waders that breed farther north.

Rarities regularly turn up here including ducks, herons and waders, and the Washes are worth visiting at any time of the year.

Access: there are two major access points, plus the excellent area at Welney that can be seen from the road. In the southern section the RSPB reserve is centred on Welches Dam, with a series of hides situated along the western embankment that are best visited in the afternoon when the light is better. As this side of the Washes floods first, it is better to visit it when the water level is low rather than high. Head southwards from Manea to the visitor centre. The Wildfowl Trust Refuge, too, is better at times of lower water levels, for here has been created a series of artificial pools that conveniently concentrates the birds immediately in front of a series of hides. Members of the Trust can enjoy the luxury of large glass windows in what is probably Britain's most comfortable hide. Feeding brings wild swans almost within touching distance, enabling individuals to be recognized year after year. The Refuge is reached by heading across the Washes from Welney and turning left on the far bank.

Permits: there is an admission charge to non-members of the Wildfowl Trust to the hide at Welney; in summer it is also possible to take a 2-mile walk across part of the Washes. The RSPB centre is open at weekends, but the hides are free throughout the year.

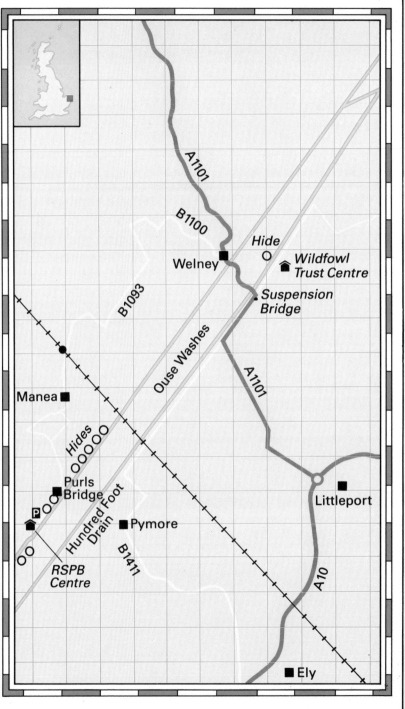

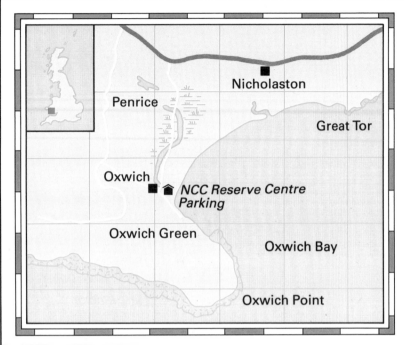

OXWICH BAY, WEST GLAMORGAN OS 159

Location: this delightful area lies on the south coast of the beautiful Gower Peninsula, about 10 miles west of Swansea.

Habitats: Oxwich is enclosed by limestone hills and consists of a low-lying valley floor contained by a broad sandy beach, backed by dunes, which partially dams the drainage stream. There are large reed beds broken by open pools, shallow marshes and dense thickets of willow. The whole area is a National Nature Reserve.

Birds: Oxwich is the major western stronghold of Reed Warbler in Britain and the reed beds also hold breeding Cetti's Warbler and Bearded Tit. Grasshopper Warblers, Sedge Warblers and Water Rail breed, too and Buzzards nest in the woods, along with Sparrowhawk and all three British woodpecker species. Regular migrants include harriers, Osprey and Hobby. In winter there are gulls, divers, seaducks and waders. A few Blackcap and Chiffchaff overwinter.

Access: leave Swansea on the A4118 and turn left on a minor road to Oxwich village. The National Nature Reserve centre, on the seaward side of the village is open on weekdays all year, and at weekends as well from spring to autumn; it has access maps.

Permits: obtain permission from the warden to use the hide (although this is not available in July and August).

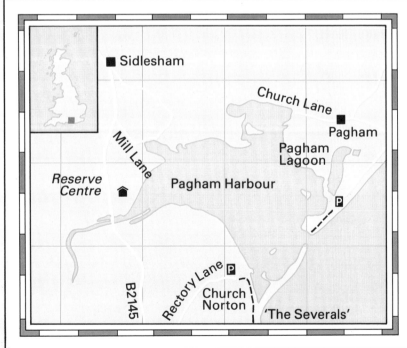

PAGHAM HARBOUR, WEST SUSSEX OS 197

Location: this tidal inlet lies on the western side of Selsey Bill immediately west of Bognor Regis.

Habitats: at low tide banks of mud, sand and shingle attract a wide variety of birds to feed. The mouth is narrow and has its own special birds. Sidlesham Ferry Pool is a tiny backwater that is superb during passage periods, while Pagham Lagoon is an abandoned gravel pit with a fen-like annexe at the northern end.

Birds: in summer Pagham is a major haunt of Little Tern, along with Ringed Plover and Shelduck. In winter there are regular Red-throated Diver, Slavonian Grebe, Brent Goose, Goldeney, Red-breasted Merganser and Eider. Waders winter as well, with Black-tailed Godwit and Ruff regular in small numbers. Spring and autumn passage waders include many Spotted Redshank, Greenshank, Little Stint and Curlew Sandpiper. Often, small numbers of these birds frequent the Ferry Pool.

Access: the West Sussex County Council has a reserve here with a centre at Sidlesham Ferry and a car park. From the Chichester by-pass follow signs to Selsey (not Pagham). Continue to Church Norton and walk to the Harbour mouth.

Permits: not required.

PAPA WESTRAY, ORKNEY OS 5

Location: situated in the extreme north of the Orkney Islands, this little island is less than a mile east of its neighbour, Westray.

Habitats: a crofting community occupies much of the central area; to north and east are maritime heath with low sandstone cliffs. The large Loch of St Tredwell is set in gently undulating country.

Birds: together with nearby Westray, these islands hold the greatest diversity of breeding seabirds in Britain. The northern part of the island is the RSPB reserve of North Hill, with over 6000 pairs of breeding Arctic Tern. Here, too, is a thriving colony of Arctic Skua, and breeding Guillemot, Razorbill, Black Guillemot, Kittiwake and Fulmar. Probably the best area is Fowl Craig on the east coast. Several pairs of Corncrake still breed here and there is a small breeding colony of Storm Petrel on the Holm of Papa. Migrants have included rarities. Sooty Shearwaters are regular in late summer.

Access: the island is easily reached by air from Westray. For details of accommodation, contact the Papa Community Co-op, Papa Westray, Orkney (Tel: 085 74 267).

Permits: none required, but contact the summer warden on arrival. Be careful not to disturb the breeding terns. By writing well before your visit, you can arrange an escorted tour of the nesting colonies.

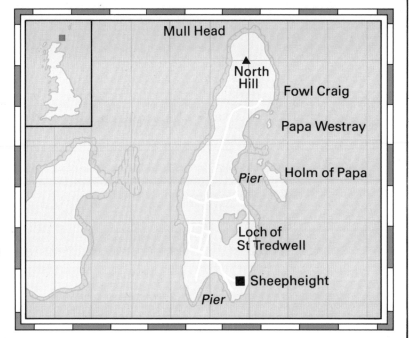

PENNINGTON MARSHES, HAMPSHIRE OS 196

Location: at the western end of the Solent, opposite the Isle of Wight, between Lymington and Keyhaven.

Habitats: an area of low-lying marshes and fields, broken up by freshwater 'borrow pits' that have gently shelving edges. On the seaward side there are also 'enclosed' areas that provide saline feeding grounds, and saltmarsh.

Birds: this is a fine area in winter, with good numbers of Brent Goose, along with Wigeon and the more widespread waders, including Grey Plover, Turnstone and Sanderling. Spotted Redshank and Ruff, on the marshes, also overwinter. During spring and autumn there is a wider variety of waders, though the two last-mentioned species, along with Greenshank, often dominate the freshwater pools. Little Stint and Curlew Sandpiper are regular in autumn and there is a good passage of Black Tern. In summer the colony of Black-headed Gulls may play host to a visiting Mediterranean Gull, and Little Tern breed.

Access: leave Lymington southwards on the A337 and turn left on Lower Pennington Lane. Continue through the village on a track past the grazing marshes, then walk to the sea-wall.

Permits: not required.

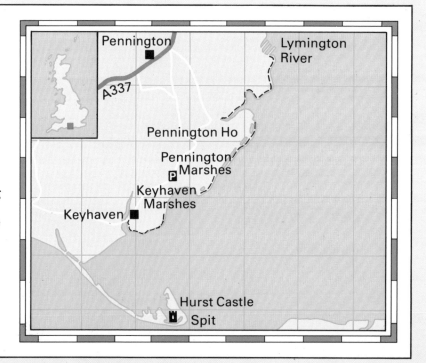

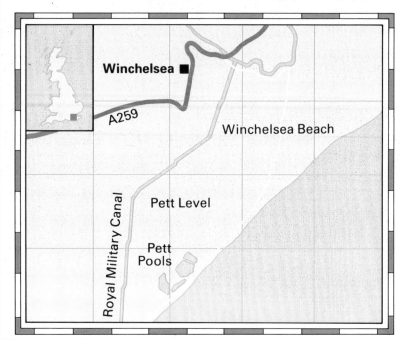

PETT LEVEL, EAST SUSSEX OS 189

Location: this wetland area lies at the eastern end of the county, about 4 miles south of Rye. It can be approached via Winchelsea Beach by taking the Fairlight road toward Hastings.

Habitats: this is an area of low-lying grazing marshes criss-crossed by a network of drainage ditches and broken by a few splashy areas that flood in winter. The sea-wall is backed by several large 'borrow pits', one of which is pumped out in mid-July each year by the Sussex Ornithological Society to expose an area of mud that attracts waders in autumn. The society maintains a small reserve here.

Birds: winter sees Brent Goose, as well as Wigeon and other ducks, along with a variety of waders that flight in at high tide. There are usually a few raptors around, too, mostly Hen Harrier and Short-eared Owl, and the sea holds Great Crested Grebe, Scoter and Eider. During the autumn passage, when the pool nearest the coast is pumped out, a fine variety of waders put in an appearance, including Little Stint, Curlew Sandpiper, Ruff, Greenshank, Knot and often a rarity. Black Tern, Little and Mediterranean Gulls and the odd Marsh Harrier usually occur each autumn.

Access: leave Rye westward on the A259. Turn left at Winchelsea on to a minor road to Winchelsea Beach. Follow this to the pools.

Permits: none required; view the site from the road.

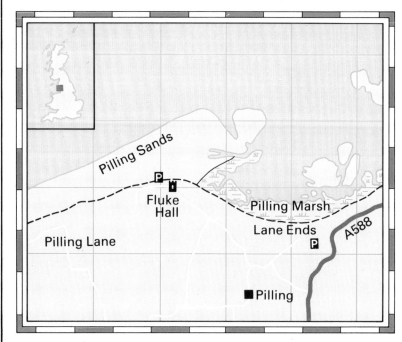

PILLING, LANCASHIRE OS 102

Location: this is another spot on the vast area of Morecambe Bay that is highly productive of both waders and wildfowl. It lies on the southern shore of the bay about 9 miles north of Blackpool.

Habitats: the vast intertidal sands are separated from the low-lying grazing and arable land by a sea-wall. Birds flight between the two different habitats.

Birds: the area between Pilling and Cockerham has long been the favourite haunt of Morecambe's flock of Pink-footed Geese, which feed on the fields here before flighting out to the sand banks to roost. They may number up to 4000 and are often accompanied by a few White-fronted Geese. Finding them is a matter of careful searching from the network of small lanes that run through the area. Pilling is also a major wader resort and in winter thousands of Knot, Dunlin, Redshank, Oystercatcher and Bar-tailed Godwit may be present.

Access: the network of lanes can be explored for geese between Pilling and Cockerham via the A588, which lies north-east of Blackpool. The geese may also be seen late in the day from the sea-wall. This is reached by driving northwards from the village to a car park, from where the waders can also be watched as they fly in to roost.

Permits: none required.

PITSFORD RESERVOIR, NORTHAMPTONSHIRE OS 141 & 152

Location: about 5 miles to the north of Northampton, between the villages of Brixworth and Holcot.

Habitats: many of the banks are gently shelving. The northern part, a nature reserve, has several sheltered bays and also some plantations and woodland. The southern part is more open.

Birds: winter brings a variety of ducks, including good numbers of Wigeon, along with Gadwall, Shoveler, Goldeneye and Pintail. There are also Bewick's Swan here, though usually they move on before the onset of hard weather. During spring and autumn passage periods waders can be interesting, particularly in autumn when Little Stint and Curlew Sandpiper are regular. Terns, including Black Terns, also pass through. In summer, there is a variety of warblers and an occasional Hobby. There are usually a few Ruddy Duck present throughout the year.

Access: Pitsford reservoir car park is found by turning left in the village. Return to Pitsford and turn left to Holcot and then left again across the causeway to view the more interesting northern half.

Permits: write (enclosing a s.a.e.) for a day permit to visit the reserve to: The Warden, c/o Northants Trust for Nature Conservation, Lings House, Billing Lings, Northampton NN3 4BE.

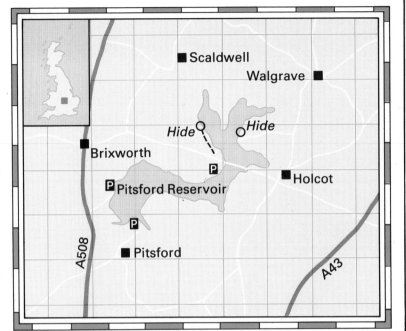

PORTLAND, DORSET OS 194

Location: the Isle of Portland extends southwards into the English Channel south of Weymouth. It is joined to the mainland by a causeway (Ferrybridge), with Portland Harbour to the east.

Habitats: Portland is a virtually treeless island of limestone rock. Birdwatching interest centres on the bird observatory at Portland Bill, as the southern tip of the island is known, the muddy foreshore at Ferrybridge and the sheltered waters of Portland Harbour.

Birds: the gardens and small fields around the Old Lower Light attract a wonderful range of small birds in spring and autumn, including many rarities. The Obelisk at the Bill is an excellent seawatch point, while to the north, Portland Harbour offers winter shelter to divers, grebes and seaducks (including Red-breasted Merganser and Eider).

Access: leave Weymouth on the A354 after checking for birds on Portland Harbour near Sandsfoot Castle. Stop on the south side of Ferrybridge at a car park on the right hand side and check the bay. Continue to Portland Bill and 'The Bill' car park.

Permits: none required. Accommodation is available at the Observatory: contact The Warden, Portland Bird Observatory, Old Lower Light, Portland Bill, Dorset DT5 2JT.

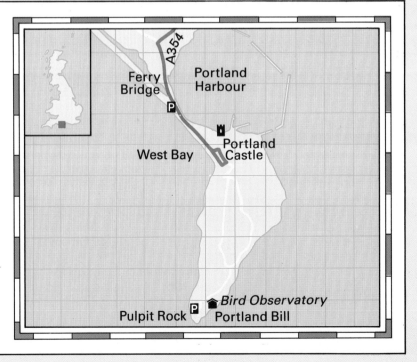

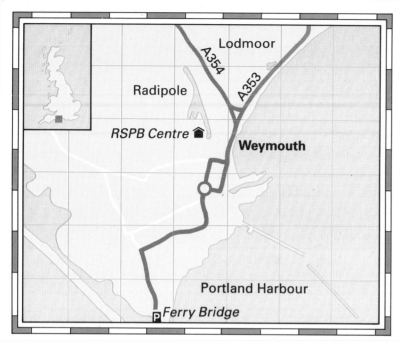

RADIPOLE AND LODMOOR, DORSET OS 194

Location: these two RSPB reserves are at Weymouth. Radipole is within the town itself, while Lodmoor lies just to the north-east.

Habitats: Radipole is the inland extension of Weymouth Harbour. Since 1924, when a bridge was built across the River Wey, this estuary has gradually become a freshwater site. It is now a reedy backwater with areas of open water, muddy banks and scrub. Lodmoor is damp grassland with marshy pools and some reed beds.

Birds: migrants have always been the main attraction, along with waders, terns, gulls: this is a prime spot for Little, Mediterranean and Ring-billed Gulls, and Black Terns are regular during both spring and autumn passage periods. Waders may include a rarity from time to time, while Garganey are present each spring. Warblers, including Cetti's, breed in the reed beds, and there are small numbers of breeding Water Rail, Kingfisher and Bearded Tit.

Access: the RSPB reserve centre is situated at the car park, near the bus station just north of Westham Bridge. For Lodmoor leave the town on the coastal A353 to the Sea Life Centre, where the entrance to the reserve and hides can be found.

Permits: car parking tickets purchased at Radipole can be used at Lodmoor. Otherwise, access is free.

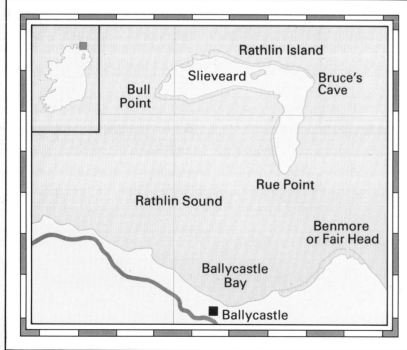

RATHLIN ISLAND, CO. ANTRIM, NORTHERN IRELAND OSNI 5

Location: Rathlin lies off the north-eastern coast of Northern Ireland and is, more or less, the nearest point of Ireland to Scotland. It is separated from the mainland by the five miles of Rathlin Sound.

Habitats: this is quite a large island extending some five miles from east to west and about four miles north to south. Extensive cliffs along the northern coast are now an RSPB reserve and, in the west, are a nature reserve of the Northern Ireland Department of the Environment. There are guest houses and caravans to be hired.

Birds: large colonies of cliff-breeding species including Guillemot, Razorbill, Black Guillemot, Fulmar and Kittiwake. There is a thriving puffinny and Manx Shearwaters breed in the same cliff-top burrows. Peregrine and Chough round off the collection. During passage periods Rathlin may attract many small migrants and has a number of rarities to its credit. It is, however, strategically sited to watch for migrant seabirds entering or leaving the Irish Sea and skuas and shearwaters are regularly seen in autumn.

Access: there is a regular boat service from Ballycastle between May and September and the local minibus service runs somewhat erratically between Church Bay and Keeble.

Permits: none required.

RHUM, HIGHLAND   OS 39

Location: Rhum is the largest of the group of islands that lies south of Skye in the Inner Hebrides. Skye is 8 miles away, and the nearest mainland port is Mallaig, 16 miles to the east.

Habitats: this is a moor-covered island rising to over 750m. There are cliff-girt shores, interrupted by sandy bays and coves, and some areas of rough pasture. A reafforestation programme is being carried out by the Nature Conservancy Council, who manage the whole of the island as a National Nature Reserve.

Birds: a few pairs of Golden Eagle, Merlin and Peregrine breed, and there are breeding Golden Plover, Short-eared Owl and Red Grouse on the moors. Other breeding birds include Dipper, Wheatear and Ring Ousel and the growing woodland is being colonized by an increasing variety of small birds. Between 1975 and 1985, 82 White-tailed Eagles were released here and, though they have spread throughout the Inner Hebrides, they may still be seen here.

Access: day visitors may land at Loch Scresort, but will have little time for exploration. Visitors can now stay at Kinloch Castle: contact Hebridean Holidays Ltd. (Tel: 0687 2026). Caledonian MacBrayne steamers leave Mallaig four times a week.

Permits: these are necessary to leave the Loch Scresort area. Write to the NCC Warden, White House, Kinloch, Isle of Rhum.

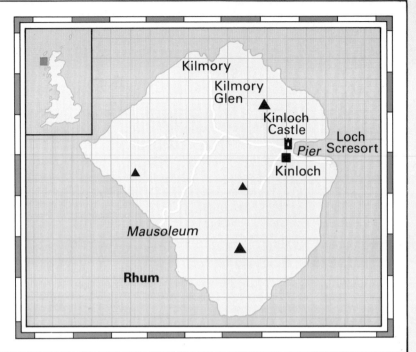

RIBBLE ESTUARY, LANCASHIRE   OS 102 & 108

Location: this estuary lies some 10 miles downstream of Preston, on the coast between Blackpool and Southport.

Habitats: the Ribble is mainly sandy. The inner estuary has vast sand banks, but they are guarded by large areas of saltmarsh that make access difficult.

Birds: this is one of Britain's most important estuaries. In winter, over 70,000 Knot and 42,000 Dunlin have been counted, along with thousands of Oystercatchers, Sanderling, Redshank and both Bar-tailed and Black-tailed Godwits. Pink-footed Geese may number 14,000 in early winter – almost a quarter of the total world population. Additionally there are Bewick's Swan, many ducks, Hen Harrier, and a fine passage of autumn waders.

Access: Southport Marine Parade is a splendid birding spot. Further in, Crossens Marsh, Bank Marsh and Hesketh Marshes can all be viewed from the sea-wall, which is accessible via minor roads off the A565. In the north St Anne's, Fairhaven and Lytham offer good watching from the promenades. Squire's Gate, south Blackpool, has a narrow shoreline, allowing superb views of divers, grebes and seaducks at high tide in autumn and winter.

Permits: none required on public rights of way.

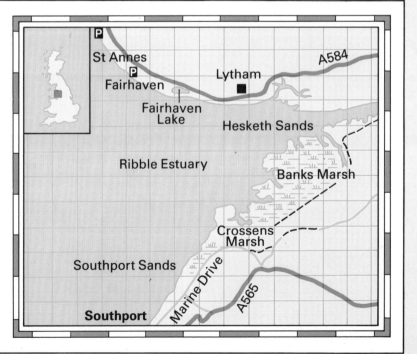

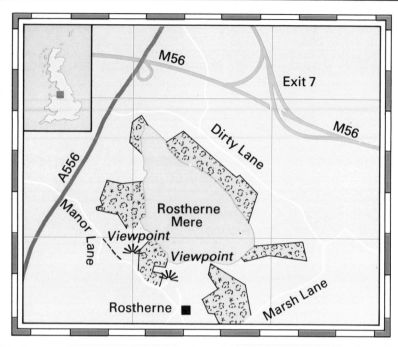

ROSTHERNE MERE, CHESHIRE OS 109

Location: this fine lake lies on the southern outskirts of Greater Manchester, about 2 miles south-west of Altrincham.

Habitats: with its surrounding reed beds and bushy scrub, Rostherne bears a remarkable resemblance to a Norfolk Broad rather than a suburban lake. It is a National Nature Reserve.

Birds: the shallow waters attract a fine variety of surface-feeding ducks, especially Mallard, Teal, Wigeon, Shoveler and Pintail. Diving ducks are also present, though generally in smaller numbers; these are mainly Tufted Duck and Pochard, though most winters see a scattering of Goldeneye and Goosander. Scarcer duck species turn up from time to time. Winter also brings Water Rail, and on passage Black Tern and other terns are regular. Breeding birds include Great Crested and Little Grebes.

Access: there is no formal access to this National Nature Reserve, but much can be seen from the surrounding lanes. Leave the M56 at Exit 7 and proceed along the A556. Turn along Manor Lane to Rostherne village where the churchyard offers a good viewpoint.

Permits: annual permits for the A. W. Boyd Memorial Observatory can be obtained from the Manchester Ornithological Society, 1 Hart Avenue, Sale, Cheshire M33 2JY.

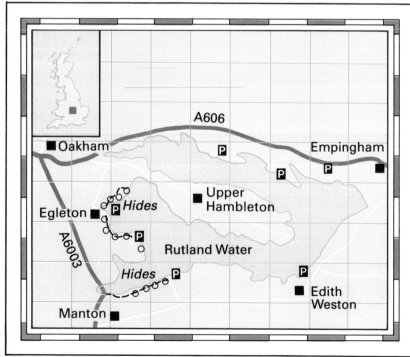

RUTLAND WATER, LEICESTERSHIRE OS 141

Location: between Leicester and Peterborough, 4 miles from the A1.

Habitats: this reservoir, England's largest, was created in 1975. Its 3000 acres and mile upon mile of gently shelving natural shoreline offer security and food for wintering ducks and passage waders and the western end of the southern area is a nature reserve of the local naturalists' trust and the Anglian Water Authority.

Birds: winter ducks include over 1000 Gadwall and reasonably regular Goosander, Smew, Ruddy Duck and Scaup. Grebes include all the regular British species, though most are more likely to be seen in autumn than in winter. The same is also true of waders. Spring and autumn passage periods regularly bring Little Stint, Curlew Sandpiper, Greenshank and Black-tailed Godwit, along with terns, including Black Tern.

Access: take the A606 towards Empingham. In the south-west the Lyndon Reserve is reached via the minor road east of Manton. The Egleton Reserve, in the west, is reached via the A6003.

Permits: are available to non-members of the Leicestershire and Rutland Trust for Nature Conservation at the centres on various days of the week: at present, on weekends throughout the year and, during the summer (May–October), also from Tuesday to Thursday.

RYE HARBOUR, EAST SUSSEX OS 189

Location: this local nature reserve lies 2 miles south of Rye. The huge promontory of Dungeness (*see page* 34) lies to the east.

Habitats: Rye Harbour is a shingle area built up by the sea at the mouth of the River Rother. A succession of old shorelines extends inland for 1–3 miles, and here the gravel-extraction industry has dug out a series of pits, now abandoned and flooded. Areas of offshore mud are exposed at low tide. There is also arable land and scrub.

Birds: breeding birds include Little Tern, plus Common and Sandwich Terns on specially constructed islands in the Ternery Pool nearest the coast. There is a thriving Black-headed Gull colony. In winter, ducks, grebes and Water Rail are regular and Hen Harrier and Merlin are often present. Spring and autumn passage brings the usual waders – high tide is best. In a good year Curlew Sandpiper, Little Stint, Spotted Redshank and Greenshank may all be abundant and in spring there is a large flock of Whimbrel. For most of the year the reserve is the major wader roost for Rye Bay.

Access: leave Rye westwards and turn left from the A259 on the outskirts of the town to Rye Harbour. Park near the nature centre and walk along the concrete track opposite to the sea and the hides.

Permits: not required, but there are collecting boxes.

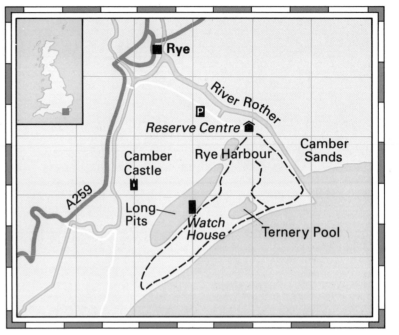

ST ABB'S HEAD, BORDERS OS 67

Location: on the east coast just north of the Scottish border and 12 miles north of Berwick-upon-Tweed; it is easily accessible to anyone travelling to and from Edinburgh on the A1.

Habitats: the cliffs here rise to 90m and are conveniently indented to offer excellent views of the breeding seabirds. The Head is also a good spot for watching seabird migration and there is a freshwater pool, Mire Loch, with plenty of bushy cover for small migrants.

Birds: the breeding seabirds here include thousands of Guillemot, Razorbill, Fulmar, Shag and Kittiwake, along with much less numerous Puffin. Though they do not breed, Gannets are regularly seen offshore and, during passage periods, they are often accompanied by marauding Great Skuas. Other skuas are regular in autumn and shearwaters, terns, seaducks and divers may also occur at this time. The latter are also present during the winter. Small migrants include the regular chats, warblers and flycatchers. A scattering of rarities is reported every year.

Access: from the A1107, turn right in Coldingham to St Abb's village on the B6438. A path leads northward to the Head, which may also be approached by the road to the lighthouse. Mire Loch lies east of this road.

Permits: none required.

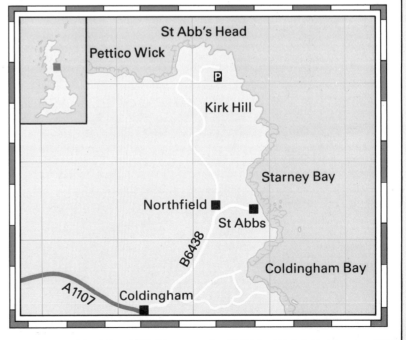

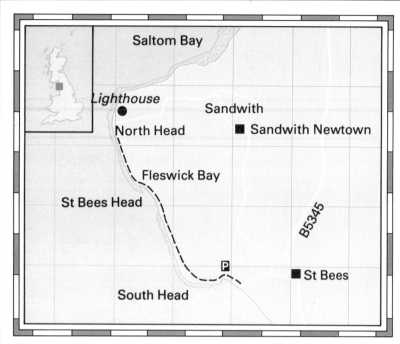

ST BEES HEAD, CUMBRIA OS 89

Location: the westernmost point of the Lake District, this headland lies just 2 miles north-west of the village of St Bees.

Habitats: the red sandstone cliffs rise to 90m and are eroded, forming perfect ledges for breeding seabirds. The tops are grassy, with clumps of gorse.

Birds: this is an RSPB reserve that contains large colonies of breeding seabirds, with Guillemot, Kittiwake and Fulmar the most numerous. Indeed, it is one of England's largest west coast seabird breeding colonies and the site of the country's only breeding Black Guillemots. Razorbill are comparatively scarce, as are Puffin, but Shag and Cormorant both breed, as do Peregrine. Seawatching can be productive, especially with south-westerly winds, when Gannet, skuas and shearwaters may all be seen.

Access: leave Whitehaven southwards on the B5345 and turn left in St Bees to the beach car park. Walk northwards along the cliff-top footpath, which has several excellent (and safe) vantage points. It is a 2½-mile walk from the car park to the lighthouse; disabled visitors only may approach the lighthouse by car on a private road from Sandwith.

Permits: a summer warden is present at the lighthouse, but no permits are required.

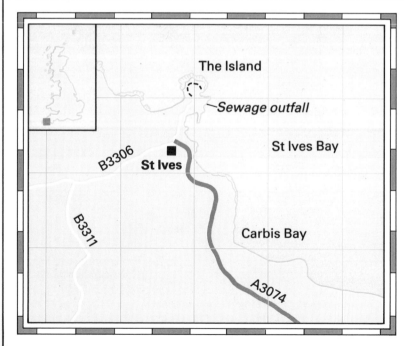

ST IVES, CORNWALL OS 203

Location: this is a flourishing seaside resort situated on the north Cornish coast near Penzance and Land's End.

Habitats: St Ives Island is actually a rocky headland, while to the south is the sewage outfall and the harbour.

Birds: this is an outstanding seabird spot at the right time and in the right conditions. Autumn, particularly September, is the right time, and north-west winds, especially following a south-westerly gale the right conditions. Both Storm and Leach's Petrels, Great and Arctic Skuas, Manx Shearwaters (including the Balearic race) and Sooty Shearwaters, thousands of Guillemots and Razorbills, Kittiwakes and Gannets and often Sabine's Gulls are to be seen; Grey Phalarope may occur in late autumn. In winter there are divers, Slavonian Grebe and often Glaucous or Iceland Gulls. The sheltered St Ives Bay has seabirds throughout the year, and nearby sites also have much to offer the birdwatcher: try the Hayle Estuary (*see page* 49), Marazion Marsh (*see page* 74), Lands End (*see page* 60), and the Isles of Scilly (*see page* 58).

Access: the Island is at the north end of the town: follow signs to the car park. The sewage outfall is just east of the car park. There is a footpath to the coastguard lookout station.

Permits: none required.

SANDWICH BAY, KENT OS 179

Location: on the east coast of Kent, immediately south of the estuary of the River Stour between the North and South Forelands.

Habitats: the offshore sand and mud banks here form part of the intertidal Pegwell Bay and the Stour estuary, immediately to the north, where there are Kent Trust for Nature Conservation and National Trust reserves. Much of the large area of dunes has been turned into famous golf courses. There are fields, hedges, marshy pools and reed beds.

Birds: this is a migration watch point, with the emphasis on seabirds and small migrant chats, flycatchers and warblers. There are, however, several areas for waders, and Kentish Plover in spring, and Little Stint and Curlew Sandpiper in autumn, are regular. It is a poor autumn that does not produce Pallas's Warbler and other eastern vagrants.

Access: the whole area is private and is accessible only via a toll road between Sandwich and Sandwich Bay. The observatory offers hostel accommodation to keen migrant watchers. There is a road northward along the coast from Sandwich Bay which gives access to the nature reserves at the mouth of the Stour.

Permits: contact The Honorary Warden, Bird Observatory, 2 Old Downs Farm, Guildford Road, Sandwich, Kent CT13 9PF.

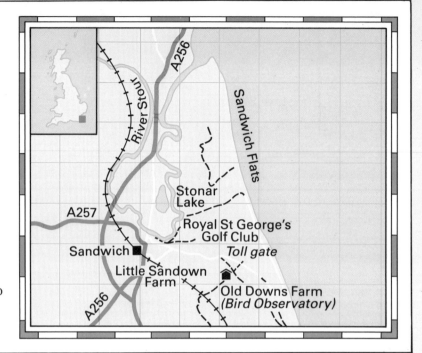

SHANNON ESTUARY, CO. LIMERICK, IRISH REPUBLIC

IOS½ 17

Location: on the west coast of Ireland, this is Ireland's largest estuary, extending for over 50 miles downstream from Limerick.

Habitats: vast mud banks are exposed at low tide, especially where the River Fergus joins the Shannon on its northern shore, at Poulnasherry Bay and the inlets east of Aughinish Island.

Birds: this is a major wetland, one of the most significant in Europe. In an average winter it holds over 10,000 wildfowl and twice as many waders, but may hold much larger numbers of both during peak spring and autumn passage periods. This is a major haunt of Black-tailed Godwit, with regular winter numbers over 8000 and a spring passage record of over 16,000 birds. Most of these concentrate at the Fergus inlet–Shannon Airport area. Here, too, are vast flocks of Dunlin (up to 30,000), Bar-tailed Godwit, Curlew, Knot and Redshank, along with up to 100 Greenshank. Wigeon are the most abundant duck, and other wildfowl include Scaup, Whooper Swan, Brent Goose and Greylag Goose.

Access: there is road access off the N18 to Shannon Airport and the R473 west of the Fergus inlet. Other access requires a detailed map.

Permits: none required.

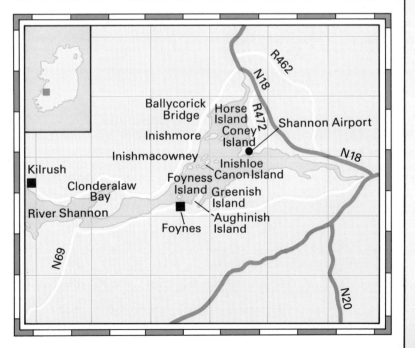

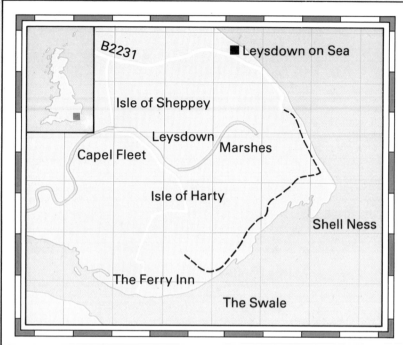

SHELL NESS, KENT OS 178

Location: on the north Kent coast at the mouth of the Swale estuary, forming the easternmost point of the Isle of Sheppey.

Habitats: Shell Ness is a headland constructed of shells by tidal action. Inland lie fields, while to the west are extensive saltmarshes.

Birds: the sea here is a regular haunt of seabirds, including winter divers and grebes, along with Brent Goose, Eider, scoters and Red-breasted Merganser. Waders are abundant, with Knot and Dunlin the most common, but with Turnstone and Sanderling also sometimes numerous. Twite and Snow Bunting are local specialities, and there are good numbers of Hen Harrier and Short-eared Owl, and the occasional Peregrine. Though passage periods bring a wider variety of species, there are other sites on the Isle of Sheppey, notably Elmley Marshes (*see page* 37), that are usually better at these times.

Access: follow the A249 on to the Isle of Sheppey, then take the B2231 to Leysdown-on-Sea. Leave Leysdown eastwards on a minor road along the coast until you reach a few houses, where it is possible to park. From here it is a short walk southwards to the Ness beyond which is a bay with roosting waders. The shoreline to the north is also productive, especially on a rising tide.

Permits: none required, but make sure you do not disturb the birds.

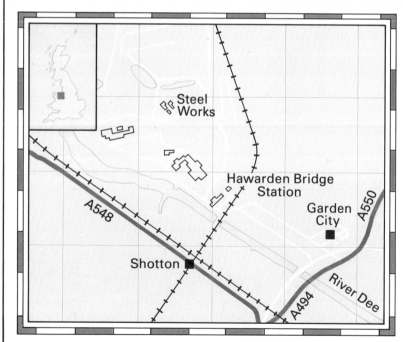

SHOTTON POOLS, CLWYD OS 117

Location: this site lies within the confines of Shotton Steelworks at the head of the Dee estuary. Chester is 10 miles to the south-east.

Habitats: the saltmarshes are surrounded by lagoons and marshes as well as several reservoirs. There are areas of reeds and several of the pools have rafts to encourage breeding and resting birds. There are also areas of farmland to add diversity to this highly successful little reserve.

Birds: the specially constructed rafts offer breeding sites to a substantial colony of Common Terns. Elsewhere, species as varied as Ringed Plover, Reed Warbler and Yellow Wagtail find a summer home. It is, however, during spring and autumn passage periods that Shotton shines. In autumn, in particular, the pools attract a wide variety of waders, with Little Stint, Curlew and Wood Sandpipers, Greenshank and Spotted Redshank among the more common and widespread species. Whimbrel are more abundant in spring. Autumn also brings a good passage of Black Terns and there is a rarity of some sort most years.

Access: The British Steel Corporation Works are signposted on the A550 and access is strictly by permit.

Permits: write to the PR Manager, BSC, Shotton Steelworks, Deeside, Clwyd. Permits are accompanied by a map showing access.

SKELLIGS, CO. KERRY, IRISH REPUBLIC IOS½ 20

Location: the Skelligs are the smallest and most isolated of the islands that lie off the rugged coast of south-west Ireland.

Habitats: these are uninhabited cliff-girt islands that rise spectacularly straight from the sea.

Birds: the Skelligs form the middle group of Kerry bird islands, between the 'Inish' group to the north and the 'Bull' group to the south. They are more isolated than either and hold some outstanding seabird colonies. All the Skellig islands are worth visiting, though none are of easy access. The best localities and their specialities are: Inishtooskert for Storm Petrel and Manx Shearwater; Inishtearaght for Puffin, Storm Petrel and Manx Shearwater; Inishabro for Storm Petrel and Manx Shearwater; Inishvickillane for Puffin, Razorbill, Storm Petrel and Manx Shearwater; and Puffin Island for its huge Manx Shearwater colony. Little Skellig itself has a huge gannetry, while Great Skellig has good colonies of Storm Petrel and Manx Shearwater.

Access: boats may be chartered from the nearby mainland fishing villages (try Ballinskelligs), but choose a calmish day, as landing is far from easy. Day trips are fun, but longer stays require a tent.

Permits: not required.

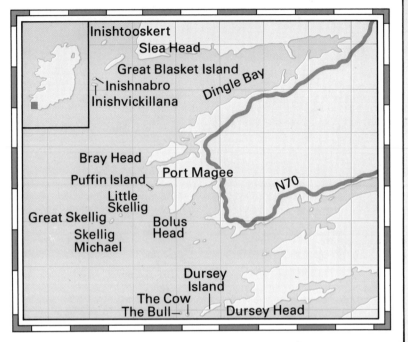

SKOMER, DYFED OS 157

Location: this is the best known and most easily accessible of the 'Pembrokeshire' islands. It lies a mile off the south-west coast of Wales about 10 miles west of Milford Haven.

Habitats: Skomer has some fine cliffs, broken by deeply cut gullies that make viewing both easy and safe. The interior is grassy and honeycombed by the burrows of rabbits and Puffins.

Birds: the three 'Pembrokeshire' islands each have their own specialities. Grassholm has a huge gannetry; Skokholm has breeding seabirds, but is primarily a migration watch point; while Skomer is a classic seabird island. Puffin, Guillemot, Razorbill, Fulmar and Kittiwake are all abundant breeders and there are breeding Shags, Buzzard, gulls and Chough as well. Inland there is a breeding colony of 100,000 pairs of Manx Shearwater.

Access: the island can be visited daily, except Monday, throughout the summer months via Martin's Haven, which is 2 miles west of Marloes towards Wooltack Point. There is an information centre and car park (fee charged) at Martin's Haven. A boat fee and landing fee are both payable and there is limited single accommodation for members of the West Wales Trust for Nature Conservation, 7 Market Street, Haverfordwest, Dyfed SA61 1NF.

Permits: Landing fee on arrival; as above to stay.

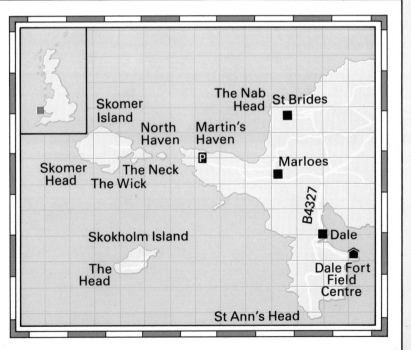

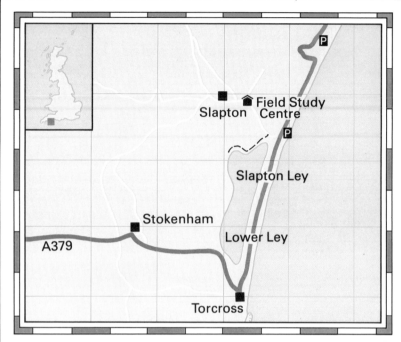

SLAPTON LEY, DEVON OS 202

Location: this large lagoon lies on the south coast of Devon between Dartmouth and Start Point.

Habitats: the shoreline of Start Bay consists of a huge shingle beach that has enclosed a series of freshwater lagoons. They are fringed by bushy scrub and there are field and woodland inland. Slapton Ley is a nature reserve of the Field Studies Council.

Birds: the reed beds here are full of Sedge and Reed Warblers in summer and Cetti's Warbler is resident. A variety of species breeds inland, including Buzzard, Sparrowhawk, Raven and Cirl Bunting (a South Devon speciality). In winter, Water Rails are often quite obvious, a variety of ducks, and perhaps the odd diver or grebe, too. Most years see a few Bittern and Bearded Tit during hard weather. On passage there are frequently terns and skuas and occasionally Sooty Shearwater; warblers, chats and flycatchers among the shoreside bushes; the occasional Marsh Harrier or Hoopoe; regular Garganey in spring; and a regular autumn arrival of Aquatic Warblers among the reeds.

Access: the coastal A379 from Dartmouth runs along the beach.

Permits: on arrival, contact Slapton Ley Field Centre for information. It also offers accommodation and study courses: write to Slapton Ley Field Centre, Slapton, Kingsbridge, Devon TQ7 2QP.

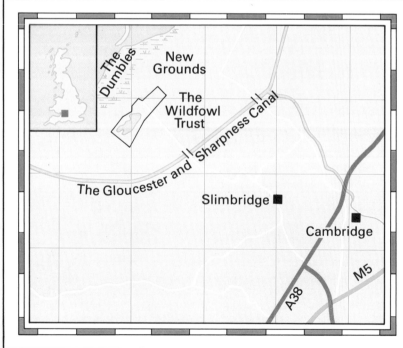

SLIMBRIDGE, GLOUCESTERSHIRE OS 162

Location: on the bank of the Severn, 10 miles from Gloucester.

Habitats: the Wildfowl Trust, founded in 1946 by Sir Peter Scott, have their headquarters here and the collection of ducks, geese, swans and flamingoes is the largest in the world. The birds are housed in enclosures with ponds or lakes. There are hedges and woodland within the collection area, while outside the sea-wall lie grassy saltmarsh and reclaimed meadows, with the tidal river beyond.

Birds: apart from the wildfowl collection, wild birds flight in. Outstanding is the wild flock of Bewick's Swan, one of the largest in the country, that swim around the Rushy Pen for most of the winter. Wild ducks are invariably present, including Wigeon, Pintail and Shoveler. White-fronted Geese regularly exceed 5000 after Christmas. Among them, the occasional Lesser Whitefront or Red-breasted Goose. Waders are less in evidence, but there are good winter numbers of the more common species as well as a wider variety on passage. A Peregrine usually winters.

Access: leave the M5 at Exit 13 or 14 and follow signs to the Wildfowl Trust on the A38. Open daily.

Permits: admission charge for non-members of the Wildfowl Trust.

SNETTISHAM, NORFOLK OS 132

Location: this RSPB reserve is situated on the eastern shore of the Wash between Kings Lynn and Hunstanton.

Habitats: shingle banks with extensive mud flats extending seawards and a hinterland of rough grazing fields. A series of old gravel pits forms a major high-tide roost for waders.

Birds: The Wash is one of Europe's major wetlands and Snettisham is one of its major high-tide wader roosts. Knot, Dunlin, Bar-tailed Godwit, Oystercatcher and Redshank are dominant, but there are always other species present, too. The pits are also used by many wildfowl, with Shoveler, Teal, Wigeon, Gadwall, Goldeneye and Red-breasted Merganser all regular. Occasional seaducks and divers also put in appearances. Both Brent and Pink-footed Geese use the area, mostly roosting on the sand and mud banks offshore. During spring and autumn passage periods, good numbers of waders use the pools as a resting and feeding ground.

Access: leave the A149 at Snettisham and take a minor road westward to the beach. Park in the public car park and walk southwards along the seaward side of the gravel pits until you reach the hides around the southernmost of the pits. Timing is crucial: arrive an hour before high tide – preferably a really high one.

Permits: none required.

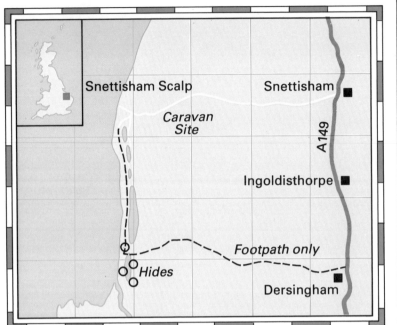

SOUTH STACK, GWYNEDD OS 114

Location: these cliffs lie at the north-western corner of Anglesey, less than 3 miles west of the port of Holyhead and the end of the A5.

Habitats: this is an RSPB reserve covering much of Holyhead Mountain and extending along a cliff-girt coast from North Stack to South Stack. There is also a separate section around Penrhyn Mawr. The area is basically heather and grass moorland, but the main birdwatching interest is centred on the seabird cliffs.

Birds: there are thousands of Guillemot, Razorbill and Kittiwake here, along with smaller numbers of Fulmar, Puffin and Shag. Outstandingly, there are several pairs of Peregrine and Chough, as well as a good population of Raven. Visitors in summer should not ignore the seawatching possibilities, for both Manx Shearwater and Gannet regularly pass by offshore.

Access: leave Holyhead and the A5 westward, signposted South Stack. There is a car park and an information centre at Ellin's Tower that is open daily throughout the summer. A network of good paths leads to North Stack, Holyhead Mountain and across the bridge to South Stack itself. A road also leads southward to another car park at Penrhosfeilw Common where there are more paths to explore.

Permits: none required, but do visit the information centre, where there is a summer warden.

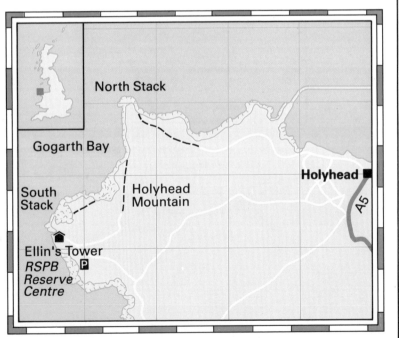

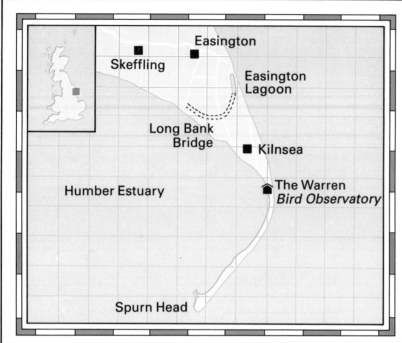

SPURN HEAD, HUMBERSIDE OS 113

Location: at the mouth of the Humber, 25 miles from Hull.

Habitats: this 3-mile long, shingle spit contains large areas of intertidal mud, including Spurn Bight, and small areas of saltmarsh lie to the west, and a sandy shore to the east. Marram grass, bushy thickets and elder scrub offer cover to migrant birds. There are lagoons and small areas of farmland and gardens.

Birds: in winter there are divers and Brent Geese, hosts of waders, winter raptors and Snow Buntings, but during spring and autumn passage periods 'Spurn' really comes into its own. Northerly winds produce skuas and shearwaters, often including Pomarine Skua and Sooty Shearwater. Terns are often numerous and waders include a sprinkling of the scarcer species. Small nocturnal migrants include chats, warblers and flycatchers, with Wryneck, Bluethroat and Barred Warbler in September, and Yellow-browed and Pallas's Warblers in October. Spurn Nature Reserve is owned by the Yorkshire Wildlife Trust, and includes the whole of Spurn Head.

Access: from the A1033 turn south at Patrington on to the B1445 to Kilnsea. A toll is payable beyond Kilnsea. Self-catering accommodation is available: write to The Warden, Spurn Bird Observatory, Kilnsea, Patrington, Hull, Humberside, HU12 0UG.

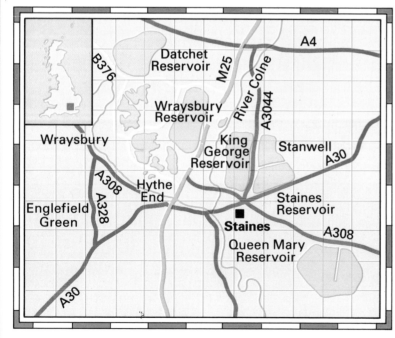

STAINES RESERVOIR, SURREY   OS 176

Location: 17 miles west of the centre of London next to Staines, very near the M4 and M25 motorways, among a maze of roads, many of them heading for Heathrow Airport.

Habitats: these are two large concrete-banked reservoir pools, separated by a public causeway, offering open water to a variety of species. Other good sites are Queen Mary Reservoir, which can be visited; Datchet Reservoir, with only partial access; Wraysbury and King George VI Reservoirs, completely out of bounds.

Birds: winter wildfowl include many Tufted and Pochard, along with fewer Goldeneye and Goosander, and the occasional rarity. There are usually a few Black-necked Grebes, reaching their highest numbers in late summer, and a few Little Gulls regularly in spring and autumn. Passage also brings small numbers of waders and terns, the latter regularly including Black Terns. When a pool is drained it may then attract a fine selection of waders.

Access: the A3044 between Staines and Colnbrook runs between the Staines and King George VI Reservoirs. On the west side is a pumping station beside the road. Park here and walk up the path opposite between railings to the causeway.

Permits: none required.

STODMARSH, KENT   OS 179

Location: in the valley of the River Stour about 5 miles north-east of Canterbury.

Habitats: mining subsidence along the valley has created a series of shallow lagoons and floods, most of which have been colonized by reeds to form the largest freshwater marsh in Kent. At Stodmarsh these have been incorporated into a National Nature Reserve.

Birds: in the 1960s colonizing Savi's Warblers chose this as their first British breeding stronghold. They were followed, in 1972, by Cetti's Warbler. Sadly, being susceptible to hard winters, both species have declined. Other attractions include Bearded Tit and Bittern, abundant Sedge and Reed Warblers, a sprinkling of Grasshopper Warblers, and often the earliest Garganey in the country. Passage brings Black Tern and many waders, especially Ruff and Black-tailed Godwit, and the odd Marsh Harrier, Osprey, Hobby and Short-eared Owl. Winter brings ducks and Hen Harrier.

Access: leave Canterbury eastwards on the A257 and turn left on an unmarked lane just past a British Telecom yard. Follow this to Stodmarsh. In the village take the turning next to the Red Lion to the Reserve car park. Walk to the Lampen Wall which runs across the marsh to the river. This path continues to Grove Ferry.

Permits: not required.

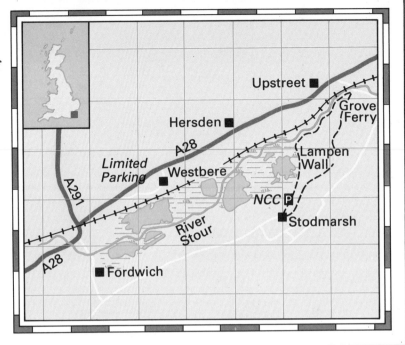

STRANGFORD LOUGH, CO. DOWN, NORTHERN IRELAND

OSNI 21

Location: this large sea lough lies on the east coast of Northern Ireland only a few miles to the south-east of Belfast.

Habitats: huge mud flats are exposed at low tide and there are many small islands. A barrage across the mouth of the River Quoile has created a freshwater which is a National Nature Reserve, and there are three reserves at the seaward end of the lough.

Birds: wintering species include Pale-bellied Brent and Wigeon. There are good numbers of Whooper Swan, Shelduck and Teal, along with smaller but significant numbers of Pintail, Goldeneye and Red-breasted Merganser. Seaducks are regular, as are grebes and Great Northern Diver. Waders, too, are abundant, with Knot, Dunlin, Oystercatcher, Curlew, Redshank and Bar-tailed Godwit all reaching four-figure populations in winter. Greenshank and Black-tailed Godwit winter regularly. There are good breeding colonies of Arctic and other terns.

Access: view from the A20 south of Newtownards. The best areas, however, lie on the western shore. Start at the Wildfowl and Wetlands Trust reserve at Castle Espie, well signposted on A22.

Permits: not required.

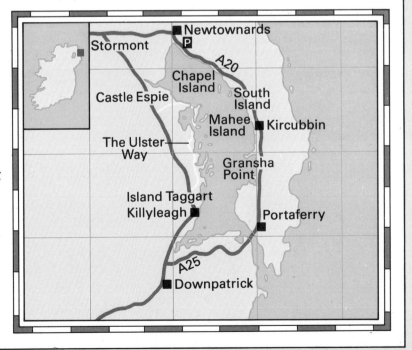

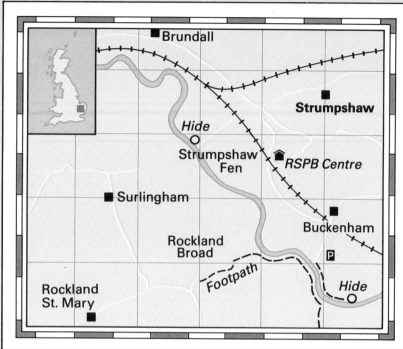

STRUMPSHAW FEN, NORFOLK

OS 134

Location: this RSPB reserve is just 5 miles east of the suburbs of Norwich, in the Yare valley, immediately north of Rockland Broad.

Habitats: this is an area of reed beds, broken by alder carr, willow scrub and areas of open water, surrounded by rough grazing fields. To the east, outside the reserve, lie Buckenham grazing marshes.

Birds: Buckenham has long been a haunt of a flock of Bean Geese. The reserve holds breeding Marsh Harrier and Bearded Tit, Water Rail, Woodcock, Kingfisher and Reed Warbler. Cetti's Warbler was common but has been affected by severe winters, but Grasshopper Warbler is still quite common. During the winter, Hen Harrier, Short-eared Owl and Great Grey Shrike occur regularly.

Access: leave Norwich on the A47 toward Great Yarmouth and turn right on to a minor road to Brundall. Beyond the village take a right towards Hassingham and then another right along Low Road. The RSPB car park is on the right, with the reception centre across a pedestrian level-crossing beyond. For Buckenham and the Bean Geese, continue eastwards from the RSPB car park, then turn right and continue to Buckenham Station. Turn right on a track to the river and car park. Walk eastwards to the mill and nearby hide.

Permits: open daily; no permits required.

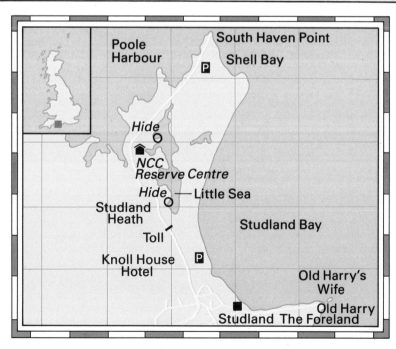

STUDLAND HEATH, DORSET

OS 195

Location: this National Nature Reserve lies on the coast between Poole Harbour and the Isle of Purbeck.

Habitats: sandy heathland with heather, gorse pines and birch scrub. In the east are extensive dunes, among which is Little Sea, a dune-slack lake. Beyond this lies the sea at Studland Bay.

Birds: like the nearby Arne Reserve of the RSPB (*see page* 11), this is a major stronghold of the scarce and highly localized Dartford Warbler. Nightjars also breed here. During passage periods there is a fine collection of waders at Little Sea. Winter brings ducks, including Red-breasted Merganser and Scoter, to the Bay and Sanderling to the beach. Avocet and Black-tailed Godwit usually winter. Bearded Tit usually occur among the reeds at Little Sea.

Access: from Wareham, in the north of the Isle of Purbeck, take the A351 southwards and turn left on to the B3351 at Corfe Castle. Follow the signs to Studland village. Alternatively, from Bournemouth, take the Sandbanks Ferry to South Haven Point. The Nature Reserve observation point lies along a minor road, Ferry Road, between Studland and South Haven Point. There are hides overlooking Little Sea and paths and tracks of free access.

Permits: none for marked paths; toll payable for Ferry Road.

TACUMSHIN LAKE, CO. WEXFORD, IRISH REPUBLIC

IOS½ 23

Location: this wetland lies at the south-eastern corner of Ireland. Wexford, about 10 miles north, is the nearest town, but the ferry terminal of Rosslare is much closer, only 6 miles to the north-west.

Habitats: until 1974 Tacumshin Lake was an area of intertidal mud, all but cut off from the sea by a narrow shingle bar. Then the exit was artificially closed and a drainage sluice dug through the beach. The result has been to reduce considerably the area of wetland and convert it from a tidal basin into a freshwater lake. In late summer the muddy edges provide food for waders.

Birds: in winter wildfowl include up to 400 Brent Geese and 100 Bewick's Swans, the latter doubtless flying in from the nearby Wexford Slobs (*see page* 105). There is also a great variety of ducks, with large numbers of Wigeon; diving ducks include Scaup. Waders are neither outstanding nor particularly numerous in winter, but usually include Ruff. During passage periods, especially autumn, American waders now almost annual.

Access: leave Wexford southward on the N25 and explore the lake from the R736 and roads to the south.

Permits: none required.

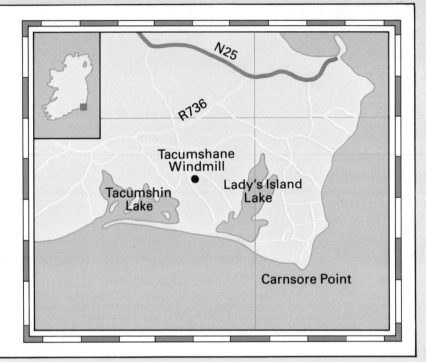

TEESSIDE AND COWPEN MARSH, CLEVELAND   OS 93 & 94

Location: this area is the estuary of the River Tees, which reaches the North Sea beyond Middlesbrough.

Habitats: the estuary has been reclaimed for industry and much is covered by oil refineries. There are, however, major intertidal banks at Seal Sands and various pools, creeks and marshes remain.

Birds: winter brings Knot, Dunlin, Sanderling, Redshank, Bar-tailed Godwit, Ruff and Shelduck. Gulls usually include Glaucous, often Iceland, and occasionally a really rare species. The gulls congregate near the mouth where divers, grebes and seaducks can also be found. Autumn usually brings Manx and Sooty Shearwaters, Great and Arctic Skuas and masses of terns, plus a fine selection of waders, with major rarities every year.

Access: Cowpen Marsh lies on the A128. This reserve of the Cleveland Nature Conservation Trust (CTNC) is open to members (and RSPB members) from February to August. The pools to the east of the A178 have walking access and from Seaton Carew there are paths to North Gare. Contact the CNCT warden on arrival or write to Cleveland Nature Conservation Trust, Old Town Hall, Mandale Road, Thornaby, Stockton-on-Tees, TS17 6AW.

Permits: see above.

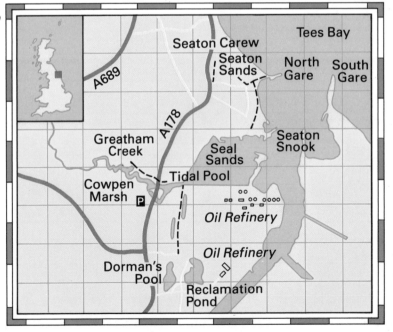

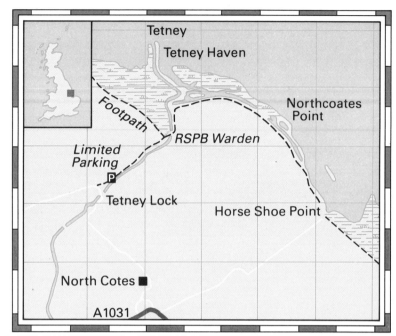

TETNEY, LINCOLNSHIRE OS 113

Location: these marshes lie at the mouth of the River Humber on its southern shore. Tetney is an RSPB reserve.

Habitats: there are large intertidal flats, areas of saltmarsh, an extensive dune system and several 'borrow pits', backed by fields.

Birds: in summer there is a major Little Tern colony here, while Oystercatcher, Redshank, Ringed Plover and Shelduck also breed. Access at this time is, however, highly restricted to protect the breeding birds. During the winter there is a major wader roost here, including Knot, Dunlin, Grey Plover, Oystercatcher and Bar-tailed Godwit. Wildfowl include Brent and Wigeon. Seaducks may include Scaup, Eider, Common and Velvet Scoters, Goldeneye and Red-breasted Merganser, and occasional Long-tailed Duck, while there are usually Red-throated Divers offshore. Merlin, Hen Harrier and Short-eared Owl are all regular winter visitors. Passage periods bring a selection of waders, especially in autumn, and many terns.

Access: leave Grimsby southwards on the A1031 to Tetney and turn left to Tetney Lock. Where the road turns left over the lock, continue on a road along the northern shore of the canal. Walk along the private road to the RSPB warden's caravan (warden present April–August). Continue to Tetney Haven and the sea-wall.

Permits: none required.

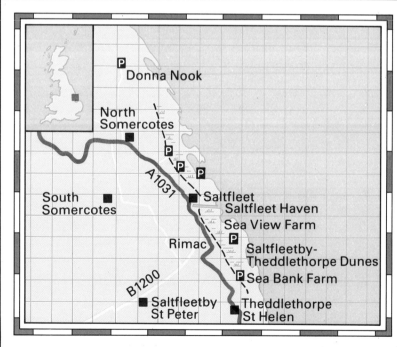

THEDDLETHORPE AND SALTFLEETBY, LINCOLNSHIRE OS 113

Location: this area lies on the coast between Grimsby and Skegness. Mablethorpe, 5 miles to the south is the nearest town.

Habitats: the whole area is a National Nature Reserve. The sand dunes have 'slacks' (damp hollows between the dunes), some having freshwater marshes with reeds and willow scrub.

Birds: Brent Geese are regular in winter and there are usually a few divers and seaducks offshore. Knot, Dunlin, Grey Plover and Oystercatcher are all present and both Marsh and Hen Harriers are regular. The beach holds Snow Bunting throughout winter. During spring and autumn passage periods there are waders and terns on the marshes and many migrant warblers, chats and flycatchers among the bushes. Shelduck, Water Rail, Ringed Plover, Snipe, Redshank and Short-eared Owl all breed.

Access: leave Mablethorpe northwards on the A1031, from which five tracks lead seawards, each with parking at the end. A footpath connects them. Look out for notices drawing attention to the danger area of the RAF bombing range.

Permits: not required.

THURSLEY COMMON, SURREY OS 186

Location: this National Nature Reserve lies roughly at the centre of a triangle with its corners at Farnham, Hindhead and Godalming, all of which give easy access.

Habitats: one of a string of heaths in this part of Surrey, Thursley is mainly dry heathland with heather and gorse, broken up by marshes and areas of birch scrub. Though offering similar habitats as Frensham and Hankley Commons to the west, it has always had a better birding reputation.

Birds: the heathland birds of southern England are fighting a losing battle, with species such as Stone-curlew, Red-backed Shrike and Woodlark all fast disappearing. Of these, only Woodlark can be found here, but there are also Dartford Warbler, Hobby, Tree Pipit, Lesser Spotted Woodpecker and Redstart. The Dartford Warbler is the main attraction, though numbers fluctuate year by year. The Hobby is usually much easier to see and late summer afternoons are generally productive.

Access: leave the A3 westwards to Thursley village; park here and walk northwards. Alternatively, continue to a T-junction and turn right to Moat Pond on the Elstead road. Keep to the paths.

Permits: not required.

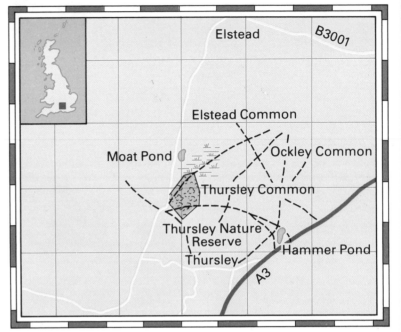

TITCHWELL, NORFOLK OS 132

Location: Titchwell lies at the eastern end of the North Norfolk coast, between Hunstanton and Burnham. The RSPB reserve is a short distance west of Titchwell village, next to the A149.

Habitats: a shallow fresh lagoon dotted with islands, a brackish lagoon, a small intertidal creek and a considerable area of reed beds with invading scrub.

Birds: the major East Anglian specialities all breed here, including Bittern, Marsh Harrier, Water Rail and Bearded Tit. Recently they have been joined by Avocet. In summer the reed beds are alive with warblers, and both Little and Common Terns breed near the beach. Spring brings many migrants, with Black Tern, Little Gull and Spoonbill all regularly present, and a good collection of waders. In autumn, waders are really excellent here. Though there are regular divers, grebes and seaducks offshore in winter, this is also an excellent season for waders on the pools. There are reasonable chances of seeing Short-eared Owl and Hen Harrier, and the beach holds Snow Buntings.

Access: leave Titchwell village westwards on the A149 and after 5 miles turn right on an inconspicuous track to the reserve centre and car park. A raised wall leads to the hides and the shore. At the end turn right to a further hide looking back into the reserve.

Permits: none required.

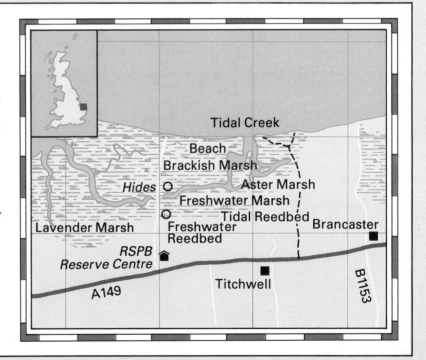

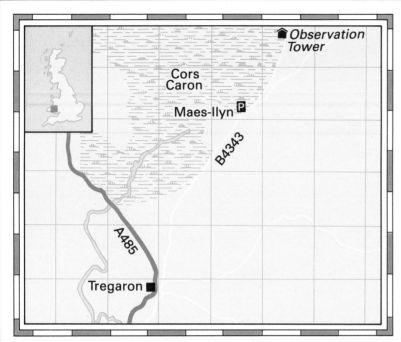

TREGARON, DYFED OS 146

Location: the small town of Tregaron lies among the hills of south-central Wales. A National Nature Reserve now known as Cors Caron (formerly Tregaron Bog) lies north of the town.

Habitats: Cors Caron is a superb raised bog, with a flat marshy landscape broken by clumps of scrub. There are several small ponds and an artificial pool bordered by reeds. The surrounding hills and stream-filled valleys are well wooded, with deciduous woodland and coniferous plantations, and open sheep pastures on the tops.

Birds: Tregaron has long been famous as Britain's most reliable place to see Red Kite. These splendid raptors are most regularly seen along the B4343 between town and reserve, and particularly from the car park, where a nature trail leads north across the bog. Another good spot is about 1 mile south of the town on the same road – look for the rubbish tip, which attracts the birds. A minor road to Llanwrtyd Wells gives further chances of seeing Red Kite. The area holds usual breeding species one would expect in upland western Britain, including Dipper, Grey Wagtail, Pied Flycatcher, Redstart, Buzzard, Sparrowhawk and, in winter, Peregrine and Hen Harrier.

Access: leave Tregaron northwards on the B4343 for 2½ miles. Park on the left and walk along the trail to a windy tower hide.

Permits: not needed, but no access other than detailed above.

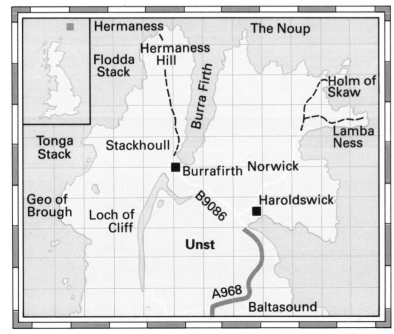

UNST, SHETLAND OS 1

Location: this is the northernmost island of the British Isles, with only a few rock stacks lying offshore further north.

Habitats: the main breeding centre for birds is the promontory of Hermaness in the north-west of Unst. This is a National Nature Reserve, with spectacular cliff scenery.

Birds: the cliffs hold all the usual breeding seabirds, including a fine gannetry, with over 10,000 pairs. The Gannets nest on the broken areas near the cliff foot as well as on the offshore stacks. Among them is a solitary Black-browed Albatross, which has summered here since 1972. There are also Guillemots, Razorbills, thousands of Puffins, Black Guillemots, Shags and Fulmars, and masses of Kittiwakes. Unfortunately, the cliffs here are broken on a dramatic scale, with many huge landslides, and are decidedly dangerous. Walk along the cliff-tops, but take great care on the steep grass slopes, which are especially slippery after rain. The moors hold both Great and Arctic Skuas in good numbers. To the south the Loch of Cliff is favoured by seabirds as a bathing site.

Access: there are regular inter-island car ferries from Yell and daily flights on weekdays from Tingwall Airstrip near Lerwick, or Mainland Shetland, by Loganair.

Permits: none required.

WALBERSWICK, SUFFOLK OS 156

Location: this is a small village on the Suffolk coast immediately south of the mouth of the River Blyth, a mile south of the small town of Southwold. There is a National Nature Reserve here.

Habitats: the shingle beach protects a low-lying area of marshy pools and extensive reed beds. There are open pools and deep dykes, and an overgrown fen, heath and coverts at the western end.

Birds: Bittern, Water Rail, Marsh Harrier and Bearded Tit are present in summer, along with masses of Sedge, Reed and Grasshopper Warblers. Both Savi's and Cetti's Warblers bred here, too. The heaths have nesting Nightjar and Woodcock, and there is still a pair or two of Stone-curlew on the stony fields. Passage waders in spring and autumn include a good collection on the shore pools, though they are much disturbed. Snow Buntings and Twite winter, though Shore Larks tend to occur only in autumn. Winter also brings Hen Harrier, Short-eared Owl and sometimes Rough-legged Buzzard.

Access: leave the A12 just south of Blythburgh, turning right on to the B1387 and following signs to Walberswick. Park at the beach car park and walk southwards along the path behind the sea-wall. Take the second embankment opposite the old windpump to reach the latter, and then head inland to Hoist Covert.

Permits: none required for rights of way.

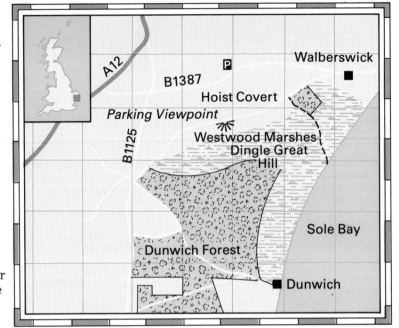

WALNEY ISLAND, CUMBRIA OS 96

Location: this large sand and shingle bar forms the north-western corner of Morecambe Bay (*see page* 76) and lies immediately offshore of Barrow-in-Furness. It is joined to the mainland by road.

Habitats: this is a low-lying island with sandy beaches and large areas of shingle broken by pools of freshwater. Cover is very limited.

Birds: Walney is one of the prime wader sites in Britain, with a massive roost of these birds that includes over 10,000 wintering Oystercatchers, yet it is renowned chiefly as a migration site for small migrants and a massive gull breeding colony. Among the latter are close to 10,000 pairs each of Lesser Black-backed and Herring Gulls, along with small numbers of Great Black-backed Gulls. Other summer breeding birds include Eider, Little Tern and Shelduck. Seawatching is also productive, especially after westerly gales. Shearwaters, skuas and petrels all occur annually and Little Auk most years. In winter Walney is good for Hen Harrier, Merlin, Peregrine (which also breed locally) and Short-eared Owl.

Access: take the bridge from Barrow and head south via Biggar to the nature reserve and observatory, where there is a nature trail and several hides. Contact the Warden, Coastguard Cottages, South Walney Nature Reserve, Barrow-in-Furness LA14 3YQ.

Permits: there is a small charge on arrival.

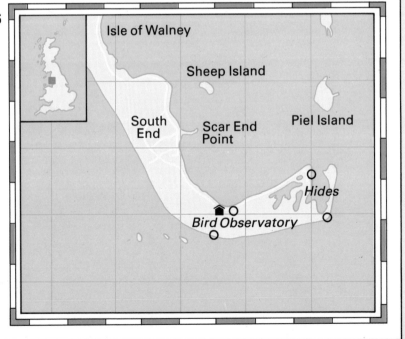

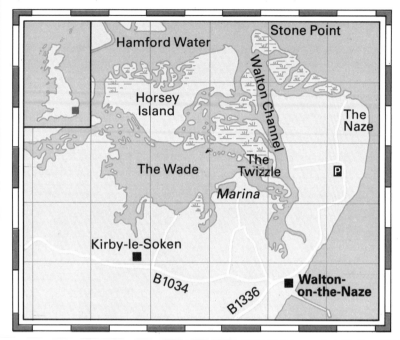

WALTON-ON-THE-NAZE, ESSEX OS 169

Location: on the Essex coast between Clacton and Harwich.

Habitats: this is a largely intertidal area with areas of saltings backed by rough grazing. The sea-wall defences have created deep dykes, but there are still several marshy pools and backwaters.

Birds: though Little Tern and Ringed Plover breed, this is mainly a winter and passage area with waders and wildfowl the main draw. Greenshank, Little Stint and Curlew Sandpiper are all regular in autumn, while in winter they are replaced by Dunlin, Curlew and Redshank. Golden Plover may be abundant but the scene is dominated by over 3000 Brent Geese. The major wader roosts are on Hamford's islands, but Stone Point regularly holds a flock of Sanderling at high tide. Bewick's Swan are regular and there are many ducks, including Wigeon. Red-breasted Merganser have a winter stronghold here and there are regular Hen Harrier, Short-eared Owl and Twite.

Access: Walton-on-the-Naze is easily reached via the A12 and Colchester. Park in the cliff-top car park. Walk northwards. Low water allows access as far as Stone Point, but wellies are essential as is good information about the timing of the tides.

Permits: none required.

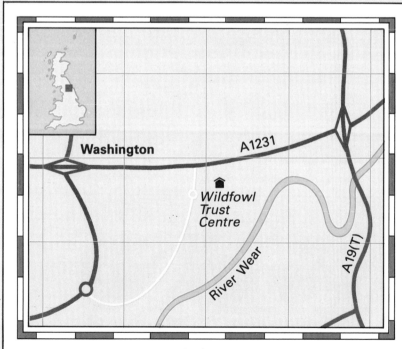

WASHINGTON WATERFOWL PARK, TYNE AND WEAR OS 88

Location: this Wildfowl Trust refuge is situated on the north bank of the River Wear, on the eastern outskirts of Washington New Town, itself a suburb of the great Tyneside conurbation.

Habitats: low-lying riverside marshes have been converted to extensive shallow pools, and imaginative landscaping has created a series of excavated ponds rising in a terraced arrangement.

Birds: this is a typical Wildfowl Trust collection, with a fine visitor centre and well laid out paths giving access and splendid views of an excellent collection of captive ducks and other wildfowl. Unlike some of the other Trust centres, there was no tradition of wildfowl use prior to the reserve's establishment, so that wild birds have had to be encouraged to use the area. The new marshy pools have certainly done so. Specially planted reeds now attract Reed Warbler in summer and Water Rail in winter. Passage periods, especially autumn, bring waders, including Wood Sandpiper, Greenshank, Black-tailed Godwit and the occasional Temminck's Stint. It can only be a matter of time before wild swans discover the area.

Access: take the A1231 to Washington New Town and follow the Wildfowl Trust signs to the refuge.

Permits: charge for non-members.

WEETING HEATH, NORFOLK

OS 144

Location: the village of Weeting lies on the Norfolk–Suffolk border within the huge area known as Breckland (or the Brecks), and about 6 miles north-west of the town of Thetford. The heath itself lies about a mile west of the village on the Hockwold road.

Habitats: dry, infertile soils have created a substantial area of poor grassland typical of what the Brecks once were. This poor sheep pasture is broken by belts of conifers, with other ungrazed areas covered by thicker ground vegetation.

Birds: typical Breckland birds here include Long-eared Owl, Nightjar, Woodcock, Grasshopper Warbler and Crossbill. Weeting Heath is also established as the top spot for Stone-curlew in Britain. Several pairs still breed here and these fine birds can be watched at leisure from the end of March well into the summer.

Access: leave the A1065 at Weeting village turning left on to a minor road westwards toward Hockwold. After 1½ miles, look out for a small car park on the left among a belt of pines. There is a warden at the caravan throughout the Stone-curlew breeding season. A marked path leads to two hides giving fine views of these exciting birds.

Permits: available for a small fee from the warden.

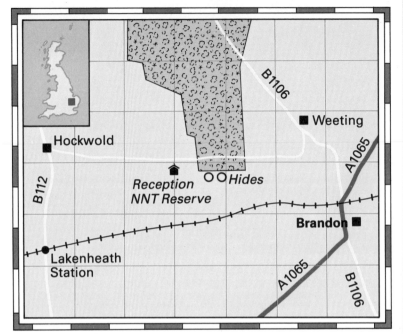

WEXFORD SLOBS, CO. WEXFORD, IRISH REPUBLIC

IOS½ 23

Location: at the south-eastern corner of Ireland, where the town of Wexford itself overlooks much of the best habitat.

Habitats: the North and South Slobs are extensive mud banks and large areas of saltmarsh that have been reclaimed and converted to low-lying grassland, intersected by a network of drainage ditches.

Birds: this is Ireland's major wetland, where the winter population of Greenland White-fronted Geese regularly exceeds 5000, representing about half the total world population. Brent Geese also winter, but in smaller numbers, with a scattering of Pink-footed and Barnacle Goose and the occasional Snow Goose, the latter are mostly regarded as genuine wild birds rather than escapees. Nearly a thousand Pintail also winter and there is a growing herd of Bewick's Swan. Bar-tailed and Black-tailed Godwits are more numerous on spring and autumn passage. Spotted Redshank are notable in autumn. Summer brings large colonies of terns on Tern Island, including Europe's major Roseate Tern colony.

Access: the best area is usually northwards from Rosslare to the Point, where there is a major wader roost.

Permits: none required.

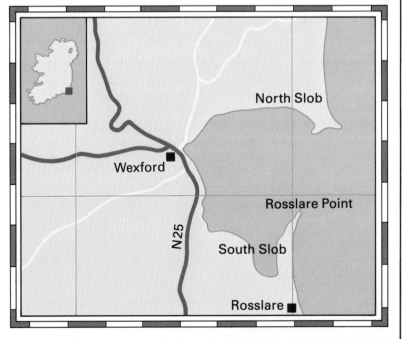

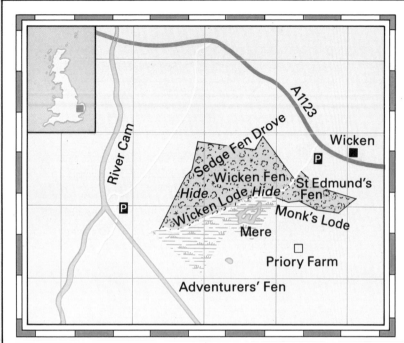

WICKEN FEN, CAMBRIDGESHIRE OS 154

Location: this area of old fenland lies about 7 miles north-west of Newmarket and is marked as 'Adventurers' Fen' on most maps.

Habitats: parts of this important reserve are the last remnants of the original Fens which, prior to drainage, covered so much of the hinterland of The Wash. Adventurers' Fen has been drained, but never with great success. It is now a mere with reed beds.

Birds: many birds breed here, but few are easily seen. They include Bearded Tit, Water Rail and the highly elusive Spotted Crake, as well as Snipe, Redshank and Woodcock, Long-eared Owl, Lesser Spotted Woodpecker and Willow Tit. Breeding warblers include Grasshopper, Cetti's and Savi's, though the latter two have declined. Winter brings many ducks, mainly Wigeon, along with Bittern, Hen Harrier, Water Rail and Short-eared Owl.

Access: leave the A45 Newmarket by-pass, turning right on to the A142 northbound towards Ely. Turn left about a mile after Fordham on to the A1123 to Wicken. On the far side of the village turn left, signposted 'Wicken Fen'. There is a car park, visitor centre and an automatic permit dispenser. Follow tracks and paths for easy exploration and hides. The tower hide is excellent in winter.

Permits: available on arrival. National Trust members enter free.

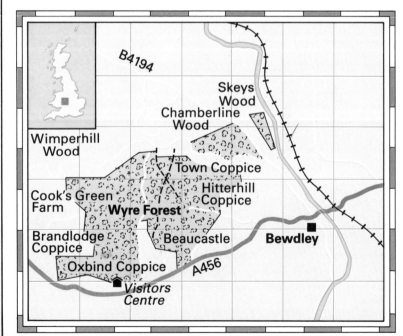

WYRE FOREST, SHROPSHIRE

OS 138 & 139

Location: this remarkably fine forest lies immediately west of the Midlands conurbation on the Shropshire–Worcestershire border and only a few miles west of Kidderminster, the nearest large town.

Habitats: this is a large forest by British standards extending over some six square miles. It is a mature, old forest dominated by deciduous trees, but with an interesting mix of conifers and open heathland. The attractive Dowles Brook bisects the area.

Birds: Wyre Forest offers a good cross-section of the woodland birds of this part of Britain with the western specialities of Pied Flycatcher, Redstart and Wood Warbler present in variable numbers. There are all three woodpeckers, Tree Pipit, Crossbill and Hawfinch to be found, with Dipper and Kingfisher along the streams. Walking the many footpaths in spring it is difficult to realise just how close one is to the great urban sprawl of Birmingham.

Access: leave Birmingham south-eastwards on the A456 to Kidderminster and continue to Bewdley. Turn right on to the B4194. After a couple of miles the forest will be signed. It is a NNR and LNR and the Forestry Commission have a centre here.

Permits: none required for the footpaths that facilitate exploration.

YNYS-HIR, DYFED OS 135

Location: this RSPB reserve lies on the southern shore of the Dyfi estuary (*see page 35*). Machynlleth lies 7 miles to the west.

Habitats: though covering a large area of the saltmarsh that flanks the estuary at this point and containing a typical selection of waders and wildfowl, Ynys-hir is also a fine site for the other birds of this part of Wales, thanks to its outcrops, grassy meadows and woods.

Birds: in summer the woods here are alive with birds and, despite its other attractions, this is probably the best time for visiting. There are breeding Lesser Spotted Woodpecker, Redstart, Pied Flycatcher and Wood Warbler, and all the other more common woodland birds. Both Buzzard and Sparrowhawk breed, too, and Whinchat, Stonechat and Tree Pipit all nest on the more open areas. Red-breasted Merganser and Common Sandpiper can be found along the streams, but Red Kite is only an irregular visitor. In winter there are White-fronted Goose, Wigeon and the more common waders, and the latter include a good selection of species during spring and autumn passage periods.

Access: leave the A487 between Machynlleth and Aberystwyth at Furnace. There is a road to the RSPB car park and information centre and a nature trail with hides. The reserve is open daily.

Permits: on arrival; there is a charge to non-members.

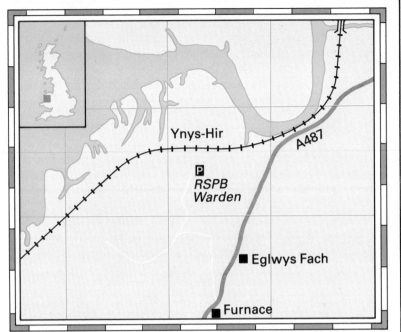

YTHAN ESTUARY, GRAMPIAN

OS 30 & 38

Location: on the Scottish east coast 12 miles north of Aberdeen, and is crossed by the A975. The village of Newburgh lies on the southern shore and the National Nature Reserve of the Sands of Forvie, on the northern shore, is included in this account.

Habitats: there are mud and sand banks at low tide. To the north lie the sandy wastes of Forvie while further north still are several lochs.

Birds: summer sees good numbers of Eider and terns at this site, all breeding at Forvie, but easily seen at the estuary mouth. The colonies of Little, Common, Arctic and Sandwich Terns attract a few skuas at all seasons, and there is usually a flock of Common Scoter offshore, often with some Velvet Scoter. During spring and autumn passage periods waders are often good, with species such as Greenshank, Ruff and sometimes Little Stint. In winter there are Greylag and Pink-footed Geese, which roost mainly on Meikle Loch, and up to 250 Whooper Swans.

Access: the A975 gives excellent views, from both village and bridge. The Sleek of Tarty, with its winter wader roost, can be examined from the bridge before crossing. From here a track leads south to the Point where a hide overlooks the ternery.

Permits: none required.

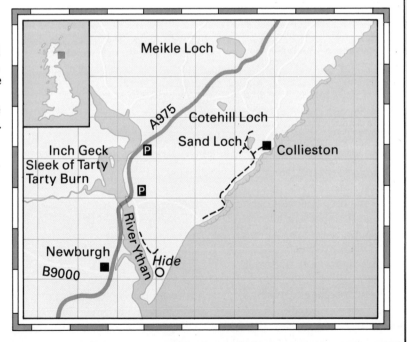

The Checklist

The official British and Irish List is determined by the Records Committee of the British Ornithologists Union (BOU) and amendments are published from time to time in the Union's journal *The Ibis*. Such records, as well as subsequent records, are also published in the annual report of the Rarities Committee of the monthly journal *British Birds*, though final acceptance of a new British bird rests with the BOU.

The BOU list is divided into four categories, A to D, and this letter code follows the name of each species in the most recent version of the list given below, which is complete to 31 December 1986. Category D species are listed separately at the end.

A Species which have been recorded in an apparently wild state in Britain or Ireland at least once within the last 50 years.

B Species which have been recorded in an apparently wild state in Britain or Ireland at least once, but not within the last 50 years.

C Species which, although introduced by man, have now established a regular feral breeding stock which apparently maintains itself without necessary recourse to further introduction.

D Species which have been recorded within the last 50 years and would otherwise appear in category A except that (1) there is a reasonable doubt that they have ever occurred in a wild state, or (2) they have certainly arrived with ship-assistance, or (3) they have only ever been found dead on the tideline; also species which would otherwise appear in category C except that their feral populations may or may not be self-supporting.

☐ **Red-throated Diver** A
Gavia stellata
Widespread breeder in north and west Scotland and in Northern Ireland though nowhere common. Regular winter visitor to most coastlines where it is usually the most common diver.

☐ **Black-throated Diver** A
Gavia Arctica
Breeds in north and west Scotland as far south as the southern uplands, but is decidedly local. Winter visitor to most coasts in small numbers, more numerous in the west.

☐ **Great Northern Diver** A
Gavia immer
Bred in 1970. Otherwise a regular winter visitor in small numbers to most coasts, though may be the dominant diver in parts of the north and west.

☐ **White-billed Diver** A
Gavia adamsii
A rare winter visitor from the Arctic that is recorded annually in Scotland and exceptionally further south.

☐ **Pied-billed Grebe** A
Podilymbus podiceps
A rare vagrant from North America that was recorded nine times up to 1986.

☐ **Little Grebe** A
Tachybaptus ruficollis
A widespread resident almost throughout Britain and Ireland with some immigration during the winter.

☐ **Great Crested Grebe** A
Podiceps cristatus
A widespread resident from the Scottish lowlands southwards. More widespread in winter with some immigration from the Continent.

☐ **Red-necked Grebe** A
Podiceps grisegena
Increasing evidence that a pair will eventually breed in southern Scotland. Otherwise a regular, if scarce, winter visitor to the east and south coasts.

☐ **Slavonian Grebe** A
Podiceps auritus
Highly localized breeder, mainly in northern Scotland, where some 60–80 pairs can be found. Elsewhere mainly a winter visitor in small numbers to coasts, and tend to return to favoured haunts.

☐ **Black-necked Grebe** A
Podiceps nigricollis
Scarcer breeder in England and especially southern Scotland, and in western Ireland. Otherwise scarce winter visitor and passage migrant to coasts and reservoirs.

☐ **Black-browed Albatross** A
Biomedea melanophris
Exceptional vagrant from the southern hemisphere. One individual has been resident every summer at Hermaness in Shetland since 1971.

☐ **Fulmar** A
Fulmarus glacialis
Common breeder along almost every stretch of cliffs in Britain and Ireland. Widespread at sea outside the breeding season.

☐ **Capped Petrel** (A) B
Pterodroma lasitata
Exceptional vagrant. One found long dead at Barmiston, Humberside in 1984. Only previous record was in 1850.

☐ **Bulwer's Petrel** A
Bulweria bulwerii
Exceptional vagrant with only four records.

☐ **Cory's Shearwater** A
Calonectris diomedia
Very scare, but regular, migrant mainly in autumn to the western approaches that may be seen from southern Irish seawatch stations and occasionally elsewhere.

☐ **Great Shearwater** A
Puffinus gravis
Scarce autumn visitor from South Atlantic to western approaches that may be seen from Irish seawatch stations and elsewhere. Often seen from "western" ferries and pelagic trips, sometimes in good numbers.

☐ **Sooty Shearwater** A
Puffinus griseus
Regular late summer and autumn visitor in small numbers to most seawatch stations.

☐ **Manx Shearwater** A
Puffinus puffinus
The most abundant shearwater around out coasts with large, but highly concentrated, breeding colonies, especially in the north and west. Scarce, mainly autumn, migrant elsewhere.

☐ **Little Shearwater** A
Puffinus assimilis
Rare autumn visitor to main seawatch stations that is difficult to identify and for which reports are often rejected.

☐ **Wilson's Petrel** A
Oceanites oceanicus
Exceptionally rare vagrant from southern hemisphere that is probably present offshore in the western approaches, but which is hardly ever seen from land.

☐ **White-faced Petrel** B
Pelagodroma marina
No records for over 50 years.

☐ **Storm Petrel** A
Hydrobates pelagicus
Breeds on isolated islands in north and west. Otherwise mainly storm-driven autumn visitor to the top seawatch stations, and may then occur inland.

☐ **Leach's Petrel** A
Oceanodroma leucorhoa
Breeds at a handful of isolated island sites in the extreme north-west and also probably in Ireland. Elsewhere only storm-driven in autumn.

☐ **Madeiran Petrel** A
Oceanodroma castro
Extremely rare vagrant from the Atlantic that has not been recorded in the past 50 years.

☐ **Gannet** A
Sula bassana
Fast increasing and spreading as a breeding bird, though still mainly confined to large colonies in the north and west. Elsewhere regularly seen offshore.

☐ **Cormorant** A
Phalacrocorax carbo
Widespread resident that breeds along most of the west coasts of Britain and Ireland and occasionally inland. More widespread on all coasts in winter.

☐ **Shag** A
Phalacrocorax aristotelis
Breeds at many places along the north and west coasts, often in large colonies. Mainly resident, but some birds wander to reach most coastlines in winter.

☐ **Magnificent Frigatebird** A
Frigata magnificens
Exceptional. One record, plus two other frigatebirds not specifically identified.

☐ **Bittern** A
Botaurus stellaris
Slowly declining resident that is confined to a few sites in East Anglia and one in Cumbria. Elsewhere only a very rare winter rarity.

☐ **American Bittern** A
Botaurus lentiginosus
Exceptional transatlantic vagrant that has occurred on 58 occasions, most recently in 1982.

☐ **Little Bittern** A
Ixobrychus minutus
First proved to breed at South Potteric Carr, Yorkshire in 1984 after years of rumour elsewhere. Otherwise only a summer vagrant, mainly in late spring, to Southern England.

☐ **Night Heron** A
Nycticorax nycticorax
Irregular vagrant mainly to southern England with about five records a year, though sometimes considerably more.

☐ **Green Heron** A
Butorides striatus
No records since 1889 until one was found at Stone Creek, Humberside on 27 November 1982.

☐ **Squacco Heron** A
Ardeola ralloides
Vagrant northwards from southern Europe mainly to southern England. Some 119 have been recorded, but it is by no means of annual occurrence.

☐ **Castle Egret** A
Bubulcus ibis
Spreading outwards as a breeding bird from its Iberian stronghold, this small heron is slowly becoming more regular in Britain. Though there are only 44 records, no less than 9 were in 1986.

☐ **Little Egret** A
Egretta garzetta
Rare, but annual, visitor, mainly in spring, to southern England, with 20 or more records a year.

☐ **Great White Egret** A
Egretta alba
Rare, but annual, visitor with one or two records each year.

☐ **Great Heron** A
Ardea cinerea
Widespread resident throughout Britain and Ireland. Some immigrants spend the winter here.

☐ **Purple Heron** A
Ardea purpurea
Regular visitor in small numbers that everyone expects to breed in the future. Most regular along the Suffolk coast and elsewhere in southern England.

☐ **Black Stork** A
Ciconia nigra
Vagrant northwards in tiny numbers most years. Maximum was eight in 1985.

☐ **White Stork** A
Ciconia circonia
Irregular summer visitor that occurs almost every year in small numbers, mainly in the spring.

☐ **Glossy Ibis** A
Plegadis falcinellus
Irregular vagrant from south-eastern Europe that occurs most years, but with a major influx in 1986. One or two birds have been apparently resident along the east coast southward to Kent in recent years.

☐ **Spoonbill** A
Platalea leucorodia
Regular, if scarce, passage migrant and exceptional winter visitor, mainly to south and east England presumably *en route* to and from Dutch breeding colonies.

☐ **Mute Swan** A
Cygnus olor
Resident throughout Britain and Ireland save for the major upland regions in the north and west. Slow decline apparently due to lead poisoning.

☐ **Bewick's Swan** A
Cygnus columbianus
Regular, but localized, winter visitor. Most large herds tend to occur in southern and eastern England.

☐ **Whooper Swan** A
Cygnus cygnus
Widespread winter visitor to Scotland and Ireland that is more localized in England and Wales. Most birds are apparently of Icelandic origin. Feral pairs have bred in Scotland in recent years.

☐ **Bean Goose** A
Anser fabalis
Regular, but highly localized, winter visitor from northern Europe with only a handful of traditional haunts. Recent increases in East Anglia, which is now the stronghold in Britain.

☐ **Pink-footed Goose** A
Anser brachyrhynchus
The most abundant of our winter geese with the entire Icelandic population, plus birds from Greenland, wintering in Scotland and at a few major sites in England.

☐ **White-fronted Goose** A
Anser albifrons
Widespread winter visitor to many parts of the country. Birds in Ireland and western Scotland come from Greenland. Those in England are from Russia. Welsh birds originate from both directions, but keep quite separate.

☐ **Lesser White-fronted Goose** A
Anser erythropus
Rare, but almost annual, vagrant from eastern Europe, most often found among large flocks of winter Whitefronts.

☐ **Greylag Goose** A
Anser anser
Widespread resident as a result of reintroductions. Original native stock confined to Outer Hebrides and other parts of north-west Scotland. Common winter visitor mainly to Scotland.

☐ **Snow Goose** A
Anser caerulescens
A regular straggler from North America that also escapes from wildfowl collections. Birds in Ireland tend to be regarded as genuine migrants, those in southern England are often suspect.

☐ **Canada Goose** A
Branta canadensis
Widespread resident in England and locally elsewhere. Originally introduced, the species is prospering and has developed a pattern of moult migration. Genuine vagrants occur in Ireland and western Scotland annually.

☐ **Barnacle Goose** A
Branta leucopsis
Locally abundant winter visitor. Greenland birds winter in Ireland and north-west Scotland; Spitzbergen birds on the Scottish Solway. Siberian birds now occur in small numbers annually in south-east England.

☐ **Brent Goose** A
Branta bernicla
Increasing winter visitor to many coasts and estuaries. The dark-bellied form which comes from the Soviet Union frequents east and south coasts: the pale-bellied from Greenland occurs in Ireland. Pale-bellied Spitzbergen birds are found in north-east England.

☐ **Red-breasted Goose** A
Branta ruficollis
Vagrant from eastern Europe that is now of annual occurrence, most often with flocks of Brent Geese, one of two per year, but probably increasing.

☐ **Egyptian Goose** C
Alopochen aegyptiacus
Introduced in the eighteenth century and now well established in Norfolk where the population is self-supporting.

☐ **Ruddy Shelduck** A
Tadorna ferruginea
Widely kept in wildfowl collections, these ducks are mostly regarded as escapees, though a few are probably truly wild birds from north-west Africa and southern Eurasia.

☐ **Shelduck** A
Tadorna tadorna
Resident breeding bird along many stretches of coastline and inland in some areas. More widespread, but still mainly coastal, in winter.

☐ **Mandarin** C
Aix galericulata
Introduced from China where it is now decidedly rare and may be endangered. Highly localized with most populations resident in south and east England.

☐ **Wigeon** A
Anas penelope
Widespread, often abundant, winter visitor to coastal and lowland areas throughout Britain and Ireland. Breeds in the north and at several places southward to Kent.

☐ **American Wigeon** A
Anas americana
Regular transatlantic vagrant in small numbers to Ireland, but also to Britain. Several birds have been shot bearing American rings.

☐ **Gadwell** A
Anas strepera
Originally introduced to Britain, but with genuine wild birds occurring additionally as winter visitors. Now breeds at scattered localities throughout these islands with dispersal in winter elsewhere. Rather local in Ireland.

☐ **Baikal Teal** A
Anas formosa
Extremely rare vagrant from Siberia with a total of ten records, two of which at least are regarded as genuine wild birds. The last was in southern Scotland in 1973.

☐ **Teal** A
Anas crecca
Widespread breeding bird mainly in the north and west, but also elsewhere in suitable habitats. Abundant winter visitor to all parts of Britain and Ireland.

☐ **Mallard** A
Anas platyrhynchos
Abundant and widespread breeding bird and winter visitor.

☐ **Black Duck** A
Anas rubripes
Rare transatlantic vagrant. Females show a remarkable tendency to pair with male Mallard and produce confusing hybrid young.

☐ **Pintail** A
Anas acuta
Widespread winter visitor, mainly to coastal areas, with large flocks confined to traditional sites. Scattered breeding in several parts of Britain and Ireland in small numbers.

☐ **Garganey** A
Anas querquedula
Summer visitor, mainly to southern England, from Africa, south of the Sahara. Regular spring and autumn passage migrant in Ireland and southern Scotland.

☐ **Blue-winged Teal** A
Anas discors
Rare transatlantic vagrant that is now recorded every year in small numbers.

☐ **Shoveler** A
Anas clypeata
Widespread breeding bird in England and eastern Scotland. More localized in Ireland and largely absent from Wales and the south-west. Large number of immigrants from Iceland and northern Europe in winter.

☐ **Red-crested Pochard** A
Netta rufina
Scarce autumn and winter visitor mainly to south-eastern England, though status confused by frequent escapes from wildfowl collections.

☐ **Pochard** A
Aythya ferina
Widespread breeding bird to most of Britain and Ireland except for the hill regions of the north and west. Abundant winter visitor, particularly to lowland reservoirs.

☐ **Ring-necked Duck** A
Aythya collaris
Scarce, though regular transatlantic vagrant that is now of annual occurrence and often long-staying. Numbers vary from six to 35 per year.

☐ **Ferruginous Duck** A
Aythya nyroca
Rare annual visitor to south and east England from south-eastern Europe mainly between autumn

and spring. Beware relatively common escapees.

☐ Tufted Duck A
Aythya fuligula
Common breeding bird throughout most of Britain and Ireland and abundant winter visitor that forms large flocks on suitable inland waters.

☐ Scaup A
Aythya morila
Locally common winter visitor to suitable coasts and sheltered bays. May form really large flocks at favoured localities.

☐ Eider A
Somateria mollissima
Common breeding bird along the coasts of Scotland and Northern Ireland. Disperses along most coasts in winter, though most birds are resident. Some immigration across the southern North Sea.

☐ King Eider A
Somateria spectabilis
Rare, but annual, vagrant from the Arctic, mainly to northern Britain. Most are males and many are long-staying.

☐ Steller's Eider A
Polysticta stelleri
Extremely rare vagrant that has occurred 13 times mostly in northern Britain. The last was a long-stay individual in the Outer Hebrides from 1972 to 1984.

☐ Harlequin Duck A
Histrionicus histrionicus
An extremely rare vagrant that breeds as near as Iceland, but which has wandered southwards to northern Britain in winter on nine occasions.

☐ Long-tailed Duck A
Clangula hyemalis
A widespread winter visitor to most coastlines with major

populations concentrated in the north and north-east. Occasionally found inland and has bred on occasion.

☐ Common Scoter A
Melanitta nigra
Widespread and common winter visitor to most coastlines, with flocks of subadults present in many areas throughout the year. Breeds in small numbers in north-western Scotland and Ireland.

☐ Surf Scoter A
Melanitta perspicillata
Scarce, but annual, visitor in small numbers to the north and west, several of which have proved long stayers. Breeds in Arctic North America.

☐ Velvet Scoter A
Melanitta fusca
Winter visitor from northern Europe to most coastlines, though absent from western Ireland. Generally outnumbered by Common Scoter, with which it associates.

☐ Buffhead A
Bucephala albeola
Extremely rare vagrant from North America that has occurred only six times, most recently in the Outer Hebrides in 1980.

☐ Goldeneye A
Bucephala clangula
Scarce, but increasing, breeder in specially erected nest boxes in the Scottish Highlands, about seventy pairs in 1985. Widespread and common winter visitor to most of Britain and Ireland, both inland and along the coasts.

☐ Hooded Merganser A
Mergus cucullatus
Extremely rare transatlantic vagrant that has occurred only five times, mostly in Ireland in winter.

☐ Smew A
Mergus albellus
Scarce, but regular, winter visitor mainly to south-eastern England, mostly seen on gravel pits and reservoirs, particularly early in the year. May occasionally summer in far north, but not breeding as yet.

☐ Red-breasted Merganser A
Mergus serrator
Breeds in northern Britain as far south as North Wales and in north and west of Ireland. Widespread along most coasts in winter when there is some immigration.

☐ Goosander A
Mergus merganser
Breeds in northern Britain, but absent from Ireland. Mainly resident, but immigrants from the Continent are found at many inland waters in England in winter.

☐ Ruddy Duck A
Oxyura jamaicensis
Introduced from North America; escapees have bred in the wild since 1960. Nowe well established in Midlands and spreading. Wanders as far as Kent in winter.

☐ Honey Buzzard A
Pernis apivorus
Very rare summer visitor that breeds in small numbers every year. Total pairs less than a dozen.

☐ Black Kite A
Milvus migrans
Rare vagrant, mainly in late spring, with most records from southern England. Apparently increasing with 13 records in 1986.

☐ Red Kite A
Milvus milvus
Slow, steady increase from the verge of extinction as resident breeding bird in central Wales. Maximum 50 pairs in 1985, but

still robbed every year. Rare, but annual, vagrant elsewhere.

☐ White-tailed Eagle A
Haliaeetus albicilla
Has bred once more following a ten-year reintroduction scheme centred on Rhum in the Inner Hebrides. Four pairs laid eggs in 1985. Elsewhere, extremely rare vagrant, mainly in winter.

☐ Egyptian Vulture B
Neophron percnopterus
Rare vagrant from southern Europe that has not occurred for over 50 years.

☐ Griffon Vulture B
Gyps fulvus
Rare vagrant from southern Europe that has not occurred for over 50 years.

☐ Marsh Harrier A
Circus aeruginosus
Scarce breeding bird that is steadily building up its numbers after a period of near extinction. Some 31 nests in 1985 was a new peak in this century. More widespread on passage and in winter.

☐ Hen Harrier A
Circus cyaneus
Increasing and spreading as a breeding species, from an all time low between the wars, when it was more or less confined to the Orkneys. Now breeds as far south as Wales. Widespread winter visitor to coasts and heaths.

☐ Pallid Harrier A
Circus macrourus
Exceptional vagrant from eastern Europe that has occurred only three times.

☐ Montagu's Harrier A
Circus pygargus
Very rare summer visitor mainly to eastern England that has not exceeded ten pairs in the past

decade. Otherwise a scarce passage migrant.

☐ **Goshawk** A

Accipiter gentilis

Slowly increasing as a breeding bird, mainly as a result of escapees from falconry. Widespread, with 35–65 breeding pairs, but still robbed annually.

☐ **Sparrowhawk** A

Accipiter nisus

Widespread breeder throughout Britain and Ireland and mainly resident. Considerable increase since the pesticide fiasco of the 1960s.

☐ **Buzzard** A

Buteo buteo

Widespread and common resident in north and west Britain, but highly local in Ireland and in south and eastern England. Regular winter visitor and passage migrant in small numbers elsewhere.

☐ **Rough-legged Buzzard** A

Buteo lagopus

Scarce winter visitor, mainly to the east coast, in variable numbers each year. Tendency to reach peak every five or six years.

☐ **Spotted Eagle** A

Aquila clanga

Extremely rare vagrant from eastern Europe that has not occurred within the past 50 years.

☐ **Golden Eagle** A

Aquila chrysaetos

Healthy population resident in Scottish Highlands and Islands with several pairs in the Southern Uplands and, more recently, a pair in the Lake District.

☐ **Osprey** A

Pandion haliaetus

Gradual increase as breeder since recolonization. In 1985 there were 34 pairs, of which 28 bred, rearing 53 young. Elsewhere an increasing passage migrant throughout Britain and Ireland.

☐ **Lesser Kestrel** A

Falco naumanni

Extrmeley rare vagrant from southern Europe where it is declining. There have been 20 records, the last in 1983 in Humberside.

☐ **Kestrel** A

Falco tinnunculus

The most widespread and abundant British and Irish bird of prey.

☐ **American Kestrel** A

Falco sparverius

Exceptional transatlantic vagrant with only two records, both in 1976, from Cornwall in June and Fair Isle in May.

☐ **Red-footed Falcon** A

Falco vespertinus

Rare passage migrant, that occurs in small numbers annually, mostly in late spring, sometimes in small flocks.

☐ **Merlin** A

Falco columbarius

Widespread, but uncommon, resident in mostly hilly districts of the north and west. Winter visitor in small numbers to most coastlines.

☐ **Hobby** A

Falco subbuteo

Summer visitor to southern England, that is steadily increasing in numbers after years of persecution by egg-collectors. Passage migrant elsewhere

☐ **Eleonora's Falcon** A

Falco eleonorae

Exceptionally rare vagrant northwards from the Mediterranean that has appeared on only two occasions; in 1977 on Merseyside, and in 1981 on Humberside – the latter dead in a cabbage patch!

☐ **Gyrfalcon** A

Falco rusticolus

Rare, but annual, vagrant averaging about three a year, mainly in winter and mainly in the north of Britain.

☐ **Peregrine** A

Falco peregrinus

Breeds in most mountain and cliff-girt coastal districts of the north and west and has made a significant recovery since its numbers were decimated by pesticides. Elsewhere mainly a coastal passage migrant and winter visitor.

☐ **Red Grouse** A

Lagopus lagopus

Resident in all hill districts of the north and west. Unknown elsewhere.

☐ **Ptarmigan** A

Lagopus mutus

Resident among the highest ranges of the Scottish Highlands. Unknown elsewhere.

☐ **Black Grouse** A

Tetrao tetrix

Resident in hilly districts of north and west. Unknown Ireland and elsewhere.

☐ **Capercaillie** A

Tetrao urogallus

Exterminated in eighteenth century, reintroduced from Sweden in the mid-nineteenth century. Resident in Scottish Highlands and unknown elsewhere.

☐ **Red-legged Partridge** C

Alectoris rufa

Introduced in eighteenth century, now well established resident in eastern and central England, and in eastern Scotland.

☐ **Grey Partridge** A

Perdix perdix

Resident almost throughout Britain and Ireland, though steady decline in numbers continues, despite artificial rearing.

☐ **Quail** A

Coturnix coturnix

Summer visitor that has a patchy distribution throughout Britain and Ireland, but which has become decidedly rare in many areas.

☐ **Pheasant** C

Phasianus colchicus

Introduced from Asia possibly by the Romans, but certainly since Norman times. Now widespread and common resident throughout Britain and Ireland, including huge numbers artificially reared – and shot – every year.

☐ **Golden Pheasant** A

Chrysolophus pictus

Introduced in late nineteenth century, mainly in the Brecks and western Norfolk, but also in Galloway. Continued introductions today, but highly confined distribution.

☐ **Lady Amherst's Pheasant** C

Chrysolophus amherstiae

Introduced at the turn of the century with a self-supporting feral population now established in Bedfordshire.

☐ **Water Rail** A

Rallus aquaticus

Widespread resident, except in the hilly districts, and winter visitor from the Continent. Nowhere common.

☐ **Spotted Crake** A

Porzana porzana

Rare summer visitor that probably breeds every year in very small numbers. Equally scare passage migrant.

☐ **Sora Rail** A

Porzana carolina

Exceptionally rare transatlantic vagrant, mainly in autumn. The total of 11 includes the latest in West Sussex in 1985.

☐ **Little Crake** A

Porzana parva

Rare vagrant from southern Europe, mainly in early spring. The latest was in East Sussex in 1985.

☐ **Baillon's Crake** A

Porzana pusilla

Rare vagrant from southern Europe, mostly in late winter or early spring. There have been no records since 1976 until when it has been more or less of annual occurrence.

☐ **Corncrake** A

Crex crex

Once widespread, this bird has declined rapidly this century due to changing agricultural techniques. It is now a summer visitor only to north-west Scotland and Ireland in any numbers. Elsewhere a scarce passage migrant.

☐ **Moorhen** A

Gallinula chloropus

Widespread and abundant resident throughout Britain and Ireland.

☐ **Allen's Gallinule** B

Porphyrula alleni

Exceptionally rare vagrant that has not occurred within the past 50 years.

☐ **American Purple Gallinule** A

Porphyrula martinica

Exceptional transatlantic vagrant that has occurred once in the Isles of Scilly.

☐ **Coot** A

Fulica atra

Widespread and numerous resident and abundant winter visitor.

☐ **American Coot** A

Fulica americana

Exceptional transatlantic vagrant. One found at Ballycotton in Ireland in 1981.

☐ **Crane** A

Grus grus

Rare passage migrant, mainly in small numbers, but with the occasional large autumn influx. Breeds in Scandinavia, winters from France through to Spain. A small group is at present resident in east Norfolk.

☐ **Sandhill Crane** A

Grus canadensis

Exceptional transatlantic vagrant with only two records: Co. Cork in 1905 and Fair Isle in 1981.

☐ **Little Bustard** A

Tetrax tetrax

Rare vagrant from south or east, mainly in winter. Formerly reasonably regular, it is now quite exceptional. (One in Hampshire on New Year's Eve 1987 broke the duck for hundreds of observers.)

☐ **Husbara Bustard** A

Chlamydotis undulata

Exceptionally rare vagrant from Middle East or North Africa. There are five records, the last in Suffolk in 1962.

☐ **Great Bustard** A

Otis tarda

Rare vagrant from southern and eastern Europe that averages about one record a year at the present time. Mostly winter.

☐ **Oystercatcher** A

Haematopus ostralegus

Widespread and common shoreline breeder, found inland in summer in northern England and Scotland. Abundant on estuaries in winter.

☐ **Black-winged Stilt** A

Himantopus himantopus

Regular, if scarce, passage migrant mainly to the south in spring, usually at the beginning of May. Bred in Nottinghamshire in 1945 (and again in Norfolk in 1987).

☐ **Avocet** A

Recurvirostra avosetta

Steadily increasing and spreading as a breeding bird since its war time recolonization. In 1985 there was a record 269 pairs at 14 sites, including some that were not bird reserves. Elsewhere, a scarce passage migrant and a winter visitor to the south-east.

☐ **Stone-curlew** A

Burhinus oedicnemus

A scarce summer visitor to south and east England that is steadily declining in numbers due to agricultural destruction, egg collecting and disturbance.

☐ **Cream-coloured Courser** A

Cursorius cursor

Very rare vagrant from North Africa, that has occurred on 33 occasions, most recently in Essex in 1984.

☐ **Collared Pratincole** A

Glareola pratincola

Vagrant northwards from southern Europe that occurs most years in late spring, usually in the south.

☐ **Black-winged Pratincole** A

Glareola nordmanni

Rare vagrant northwards from south-eastern Europe that is of less than annual occurrence, mainly in autumn.

☐ **Little Ringed Plover** A

Charadrius dubius

First bred in 1938 and now established as a regular summer visitor to England, though with a decidedly eastern bias. Elsewhere a passage migrant, mostly inland.

☐ **Ringed Plover** A

Charadrius hiaticula

Breeds along most coasts and in many hilly districts in good numbers. Abundant along many shorelines on passage, but numbers are smaller in winter.

☐ **Semipalmated Plover** A

Charadrius semipalmatus

Exceptional transatlantic vagrant. One on Scilly in 1978.

☐ **Killdeer** A

Charadrius vociferus

Rare transatlantic vagrant that is recorded in very small numbers most winters. Last was in Herefordshire in 1985.

☐ **Kentish Plover** A

Charadrius alexandrinus

Formerly bred in small numbers in western Kent and adjacent Sussex. Now mainly a scarce passage migrant, mainly in spring, but bred again in 1979.

☐ **Greater Sand Plover** A

Charadrius leschenaultii

Exceptional vagrant from the Middle East that was first recorded in 1978 and has appeared six times since, the last being in Norfolk in 1985.

☐ **Caspian Plover** B

Charadrius asiaticus

Exceptionally rare vagrant that has not been recorded within the past 50 years.

☐ **Dotterel** A

Charadrius marinellus

Regular summer visitor to the highest of the Scottish hills where some 15–30 pairs regularly breed.

Otherwise a scarce passage migrant that has the habit of stopping off at the same spots at the same time each year.

☐ **American Golden Plover** A
Pluvialis dominica
A rare transatlantic vagrant that occurs most years mainly in late summer and autumn.

☐ **Pacific Golden Plover** A
Pluvialis fulva
A rare vagrant from north-east Asia that has recently been 'split' from the American Golden Plover and which had been identified on only four occasions until 1986. Non-specific records of American/Pacific Golden Plovers, previously lumped as Lesser Golden Plover, may include this species.

☐ **Golden Plover** A
Pluvialis apricaria
Widespread breeder among hills of north and west. Abundant winter visitor over much of lowland Britain and Ireland.

☐ **Grey Plover** A
Pluvialis squatarola
Numerous passage migrant and winter visitor to most coasts and estuaries.

☐ **Sociable Plover** A
Chettusia gregaria
Rare vagrant from south-east Russia and Central Asia, mainly in October to southern England that is now almost of annual occurrence. There were 29 records up to 1986.

☐ **White-tailed Plover** A
Chettusia leucura
An exceptionally rare vagrant westwards from Russia and the Middle East that has occurred on four occasions, most recently in 1984.

☐ **Lapwing** A
Vanelus vanellus
Widespread and abundant breeding bird, passage migrant and winter visitor.

☐ **Knot** A
Calidris canutus
Abundant winter visitor, particularly to favoured estuaries, though in smaller numbers along most coastlines.

☐ **Sanderling** A
Calidris alba
Common winter visitor to most shorelines, with largest numbers usually present in the west in spring.

☐ **Semipalmated Sandpiper** A
Calidris pusilla
Rare transatlantic vagrant that was recorded 49 times up to 1986, mainly in autumn.

☐ **Western Sandpiper** A
Calidris mauri
Exceptionally rare transatlantic vagrant that was recorded on only seven occasions up to 1986. The last was in 1975.

☐ **Little Stint** A
Calidris minuta
Widespread passage migrant, mainly in autumn, that occasionally overwinters in small numbers.

☐ **Temminck's Stint** A
Calidris temminckii
Scarce double passage migrant that is more regular in spring than autumn. Tiny numbers have bred in northern Scotland during the past decade, but permanent colonization seems far away.

☐ **Long-toed Stint** A
Calidris subminuta
Extremely rare vagrant from Asia that occurred on only one occasion up to 1986, in Cleveland in 1982.

☐ **Least Sandpiper** A
Calidris minutilla
A very rare transatlantic vagrant that was recorded 27 times prior to 1986, when one was reported from Cornwall. Most have been in autumn, though the 1986 bird was present from February to April.

☐ **White-rumped Sandpiper** A
Calidris fuscicollis
Regular transatlantic vagrant, mainly in autumn, usually with up to 20 records a year.

☐ **Baird's Sandpiper** A
Calidris bairdii
More or less annual transatlantic vagrant in small numbers, mainly in autumn.

☐ **Pectoral Sandpiper** A
Calidris melanotus
Scarce but regular transatlantic passage migrant every autumn. Regular sightings in spring suggest that this species may become established this side of the Atlantic.

☐ **Sharp-tailed Sandpiper** A
Calidris acuminata
Exceptionally rare vagrant from north-eastern Siberia, mainly in autumn. There were 18 records up to 1986.

☐ **Curlew Sandpiper** A
Calidris ferruginea
Widespread passage migrant, especially in autumn, to coastal and inland marshes. Occasional in winter.

☐ **Purple Sandpiper** A
Calidris maritima
Regular winter visitor to rocky shorelines, mostly in small numbers. Since 1978 has bred in Scotland, with a maximum of three pairs in 1985.

☐ **Dunlin** A
Calidris alpina
Abundant along shores, estuaries and inland marshes in winter and on passage. Widespread breeder among northern and western moors.

☐ **Broad-billed Sandpiper** A
Limicola falcinellus
Rare passage migrant in small numbers in May and June most years. The best ever year was 1984 with 12 records.

☐ **Stilt Sandpiper** A
Micropalama himantopus
A very rare transatlantic vagrant that occurred on only 17 occasions until 1986, the last in Kent in 1985. Most are in autumn, in the south.

☐ **Buff-breasted Sandpiper** A
Tryngites subruficollis
A regular transatlantic migrant in small numbers, mostly in autumn, often to golf courses, airfields and similar grasslands.

☐ **Ruff** A
Philomachus pugnax
A common and widespread passage migrant throughout Britain and Ireland, that now winters regularly in smallish numbers at several sites and which has returned to breed irregularly over the past 20 years.

☐ **Jack Snipe** A
Lymnocryptes minimus
A scarce winter visitor and passage migrant throughout Britain and Ireland.

☐ **Snipe** A
Gallinago gallinago
Widespread resident and abundant winter visitor to all parts of Britain and Ireland.

☐ **Great Snipe** A
Gallinago media
Rare autumn vagrant mainly to Fair Isle and the east coast with

no more than one or two records in most recent years.

Short-billed Dowitcher A
Limnodromus griseus
Exceptionally rare vagrant from America that was positively identified on only five occasions up to 1986. Many dowitchers are not identified as to species.

Long-billed Dowitcher A
Limnodromus scolopaceus
Rare transatlantic vagrant, mainly in autumn, that also stays on to winter on occasion. Averages some half dozen records a year at present.

Woodcock A
Scolopax rusticola
Widespread resident in damp woodlands that is also a passage migrant and winter visitor from the Continent.

Black-tailed Godwit A
Limosa limosa
Scarce and localized breeding bird with some 36–90 pairs grouped in 5–13 localities, mostly in England. Regular and widespread passage migrant and winter visitor.

Hudsonian Godwit A
Limosa haemastica
Exceptional vagrant from America. One on Humberside in 1981 was also seen (presumed the same bird) in 1983.

Bar-tailed Godwit A
Limosa lapponica
Widespread and common passage migrant and winter visitor to many estuaries and shorelines.

Little Whimbrel A
Numenius minutus
Extremely rare vagrant from Asia that was first recorded in Glamorgan in 1982 and subsequently in Norfolk in 1985. These were the only records up to 1986.

Eskimo Curlew B
Numerius borealis
Transatlantic vagrant last century that is all but extinct and highly unlikely to occur again.

Whimbrel A
Numenius phaeopus
Regular double passage migrant, especially in spring, that breeds in small numbers in the Scottish islands.

Curlew A
Numenius arquata
Common and widespread summer visitor to much of Britain and Ireland, and is also common around most coasts and estuaries on passage and in winter.

Upland Sandpiper A
Bartramia longicauda
Rare transatlantic vagrant that occurred 39 times up to 1986. Now regarded as more or less annual in October on the Isles of Scilly.

Spotted Redshank A
Tringa erythropus
Regular double passage migrant mainly in the south and east that has definite favoured areas. Small numbers also winter.

Redshank A
Tringa totanus
Widespread breeding bird that is an abundant winter visitor and passage migrant.

Marsh Sandpiper A
Tringa stagnatilis
Rare vagrant from eastern Europe that is now recorded annually in small numbers, mostly in summer. Total of 59 records up to 1986.

Greenshank A
Tringa nebularia
Regular and widespread double passage migrant that breeds in small numbers in Scotland and Ireland. Small numbers in winter, mainly in the south-west.

Greater Yellowlegs A
Tringa melanoleuca
Very rare transatlantic vagrant, mostly in autumn, that occurred only 28 times up to 1986, most recently in 1985.

Lesser Yellowlegs A
Tringa flavipes
Rare transatlantic visitor that occurs in tiny numbers every year, mostly in autumn.

Solitary Sandpiper A
Tringa solitaria
Very rare transatlantic vagrant that occurred only 24 times up to 1986, mostly in autumn. Most recent was on Scilly in 1985, where about half the records now derive.

Green Sandpiper A
Tringa ochropus
Widespread passage migrant and scarce winter visitor that has bred on occasion.

Wood Sandpiper A
Tringa glareola
Widespread passage migrant, particularly in autumn, that has bred in northern Scotland in small numbers in recent years.

Terek Sandpiper A
Xenus cinereus
Rare vagrant from eastern Europe that is mainly a late spring and early summer visitor to the south and east coasts. Only 28 were recorded until 1986, when no less than four were found.

Common Sandpiper A
Actitis hypoleucos
Widespread summer visitor to the hilly districts of the north and west, and elsewhere a common passge migrant to fresh waters and marshes. A few winter in the south-west.

Spotted Sandpiper A
Actitis macularia
Rare transatlantic vagrant, mostly in autumn, but also in winter. Now recorded in small numbers every year and has bred once in Scotland in 1975.

Grey-tailed Tattler A
Heteroscelus brevipes
Exceptional vagrant from Siberia that was first recorded on the Dyfed-Gwynedd borders in 1981. This remains the only record.

Turnstone A
Arenaria interpres
Widespread winter visitor and passage migrant to all coastlines.

Wilson's Phalarope A
Phalaropus tricolor
Rare transatlantic vagrant that has occurred with increasing frequency in recent years, even in summer.

Red-necked Phalarope A
Phalaropus lobatus
Scarce breeding bird in extreme north and west. Double passage migrant, mainly in autumn and particularly after gales when it may be widespread inland.

Grey Phalarope A
Phalaropus fulicarius
Regular autumn migrant, especially after autumn storms. Rare at other times.

Pomarine Skua A
Stercorarius pomarinus
Regular double passage migrant in small numbers, mainly to north-west and south coasts in spring and to the east coast in autumn.

Arctic Skua A
Stercorarius parasiticus
Breeds in the far north in good numbers. Elsewhere, a regular double passage migrant and the most common of the skuas along all coastlines.

☐ **Long-tailed Skua** A
Stercorarius longicaudus
Scarcest of the four skuas and only a rare passage migrant in spring and autumn to our coasts.

☐ **Great Skua** A
Stercorarius skua
Scarce breeding bird in far north. Elsehwere a scarce passage migrant.

☐ **Great Black-headed Gull** A
Larus ichthyaetus
Extremely rare vagrant from southern Russia that has not occurred since 1932, though a few have been claimed.

☐ **Mediterranean Gull** A
Larus melanocephalus
Regular, but scarce, visitor throughout the year that has bred erratically on the south coast over the past two decades.

☐ **Laughing Gull** A
Larus atricilla
Rare transatlantic vagrant that is now recorded in small numbers every year.

☐ **Franklin's Gull** A
Larus pipixcan
Very rare transatlantic vagrant that was recorded 11 times up to 1986, but which is now recognised most years.

☐ **Little Gull** A
Larus minutus
Regular double passage migrant throughout England, Wales, southern Scotland and south-eastern Ireland, that may form quite large flocks in favoured areas. Scarce in winter, and attempted to breed in 1975 and 1978.

☐ **Sabine's Gull** A
Larus sabini
Passage migrant through south-western approaches that may be blown onshore by autumn storms.

Probably more abundant at sea than status indicates.

☐ **Bonaparte's Gull** A
Larus philadelphia
Rare transatlantic vagrant, mainly to the south-west, that is becoming of annual occurrence.

☐ **Black-headed Gull** A
Larus ridibundus
The most abundant and widespread of the gulls in most parts of the country. Breeds in many areas, including inland, and is an abundant winter visitor.

☐ **Slender-billed Gull** A
Larus genei
Extremely rare vagrant from southern Europe, with only a handful of records. (Two appeared in Norfolk in 1987.)

☐ **Ring-billed Gull** A
Larus delawarensis
First recorded only in 1973 as a transatlantic vagrant. Now regarded as a scarce but regular visitor, mainly in early spring, with up to 50 records each year. Many reports are still rejected.

☐ **Common Gull** A
Larus canus
Widespread breeding bird in the north and west and abundant winter visitor and passage migrant throughout Britain and Ireland.

☐ **Lesser Black-backed Gull** A
Larus fuscus
Breeds in large numbers at many places, particularly around the coasts. Common passage migrant and numerous winter visitor.

☐ **Herring Gull** A
Larus argentatus
Breeds commonly along most cliff-bound coastlines, particularly in the north and west. Abundant winter visitor to all areas.

☐ **Iceland Gull** A
Larus glaucoides
Scarce winter visitor that may occur along any coastline, but which is primarily a bird of the far north.

☐ **Glaucous Gull** A
Larus hyperboreus
Widespread, but scarce, winter visitor to all coastlines. Outnumbers Iceland Gull in all areas. Some individuals return to regular wintering area year after year.

☐ **Great Black-backed Gull** A
Larus marinus
Widespread breeding bird in north and west, and is a regular winter visitor elsewhere, though largely confined to the coast.

☐ **Ross's Gull** A
Rhodostethia rosea
Rare winter visitor from the far north, mainly to northern Britain that occurred 46 times up to 1986, but which is becoming annual.

☐ **Kittiwake** A
Rissa tridactyla
Breeds along most cliff-girt coastlines, thus mainly in the north and west. Pelagic outside the breeding season, but occurs off all shorelines in winter.

☐ **Ivory Gull** A
Pagophila eburnea
Very rare vagrant from the Arctic that occasionally appears, usually in the far northern islands. Becoming even more irregular despite increasing gull-watching.

☐ **Gull-billed Tern** A
Gelochelidon nilotica
Rare passage migrant, mainly to the south-east, in spring and autumn with 1–13 records each year. Breeds as near as the Baltic.

☐ **Caspian Tern** A
Sterna caspia
Rare passage migrant that occurs in tiny numbers each year, mainly on the south and east coasts. Breeds in the Baltic.

☐ **Royal Tern** A
Sterna maxima
Extremely rare vagrant from the tropics that has occurred only four times, most recently in south Wales in 1979. Easily confused with Lesser Crested Tern.

☐ **Lesser Crested Tern** A
Sterna bengalensis
Extremely rare vagrant that has been seen annually since first recorded in 1982. It is possible that all records refer to the single individual that was seen on television on the Farne Islands.

☐ **Sandwich Tern** A
Sterna sandvicensis
Widespread, but local, summer visitor to many coastal areas and regular passage migrant along all shorelines.

☐ **Roseate Tern** A
Sterna dougallii
Very localized summer visitor, mainly to Ireland, with small colonies in eastern Scotland and north-eastern England. Elsewhere a scarce passage migrant to coasts. Slowly declining.

☐ **Common Tern** A
Sterna hirundo
Widespread and numerous summer visitor to coasts and inland wetlands. Common passage migrant elsewhere.

☐ **Arctic Tern** A
Sterna paradisaea
Abundant summer visitor to coasts of north and west with smaller numbers south to East Anglia. Widespread passage migrant to other coasts.

☐ **Aleutian Tern** A
Sterna aleutica
Exceptionally rare vagrant. One record of one in Northumberland in 1979.

☐ **Forster's Tern** A
Sterna forsteri
Exceptionally rare vagrant, first recorded as recently as 1980, that is now seen annually in late autumn and winter. There were 13 records until 1986.

☐ **Bridled Tern** A
Sterna anaethetus
Exceptional vagrant from tropical waters that was seen only ten times up to 1986, most recently with two in 1984.

☐ **Sooty Tern** A
Sterna fuscata
Extremely rare vagrant from the tropics that occurred 26 times up to 1986, most recently in Kent and East Sussex in 1984.

☐ **Little Tern** A
Sterna albifrons
Scarce, but widespread, summer visitor to many coastlines, that is declining in many areas. Passage migrant elsewhere.

☐ **Whiskered Tern** A
Chlidronias hybridus
Rare vagrant that occurs in tiny numbers most years, mainly along the south coast in spring.

☐ **Black Tern** A
Chlidonias niger
Regular double passage migrant, mainly to south and east England, that occasionally breeds.

☐ **White-winged Black Tern** A
Chlidonias leucopterus
Rare double passage migrant in small numbers each year, mainly to south and east England.

☐ **Guillemot** A
Uria aalge
Confined to cliffs of north and west where large numbers form dense breeding colonies. Found in small numbers along all coasts in winter.

☐ **Brünnich's Guillemot** A
Uria lomvia
Exceptionally rare vagrant from the Arctic that occurred 21 times until 1986, mainly in the far northern islands in winter. Most were dead when found.

☐ **Razorbill** A
Alca torda
Breeds among the cliffs of the north and west, but is nowhere as abundant as the Guillemot. Found in small numbers along many coasts in winter.

☐ **Great Auk** A
Pinguinus impennis
Extinct. Last British birds were killed on St Kilda about 1840. Final World Extinction on Eldey, Iceland on 4 June 1844.

☐ **Black Guillemot** A
Cepphus grylle
Widespread breeder in north-west, though nowhere very numerous. Mainly resident and decidedly rare in south and east.

☐ **Little Auk** A
Alle alle
Regular autumn passage migrant that is blown onshore by gales in late October and November and which may then occur inland. Scarce at other times.

☐ **Puffin** A
Fratercula arctica
Localized breeding bird on north and west coasts. Forms dense colonies on many offshore islands. Seen in winter in small numbers elsewhere.

☐ **Pallas's Sandgrouse** A
Syrrhaptes paradoxus
Irregular visitor, sometimes in significant numbers, at the beginning of this century, that exceptionally stayed on to breed in subsequent years. Last irruption was 1909 and only six have been recorded since.

☐ **Rock Dove** A
Columba livia
Widespread and numerous as 'Feral Pigeon'. Genuine Rock Doves probably now confined to the extreme north and west.

☐ **Stock Dove** A
Columba oenas
Widespread resident throughout Britain, except the north-western Highlands

☐ **Woodpigeon** A
Columba palumbus
Common and widespread resident throughout Britain and Ireland and abundant winter visitor.

☐ **Collared Dove** A
Streptopelia decaocto
Widespread resident throughout Britain and Ireland after first colonization in 1955.

☐ **Turtle Dove** A
Streptopelia turtur
Summer visitor to south, central and eastern England and eastern Wales. Passage migrant elsewhere.

☐ **Rufous Turtle Dove** A
Streptopelia orientalis
Exceptional vagrant from the east that occurred on only eight occasions up to 1968, most recently in Cornwall in 1978.

☐ **Rose-ringed Parakeet** C
Psittacula krameri
Thinly spread and rather localized resident over much of England as far north as eastern Scotland after introduction in the 1960s.

☐ **Great Spotted Cuckoo** A
Clamator glandarius
Very rare vagrant, mainly to southern England in spring. There were 28 records up to 1986, the latest being on the Ise of Wight in that year.

☐ **Cuckoo** A
Cuculus canorus
Widespread summer visitor to Britain and Ireland

☐ **Black-billed Cuckoo** A
Coccyzus erythrophthalmus
Exceptional transatlantic vagrant that occurred only 12 times up to 1986. The latest was typically in autumn 1985 in Scilly.

☐ **Yellow-billed Cuckoo** A
Coccyzus americanus
Rare transatlantic vagrant mainly in autumn. The latest was in 1986 in Co. Cork.

☐ **Barn Owl** A
Tyto alba
Widespread, but declining, resident throughout Britain and Ireland, save for the extreme north and west.

☐ **Scops Owl** A
Otus scops
Rare vagrant from southern Europe, mostly in early summer. There were 78 records by 1986, the most recent being one in Wiltshire in 1982.

☐ **Eagle Owl** B
Bubo bubo
Exceptional vagrant that has not been recorded in the past 50 years.

☐ **Snowy Owl** A
Nyctea scandiaca
Irregular autumn and winter visitor that bred in Shetland from 1967 until 1975. Several females have been resident there since. Vagrant elsewhere.

☐ **Hawk Owl** A
Surnia ulula
Exceptional vagrant from the north-east that was recorded 11 times up to 1986, most recently in Shetland in 1983.

☐ **Little Owl** A
Athene noctua
Widespread resident in England and in north and south Wales. Winter visitor to central Wales, vagrant elsewhere. Originally introduced in late nineteenth century.

☐ **Tawny Owl** A
Strix aluco
Common and widespread resident, but absent from Ireland.

☐ **Long-eared Owl** A
Asio otus
Widespread resident, though absent from many parts of southern England. Winter visitor elsewhere.

☐ **Short-eared Owl** A
Asio flammeus
Resident in hilly regions of north and west and along coasts of East Anglia. Elsewhere, widespread winter visitor.

☐ **Tengmalm's Owl** A
Aegolius funereus
Rare vagrant from the Continent that has occurred 57 times, most recently in Orkney in 1986.

☐ **Nightjar** A
Caprimulgus eruopaeus
Widespread summer visitor, mainly to southern Britain, and passage migrant elsewhere.

☐ **Red-necked Nightjar** B
Caprimulgus ruficollis
Exceptional vagrant from southern Europe that has not been recorded within the last 50 years.

☐ **Egyptian Nightjar** B
Caprimulgus aegyptius
Exceptional vagrant from Africa

and Asia that has not been recorded within the past 50 years.

☐ **Common Nighthawk** A
Chordeiles minor
Exceptional transatlantic vagrant that occurred on 13 occasions up to 1986. The most recent was on Merseyside in 1985. Most are seen in the south-west in October.

☐ **Chimney Swift** A
Chaetura pelagica
Exceptional transatlantic vagrant that was recorded only three times up to 1986. Two were seen in Cornwall in 1982, and one in Scilly in 1986.

☐ **Needle-tailed Swift** A
Hirundapus caudacutus
Exceptionally rare vagrant from Siberia that was recorded six times up to 1986, most recently in Yorkshire in 1985.

☐ **Swift** A
Apus apus
Common and widespread summer visitor to almost all parts of Britain and Ireland.

☐ **Pallid Swift** A
Apus pallidus
Exceptional vagrant from southern Europe that occurred only on six occasions up to 1986, no less than four of which were in November 1984.

☐ **Pacific Swift** A
Apus pacificus
Exceptional vagrant from eastern Asia that occurred only once, on a North Sea gas platform in 1981.

☐ **Alpine Swift** A
Apus melba
Rare vagrant from southern Europe in spring and summer, mainly to southern England. Now regarded as annual in small numbers.

☐ **Little Swift** A
Apus affinis
Exceptional vagrant from North Africa that occurred only seven times up to 1986. The first was in Co. Cork in 1981.

☐ **Kingfisher** A
Alcedo atthis
Widespread resident as far north as central Scotland. Recent decline due to hard winters and river pollution.

☐ **Belted Kingfisher** A
Ceryle alcyon
Exceptional transatlantic vagrant that was recorded only five times up to 1986. Most recent was in Co. Tipperary in 1985.

☐ **Blue-cheeked Bee-eater** A
Merops superciliosus
Exceptionally rare vagrant that was seen on only three occasions up to 1986. The most recent was in a lorry park in Cambridgeshire in September 1982.

☐ **Bee-eater** A
Merops apiaster
Vagrant northwards from the Mediterranean, mostly to southern England in the early summer, often in small flocks.

☐ **Roller** A
Coracias garrulus
Rare vagrant northwards from southern Europe that is almost of annual occurrence in very small numbers.

☐ **Hoopoe** A
Upupa epops
Rare spring and autumn visitor that exceptionally nests in southern England.

☐ **Wryneck** A
Jynx torquilla
Formerly a scarce breeder in southern England that has now colonized Scotland where a few pairs probably breed each year.

☐ **Great Spotted Woodpecker** A
Dendrocopos major
Widespread and common resident except in northernmost Scotland and in Ireland.

☐ **Lesser Spotted**
Otherwise a scarce passage migrant mainly to the south and east coasts.

☐ **Green Woodpecker** A
Picus viridis
Widespread and common resident in England, Wales and the southern half of Scotland. Unknown in Ireland.

☐ **Yellow-bellied Sapsucker** A
Sphyrapicus varius
Exceptional transatlantic vagrant that has found its way to the Isles of Scilly once.

☐ **Woodpecker** A
Dendrocopos minor
Widespread resident over most of England and Wales that is easily overlooked.

☐ **Calandra Lark** A
Melanocorypha calandra
Exceptional vagrant northward from southern Europe that occurred only three times in Britain up to 1986.

☐ **Bimaculated Lark** A
Melanocorypha bimaculata
Exceptional vagrant from south-eastern Europe that occurred only three times up to 1986.

☐ **White-winged lark** A
Melanocorypha leucoptera
Exceptional vagrant from Russia that occurred only five times up to 1986, most recently in Norfolk in 1981.

☐ **Short-toed Lark** A
Calandrella brachydactyla
Scarce annual visitor from Africa and southern Eurasia in small numbers, mainly in autumn.

☐ **Lesser Short-toed Lark** A
Calandrella rufescens
Exceptionally rare visitor to western Ireland in the early part of the year. Only four records, though 42 birds were involved.

☐ **Crested Lark** A
Galerida cristata
Exceptional vagrant from across the Channel. There were 19 records up to 1986, the latest in Gwynedd in 1982.

☐ **Woodlark** A
Lullula arborea
Scarce and declining resident in southern England and East Anglia; rare elsewhere

☐ **Skylark** A
Alauda arvensis
Common and widespread resident, passage migrant and winter visitor throughout Britain and Ireland.

☐ **Shore Lark** A
Eremophila alpestris
Scarce winter visitor to the east coast that is apparently declining. Bred on at least two occasions in the 1970s.

☐ **Sand Martin** A
Riparia riparia
Widespread summer visitor to all parts of Britain and Ireland except the northern and western isles. Serious decline in 1980s due to drought in wintering zone.

☐ **Swallow** A
Hirundo rustica
Common and widespread summer visitor.

☐ **Red-rumped Swallow** A
Hirundo daurica
Rare vagrant northwards from southern Europe that is spreading northwards and has become of annual occurrence in recent years.

☐ **Cliff Swallow** A
Hirundo pyrrhonota
Exceptional transatlantic vagrant. One on the Isles of Scilly in October 1983.

☐ **House Martin** A
Delichon urbica
Common and widespread summer visitor to all parts of Britain and Ireland, except north and western Scotland.

☐ **Richard's Pipit** A
Anthus novaeseelandiae
Scarce passage migrant, mainly in autumn, to most coasts in small numbers.

☐ **Blythe's Pipit** B
Anthus godlewskii
Exceptional vagrant that has not been recorded in the past 50 years.

☐ **Tawny Pipit** A
Anthus campestris
Scarce passage migrant, mostly in autumn, to south and east coasts of England.

☐ **Olive-backed Pipit** A
Anthus hodgsoni
Rare vagrant from Russia that has been increasingly identified over the past 20 years. Now averages about three records a year.

☐ **Tree Pipit** A
Anthus trivalis
Widespread summer visitor to most of England, Wales and Scotland. Only a passage migrant to southern and eastern Ireland.

☐ **Pechora Pipit** A
Anthus gustavi
Very rare vagrant from Russia, mainly in September and October, mostly to Fair Isle. Total up to 1986 was 29.

☐ **Meadow Pipit** A
Anthus pratensis
Widespread and common resident throughout. Also common passage migrant and winter visitor.

☐ **Red-throated Pipit** A
Anthus cervinus
Rare vagrant from eastern Europe that occurs in variable numbers each year, mainly in autumn.

☐ **Rock Pipit** A
Anthus petrosus
Resident along most rocky shorelines. Also passage migrant and winter visitor.

☐ **Water Pipit** A
Anthus spinoletta
Scarce winter visitor from the Continent, most often found inland on watercress beds.

☐ **American Pipit** A
Anthus rubescens
Rare transatlantic vagrant that has only recently been accorded the status of a separate species.

☐ **Yellow Wagtail** A
Motacilla flava
Common and widespread summer visitor to England, the Welsh lowlands and lowland Scotland. Elsewhere, including Ireland, double passage migrant.

☐ **Citrine Wagtail** A
Motacilla citreola
Rare vagrant from Russia that occurs in small numbers most years, mostly on the east and south coasts. Expanding range westwards and males have summered.

☐ **Grey Wagtail** A
Montacilla cinerea
Resident over most of southern Britain and Ireland, and summer visitor to northern Scotland.

☐ **Pied Wagtail** A
Montacilla alba
Common and widespread resident. White Wagtail *M. a. alba* is a regular double passage migrant.

☐ **Waxwing** A
Bombycilla garrulus
Irregular autumn and winter visitor in variable numbers, mainly to eastern Britain. Irrupts from Scandiavia.

☐ **Dipper** A
Cinclus cinclus
Resident along suitable streams in all hilly districts of the north and west. Few winter vagrants from the Continent each year.

☐ **Wren** A
Troglodytes troglodytes
Common and widespread resident.

☐ **Brown Thrasher** A
Toxostoma rufum
Exceptional transatlantic vagrant. One in Dorset in 1966–67.

☐ **Grey Catbird** A
Dunetella carolinensis
Exceptional transatlantic vagrant. One on Co. Cork in November 1986.

☐ **Dunnock** A
Prunella modularis
Common and widespread throughout Britain and Ireland.

☐ **Alpine Accentor** A
Prunella collaris
Very rare vagrant from mountains of south and central Europe that has occurred on 35 occasions, but which remains as irregular as ever. Last records were in Dorset and Norfolk in 1978.

☐ **Rufous Bush Robin** A
Cercotrichas galactotes
Exceptionally rare vagrant northwards from the Mediterranean that has occurred on 11 occasions, most recently in Devon in 1980.

☐ **Robin** A
Erithacus rubecula
Common and widespread resident and winter visitor.

Thrush Nightingale A
Luscinia luscinia
Rare vagrant from eastern Europe, with most birds trapped for ringing in spring and autumn.

Nightingale A
Luscinia megarhynchos
Widespread summer visitor to southern, central and eastern England.

Siberian Rubythroat A
Luscinia calliope
Exceptionally rare vagrant from north-eastern Europe that occurred on eight occasions up to 1986, most recently in Lincolnshire in 1978.

Bluethroat A
Luscinia svecica
Scarce double passage migrant, but mainly in autumn on the east coast. A nest and eggs were found in 1968, and a pair bred successfully in 1985. Both were in northern Scotland.

Red-flanked Bluetail A
Tarsiger cyanurus
Exceptionally rare vagrant from Asia that occurred on ten occasions up to 1986, most recently on Fair Isle in 1984.

White-throated Robin A
Irania gutturalis
Exceptional vagrant from Asia Minor. One on the Isle of Man in 1983.

Black Redstart A
Phoenicurus ochruros
Localized summer visitor to south, central and eastern England, but a more widespread double passage migrant.

Redstart A
Phoenicurus phoenicurus
Widespread summer visitor, though highly localized in Ireland, and double passage migrant.

Whinchat A
Saxicola rubetra
Widespread summer visitor and double passage migrant in good numbers.

Stonechat A
Saxicola torquata
Widespread resident, particularly in the west, passage migrant and scarce winter visitor.

Isabelline Wheatear A
Oenanthe isabellina
Exceptionally rare vagrant from south-eastern Europe that occurred only four times up to 1986, the most recent was in Northumberland in 1980.

Wheatear A
Oenanthe oenanthe
Common and widespread summer visitor to hilly and coastal districts. Elsewhere, regular double passage migrant.

Pied Wheatear A
Oenanthe pleschanka
Exceptionally rare vagrant from south-east Europe that occurred ten times up to 1986, almost all in autumn.

Black-eared Wheatear A
Oenanthe hispanica
Rare vagrant from southern Europe that occurred 39 times up to 1986, mostly in spring.

Desert Wheatear A
Oenanthe deserti
Very rare vagrant that occurred only 24 times up to 1986, mostly in autumn.

White-crowned Black Wheatear A
Oenanthe leucopyga
Exceptionally rare vagrant from North Africa. One record in Suffolk in June 1982.

Black Wheatear A
Oenanthe leucura
Exceptionally rare vagrant from southern Europe that occurred only six times up to 1986.

Rock Thrush A
Monticola saxatilis
Rare vagrant northwards from the Mediterranean that occurred only 21 times up to 1986, most recently in Gwynedd in that year.

White's Thrush A
Zoothera dauma
Rare vagrant from Siberia that has occurred on 41 occasions mainly in autumn, most recently in Shetland in 1985.

Siberian Thrush A
Zoothera sibirica
Exceptional vagrant, mainly in autumn, from Siberia. Only five have been recorded, the most recent in Co. Cork in 1985.

Hermit Thrust A
Catharus guttatus
Exceptionally rare transatlantic vagrant that occurred only twice up to 1986. The first was on Fair Isle in 1975, the second on Scilly in 1984.

Swainson's Thrush A
Catharus ustulatus
Exceptional transatlantic vagrant that occurred only ten times up to 1986; all in autumn, four in Scilly.

Grey-cheeked Thrush A
Catharus minimus
Exceptionally rare transatlantic vagrant that also breeds in eastern Siberia. It was recorded on 30 occasions up to 1986, ten of which were in that year, the vast majority in October in Scilly.

Veery A
Catharus fuscescens
Exceptional transatlantic vagrant that occurred once up to 1986.

Ring Ousel A
Turdus torquatus
Summer visitor to all hilly districts of the north and west, though nowhere common. Otherwise scarce passage migrant.

Blackbird A
Turdus merula
Abundant widespread resident and winter visitor.

Eye-browed Thrush A
Turdus obscurus
Exceptional vagrant westwards from Siberia that occurred only eight times up to 1986, most recently in Orkney and Scilly in the autumn of 1984.

Dusky Thrush A
Turdus naumanni
Exceptionally rare vagrant from Siberia that occurred on only seven occasions up to 1986, most recently in Cornwall in 1983.

Black-throated (Red-throated) Thrush A
Turdus ruficollis
Exceptional Asian vagrant that occurred only 14 times up to 1986, most recently in 1983 in Greater Manchester.

Fieldfare A
Turdus pilaris
Common and widespread winter visitor that has bred most years since 1967, though numbers were fewer in 1985 than in the mid 1970s.

Song Thrush A
Turdus philomelos
Common and widespread resident and winter visitor.

Redwing A
Turdus iliacus
Common and widespread winter visitor that has bred in northern Scotland since the mid 1950s and which gradually increased in numbers until 1984.

Mistle Thrush A
Turdus viscivorus
Widespread and common resident throughout Britain and Ireland.

American Robin A
Turdus migratorius
Rare transatlantic vagrant that occurred 29 times up to 1986, mostly in autumn and winter. The most recent record was of one in Surrey that was probably killed by a Magpie.

Cetti's Warbler A
Cettia cetti
A recent colonizing and resident warbler that suffered during the bitter winters of the mid 1980s, but which maintains a good population in south and south-west England.

Fan-tailed Warbler A
Cisticola juncidis
Exceptionally rare vagrant from continental Europe that occurred only four times between 1962 and 1986.

Pallas's Grasshopper Warbler A
Locustella certhiola
Exceptionally rare vagrant from Siberia in autumn, mainly to Fair Isle, that occurred nine times up to 1986. The last was at that island in 1986.

Lanceolated Warbler A
Locustella lanceolata
Exceptionally rare autumn vagrant from Russia mainly to Fair Isle that occured 37 times up to 1986.

Grasshopper Warbler A
Locustella naevia
Widespread summer visitor throughout Britain and Ireland, except to the higher hills.

River Warbler A
Locustella fluviatilis
Exceptional vagrant from eastern Europe that occurred only ten times up to 1986. The most recent were on Fair Isle in 1984, the same year that a male was seen singing in East Anglia. The species is spreading westwards through the Continent.

Savi's Warbler A
Locustella luscinioides
Summer visitor in decreasing numbers to south and east England after successful colonization in the 1960s.

Moustached Warbler A
Acrocephalus melanopogon
Exceptional vagrant from southern Europe that occurred only ten times up to 1986, including breeding in Cambridgeshire in 1946.

Aquatic Warbler A
Acrocephalus paludicola
Regular, but scarce, autumn passage migrant along the south coast of England. Most trapped in south Devon.

Sedge Warbler A
Acrocephalus schoenobaenus
Widespread and common summer visitor, except to the hilly districts.

Paddyfield Warbler A
Acrocephalus agricola
Exceptional vagrant from Russia westwards that occurred on 13 occasions up to 1986, mostly in September on Fair Isle.

Blyth's Reed Warbler A
Acrocephalus dumetorum
Exceptional vagrant from eastern Europe that had occurred 13 times until 1986, most recently on Humberside in 1984.

Marsh Warbler A
Acrocephalus palustris
Highly localized summer visitor mainly to the west Midlands that is apparently declining at its main Worcestershire stronghold. Scarce passage migrant in south and eastern England.

Reed Warbler A
Acrocephalus scirpaceus
Widespread and common summer visitor, mainly to southern half of England.

Great Reed Warbler A
Acrocephalus arundinaceus
Scarce vagrant northwards from the Continent that appears most years in southern England, usually in spring, in small numbers.

Thick-billed Warbler A
Acrocephalus aedon
Exceptional vagrant from Asia that was recorded twice up to 1986.

Olivaceous Warbler A
Hippolais pallida
Exceptionally rare vagrant from the south and east that occurred only 14 times up to 1986, most recently in Scilly in 1985.

Booted Warbler A
Hippolais caligata
Rare vagrant from Russia that is now of almost annual occurrence, but which was recorded only 22 times up to 1986.

Icterine Warbler A
Hippolais icterina
Scarce passage migrant, mainly to the south and east coasts in autumn.

Melodious Warbler A
Hippolais polyglotta
Scarce passage migrant, mainly to the south and west coasts in autumn.

Marmora's Warbler A
Sylvia sarda
Exceptional vagrant from Mediterranean. A male was in song through the summer of 1982 on Midhope Moor, Yorkshire. This is the only record.

Dartford Warbler A
Sylvia undata
Rare resident in southern England that suffers severe population crashes during hard winters. Some 300–400 pairs probably breed in good years.

Spectacled Warbler A
Sylvia conspicillata
Exceptionally rare vagrant northwards from the Mediterranean that occurred only three times up to 1986, the last being on Fair Isle in 1979.

Subalpine Warbler A
Sylvia cantillans
Rare vagrant northwards from the Mediterranean that occurs annually in small numbers, usually in spring.

Sardinian Warbler A
Sylvia melanocephala
Extremely rare vagrant from southern Europe that occurred on 14 occasion up to 1986, the last in Lincolnshire in that year.

Ruppell's Warbler A
Sylvia rueppelli
Exceptionally rare vagrant from the eastern Mediterranean that occurred twice up to 1986. The first was in Shetland in 1977, the second on Lundy in 1979.

Desert Warbler A
Sylvia nana
Exceptionally rare vagrant from Asia that occurred only on four occasions up to 1986. The last was on Merseyside in 1979.

Orphean Warbler A
Sylvia hortensis
Exceptionally rare vagrant from southern Europe that occurred five times up to 1986. The most recent was in Aberdeen in 1982.

Barred Warbler A
Sylvia nisoria
Scarce passage migrant, mainly to the east coast in autumn.

Lesser Whitethroat A
Sylvia curruca
Widespread summer visitor to most of England. Regular passage migrant elsewhere.

Whitethroat A
Sylvia communis
Widespread summer visitor to whole of Britain and Ireland, except the highest hills of the north. Double passage migrant. Decline in numbers due to drought in wintering zone.

Garden Warbler A
Sylvia borin
Widespread summer visitor except to Scottish Highlands and much of Ireland.

Blackcap A
Sylvia atricapilla
Widespread and common summer visitor to Britain and Ireland and absent only from western Ireland and Scottish hills and extreme north. Common passage migrant that winters in small numbers in southern England and Ireland.

Green Warbler A
Phylloscopus nitidus
Exceptional vagrant from the Middle East that was first recorded on Scilly in 1983. This remains the only record.

Greenish Warbler A
Phylloscopus trochiloides
Rare, but regular, vagrant mostly in late August and mainly to the east coast. Usually four or five records each year.

Arctic Warbler A
Phylloscopus borealis
Rare vagrant, mostly in September, that averages about six records each year.

Pallas's Warbler A
Phylloscopus proregulus
Rare vagrant from Asia that is of annual occurrence in late October

– early November. Numbers vary from a handful up to 20 each year, but there was a record 116 in 1982.

Yellow-browed Warbler A
Phylloscopus inornatus
Scarce autumn visitor from Asia, mainly to the east coast, but also to the south and south-west.

Radde's Warbler A
Phylloscopus schwarzi
Rare autumn vagrant from Asia, mainly to south and east England. Occurred 51 times up to 1986, averaging two or three a season in recent years.

Dusky Warbler A
Phylloscopus fuscatus
Rare autumn vagrant from Asia, mainly to south and east coasts. Occurred 51 times up to 1986, with about three new records a year.

Bonelli's Warbler A
Phylloscopus bonelli
Rare vagrant from southern Europe, mainly in autumn, that occurred on almost a hundred occasions up to 1986.

Wood Warbler A
Phylloscopus sibilatrix
Widespread summer visitor that is common in the west of Britain, but all but absent from Ireland. Scarce passage migrant where it does not breed.

Chiffchaff A
Phylloscopus collybita
Common and widespread summer visitor that is absent from the northern hills. Passage migrant that winters in small numbers in the south-west.

Willow Warbler A
Phylloscopus trochilus
Abundant summer visitor throughout Britain and Ireland. Common double passage migrant.

Goldcrest A
Regulus regulus
Widespread resident throughout and regular winter visitor from the Continent.

Firecrest A
Regulus ignicapillus
Regular passage migrant, particularly in autumn, that winters in the south-west and breeds in small (but variable) numbers each year in southern England.

Spotted Flycatcher A
Muscicapa striata
Widespread and common summer visitor and regular double passage migrant.

Red-breasted Flycatcher A
Ficedula parva
Scarce passage migrant from eastern Europe, mainly in autumn.

Collared Flycatcher A
Ficedula albicollis
Extremely rare vagrant from the Continent that occurred on 15 occasions up to 1986, most recently in Suffolk and Yorkshire in 1985. Most records are of males in spring.

Pied Flycatcher A
Ficedula hypoleuca
Summer visitor to western hilly districts, but not Ireland. Passage migrant elsewhere, often quite common along the east coast in autumn.

Bearded Tit A
Panurus biarmicus
Highly localized resident in reed beds of the south and east of England. Usually irrupts across southern England in autumn.

Long-tailed Tit A
Aegithalos caudatus
Widespread and common resident throughout Britain and Ireland.

Marsh Tit A
Parus palustris
Common resident throughout England, Wales and south-eastern Scotland.

Willow Tit A
Parus montanus
Resident in England, Wales and southern Scotland, but somewhat local in distribution.

Crested Tit A
Parus cristatus
Resident in the pine forests of the central Scottish Highlands. Unknown elsewhere.

Coal Tit A
Parus ater
Common resident throughout Britain and Ireland.

Blue Tit A
Parus caeruleus
Common resident throughout Britain and Ireland.

Great Tit A
Parus major
Common resident throughout Britain and Ireland.

Nuthatch A
Sitta europaea
Widespread resident in England and Wales, becoming scarcer to the north.

Wallcreeper A
Tichodroma muraria
Extremely rare vagrant from high continental mountains that is mostly seen on south coast cliffs and which has overwintered. The total up to 1986 was ten, the most recent on the Isle of Wight in 1985.

Treecreeper A
Certhia familiaris
Widespread resident throughout Britain and Ireland.

Short-toed Treecreeper A
Certhia brachydactyla
Extremely rare vagrant from the Continent that occurred on seven

occasions up to 1986. The most recent were two in Kent in 1978.

☐ **Penduline Tit** A
Remiz pendulinus
Extremely rare vagrant that is expanding its range northwards on the Continent and which occurred 11 times up to 1986. The most recent was in Kent in 1984.

☐ **Golden Oriole** A
Oriolus oriolus
Rare summer visitor, mainly to East Anglia, with up to 15 pairs breeding. Otherwise scarce passage migrant.

☐ **Isabelline Shrike** A
Lanius isabellinus
Extremely rare vagrant from Asia that occurred 20 times up to 1986, mostly in autumn. The most recent were in Dorset and Gwynedd in 1985.

☐ **Red-backed Shrike** A
Lanius collurio
A fast declining summer visitor to south and east England, with a 1985 population of 6–11 pairs. Otherwise only a scarce passage migrant.

☐ **Cretzschmar's Bunting** A
Emberiza coesia
Exceptional vagrant from south-western Europe that was recorded only twice up to 1986. Both were in June on Fair Isle, in 1967 and 1979.

☐ **Yellow-browed Bunting** A
Emberiza chrysophris
Exceptionally rare vagrant from Asia that was recorded only once, on Fair Isle in 1980.

☐ **Rustic Bunting** A
Emberiza rustica
Extremely rare migrant from Scandinavia, mainly in autumn, that is recorded in single figures each year.

☐ **Little Bunting** A
Emberiza pusilla
Regular, but scarce, passage migrant mainly in October with about twenty records each year. Breeds as near as Scandinavia.

☐ **Yellow-breasted Bunting** A
Emberiza aureola
Scarce passage migrant, mainly in autumn, to the northern isles and predominantly to Fair Isle where a handful occur each year.

☐ **Reed Bunting** A
Emberiza schoeniclus
Widespread and common resident throughout Britain and Ireland.

☐ **Pallas's Reed Bunting** A
Emberiza pallasi
Exceptional vagrant from Siberia that occurred twice up to 1986. Both were on Fair Isle in autumn, in 1976 and 1981.

☐ **Black-headed Bunting** A
Emberiza melanocephala
Rare vagrant from south-western Europe that occurred 69 times up to 1986. Most have been males and may have been escapees from avaries.

☐ **Corn Bunting** A
Milaria calandra
Widespread, but localized, resident that is absent from many parts of the north and west.

☐ **Rose-breasted Grosbeak** A
Pheucticus ludovicianus
Extremely rare transatlantic vagrant, almost always in October, that occurred 18 times up to 1986. The latest was on Scilly in 1986.

☐ **Bobolink** A
Dolichonyx oryzivorus
Rare vagrant from North America that was recorded a total of 13 times up to 1986, when the latest occurred on Fair Isle in September.

☐ **Northern Oriole** A
Icterus galbula
Extremely rare transatlantic vagrant that was recorded 14 times up to 1986, most recently on Scilly in 1983.

☐ **Lesser Grey Shrike** A
Lanius minor
Decidedly rare, mainly autumn vagrant from southern Europe with three or four records a year.

☐ **Great Grey Shrike** A
Lanius excubitor
Scarce winter visitor from the Continent, mainly to the eastern side of Britain. Some individuals turn up at the same location year after year.

☐ **Woodchat Shrike** A
Lanius senator
Regular, but rare, migrant mainly in May in variable numbers.

☐ **Jay** A
Garrulus glandarius
Widespread resident that is absent only from northern Scotland, the hills and western Ireland.

☐ **Magpie** A
Pica pica
Resident throughout Britain and Ireland, though sporadically distributed in Scotland.

☐ **Nutcracker** A
Nucifraga caryocatactes
Rare winter vagrant that occasionally irrupts from its continental forest home. A total of 401 has been recorded of which 315 were in 1968. The most recent were three in 1985.

☐ **Chough** A
Pyrrhocorax pyrrhocorax
Highly localized resident along the coasts of Wales and inland in slate quarries, at Islay and along the west coast of Ireland.

☐ **Jackdaw** A
Corvus monedula
Common resident throughout Britain and Ireland.

☐ **Rook** A
Corvus frugilegus
Common resident throughout Britain and Ireland, except the Scottish mountains.

☐ **Carrion Crow** A
Corvus corone
Common resident throughout the British Isles except in Isle of Man, north-west Scotland and Ireland, where the subspecies, the Hooded Crow *C. c. cornix* replaces it. The two races interbred readily and there is a narrow overlap zone where hybrids are common.

☐ **Raven** A
Corvus corax
Resident in the hilly districts of the north and west and along adjacent coasts.

☐ **Starling** A
Sturnus vulgaris
Common and widespread resident throughout Britain and Ireland and an abundant winter visitor.

☐ **Rose-coloured Starling** A
Sturnus roseus
Rare vagrant from eastern Europe that occurs about seven or eight times a year on average, mostly in summer and autumn.

☐ **House Sparrow** A
Passer domesticus
Common and widespread resident in all areas except the Scottish Mountains.

☐ **Spanish Sparrow** A
Passer hispaniolensis
Extremely rare vagrant from the Mediterranean that occurred on only three occasions until 1986. The most recent was in Scilly in 1977.

Tree Sparrow A
Passer montanus
Widespread resident in all lowland districts of England, Scotland and Wales. Rather localized around the coasts in Ireland.

Rock Sparrow A
Petronia petronia
Exceptional vagrant from southern Europe. One was seen in Norfolk in 1981.

Philadelphia Vireo A
Vireo philadelphia
Exceptional transatlantic vagrant that was first recorded in 1985 in Co. Cork. This is the only record.

Red-eyed Vireo A
Vireo olivaceus
Rare transatlantic vagrant that is now more or less annually recorded in Scilly which boasted 15 of the 36 recorded by 1986.

Chaffinch A
Fringilla coelebs
Common resident throughout Britain and Ireland and abundant winter visitor.

Brambling A
Fringilla montifringilla
Widespread winter visitor from northern Europe that has started to breed in Scotland in small numbers during the past decade.

Serin A
Serinus serinus
Scarce migrant and summer visitor to southern England that has bred in tiny numbers for several years, mostly in Devon.

Citril Finch B
Serinus citrinella
Exceptional vagrant that has not been recorded in the past 50 years.

Greenfinch A
Carduelis chloris
Common and widespread resident, except in the Scottish mountains.

Goldfinch A
Carduelis carduelis
Common and widespread resident as far north as the Scottish lowlands. Further north it is a summer visitor or migrant.

Siskin A
Carduelis spinus
Resident in the hilly districts of the north and west and at a few places in lowland England. Elsewhere, a widespread winter visitor.

Linnet A
Carduelis cannabina
Common resident everywhere, except for northernmost Scotland, also a winter visitor.

Twite A
Carduelis flavirostris
Resident in north-western Scotland, in the Pennines and along the coasts of north-western Ireland. Winter visitor, mainly to the east coast.

Redpoll A
Carduelis flammea
Widespread resident except in south-central England, but a common winter visitor throughout Britain and Ireland.

Arctic Redpoll A
Carduelis hornemanni
Rare vagrant from northern Europe in variable numbers that occurs annually, mainly in autumn in the north and east. Exceptionally, there were 25 on Fair Isle in 1984.

Two-barred Crossbill A
Loxia leucoptera
Rare vagrant from northern Europe that occurs erratically during Common Crossbill irruptions, mainy in the north and east in autumn. There were 66 records up to 1986.

Common Crossbill A
Loxia curvirostra
Patchily distributed in England and southern Scotland as a breeding resident. More widespread following periodic irruptions from the Continent.

Scottish Crossbill A
Loxia scotica
Resident in north-central Scottish Highlands.

Parrot Crossbill A
Loxia pytyopsittacus
Rare vagrant from northern Europe, that occurs in small numbers along with irrupting Common Crossbills. A pair or two bred in East Anglia in 1983–1986.

Trumpeter Finch A
Bucanetes githagineus
Exceptionally rare vagrant from North Africa that was recorded only five times up to 1986. Most recent was in Essex in 1985.

Scarlet Rosefinch A
Carpodacus erythrinus
Scarce autumn migrant, mainly to the north, that regularly summers in Scotland in small numbers, but which has been proved to breed only in 1982.

Pine Grosbeak A
Pinicola enucleator
Extremely rare vagrant from nothern Europe that occurred only nine times up to 1986.

Bullfinch A
Pyrrhula pyrrhula
Widespread resident throughout Britain and Ireland, except for the bleakest of moors and hills.

Hawfinch A
Coccothraustes coccothrautes
Patchily distributed resident in England, Wales and southern Scotland. Nowhere common.

Evening Grosbeak A
Hesperiphona vespertina
Exceptional transatlantic vagrant that has been recorded twice: first on St Kilda in 1969; second in Highland in 1980. The possibility of escapees cannot be excluded.

Black-and-white Warbler A
Mniotilta varia
Exceptional transatlantic vagrant that occurred only ten times until 1986, most recently in Norfolk in 1985.

Tennessee Warbler A
Vermivora peregrina
Exceptional transatlantic vagrant that occurred only three times up to 1986, all in the northern isles. The most recent was in Orkney in 1982.

Northern Parula A
Parula americana
Exceptional transatlantic vagrant that occurred only ten times up to 1986. The most recent were three in October 1985 in Scilly, Cornwall and Dorset.

Yellow Warbler A
Dendroica petechia
Exceptional transatlantic vagrant that has occurred only once, in Gwynedd in 1984.

Cape May Warbler A
Dendroica tigrina
Exceptional transatlantic vagrant that has been found only once in Strathclyde in 1978.

Magnolia Warbler A
Dendroica magnolia
Exceptional transatlantic vagrant that was found on the Scillys in 1981.

Yellow-rumped Warbler A
Dendroica coronata
Exceptional transatlantic vagrant that was recorded 15 times up to 1986, most recently in 1985 when four were recorded. These

included two on Scilly, one on the Calf of Man and one in Co. Cork.

☐ **Blackpoll Warbler** A
Dendroica striata
Extremely rare transatlantic vagrant that occurred 24 times up to 1986, mostly to the south-west. Most recent were on Shetland and Co. Wexford in 1985.

☐ **American Redstart** A
Setophaga ruticilla
Exceptional transatlantic vagrant that occurred on only six occasions up to 1986, most recently in Co. Cork in 1985.

☐ **Ovenbird** A
Seiurus aurocapillus
Exceptionally rare transatlantic vagrant that occurred only three times up to 1986. The most recent was found dead in south Devon in 1985.

☐ **Northern Waterthrush** A
Seiurus noveboracensis
Exceptional transatlantic vagrant to the south-west in late September that occurred four times until 1986, most recently in Co. Cork in 1983.

☐ **Common Yellowthroat** A
Geothlypis trichas
Exceptionally rare transatlantic vagrant that was recorded only three times up to 1986, most recently in spring in Shetland and Scilly in autumn, both in 1984.

☐ **Hooded Warbler** A
Wilsonia citrina
Exceptional transatlantic vagrant that has reached here only once, in Scilly in September.

☐ **Summer Tanager** A
Piranga rubra
Exceptional transatlantic vagrant that was recorded once, in Gwynedd in September, up to 1986.

☐ **Scarlet Tanager** A
Piranga olivea
Exceptional transatlantic vagrant that occurred seven times up to 1986, most recently in Co. Cork in 1985.

☐ **Rufous-sided Towhee** A
Pipilo erythrophthalmus
Exceptional transatlantic vagrant that occurred only once, in Devon in June, up to 1986.

☐ **Savannah Sparrow** A
Ammodramus sandwichensis
Exceptional transatlantic vagrant that was added to the List in 1982 when one appeared in Dorset. It has not been recorded since.

☐ **Fox Sparrow** A
Zonotrichia iliaca
Exceptional transatlantic vagrant that was recorded only once up to 1986, in Co. Down in June.

☐ **Song Sparrow** A
Zonotrichia melodia
Exceptional transatlantic vagrant that was recorded just five times up to 1986, all in spring. The most recent was in Shetland in 1979.

☐ **White-crowned Sparrow** A
Zonotrichia leucophrys
Exceptional transatlantic vagrant that occurred only twice until 1986. Both were in spring 1977 at Humberside and Fair Isle.

☐ **White-throated Sparrow** A
Zonotrichia albicollis
Extremely rare transatlantic vagrant that occurred on 14 occasions up to 1986, most recently one that overwintered in Belfast in 1984–1985.

☐ **Slate-coloured Junco** A
Junco hyemalis
Exceptional transatlantic vagrant that was recorded just 12 times up to 1986. Most recent were three records in May 1983 in Cornwall, Dorset and Somerset.

☐ **Lapland Bunting** A
Calcarius lapponicus
Scarce winter visitor to the east coast that may form small flocks at favoured locations. Has bred erratically since 1977 in the Scottish Highlands.

☐ **Snow Bunting** A
Plectrophenax nivalis
Winter visitor to the east coasts of Britain and Ireland and passage migrant in small numbers to other coasts. Sometimes forms large flocks in favoured areas. Breeds in small numbers every year on highest Scottish mountains.

☐ **Pine Bunting** A
Emberiza leucocephalos
Extremely rare vagrant from Siberia that occurred only nine times up to 1986, most recently in Scilly and North Yorkshire in 1985, both in spring.

☐ **Yellowhammer** A
Emberiza citrinella
Widespread and common resident throughout Britain and Ireland, except to the higher hills of Scotland.

☐ **Cirl Bunting** A
Emberiza cirlus
Scarce and declining resident in southern England that has its stronghold in south Devon and a total population of no more than 60 pairs.

☐ **Rock Bunting** A
Emberiza cia
Exceptional vagrant from southern Europe that occurred only five times up to 1986.

☐ **Ortolan Bunting** A
Emberiza hortulana
Scarce passage migrant, mainly in autumn to the east coast and elsewhere in small numbers.

Category D
White Pelican
Pelicanus onocrotalus
Greater Flamingo
Phoenicopterus ruber
Wood Duck
Aix sponsa
Borrow's Goldeneye
Bucephala islandica
Bald Eagle
Haliaeetus leucocephalus
Saker
Falco cherrug
Bobwhite
Colinus virginianus
Northern Flicker
Colaptes auratus
Blue Rock Thrush
Monticola solitarius
Snow Finch
Montifringilla nivalis
Palm Warbler
Dendroica palmorum
Lark Sparrow
Chondestes grammacus
Chestnut Bunting
Emberiza rutila
Red-headed Bunting
Emberiza bruniceps
Blue Grosbeak
Guiraca caerulea
Indigo Bunting
Passerina cyanea
Painted Bunting
Passerina ciris

Index